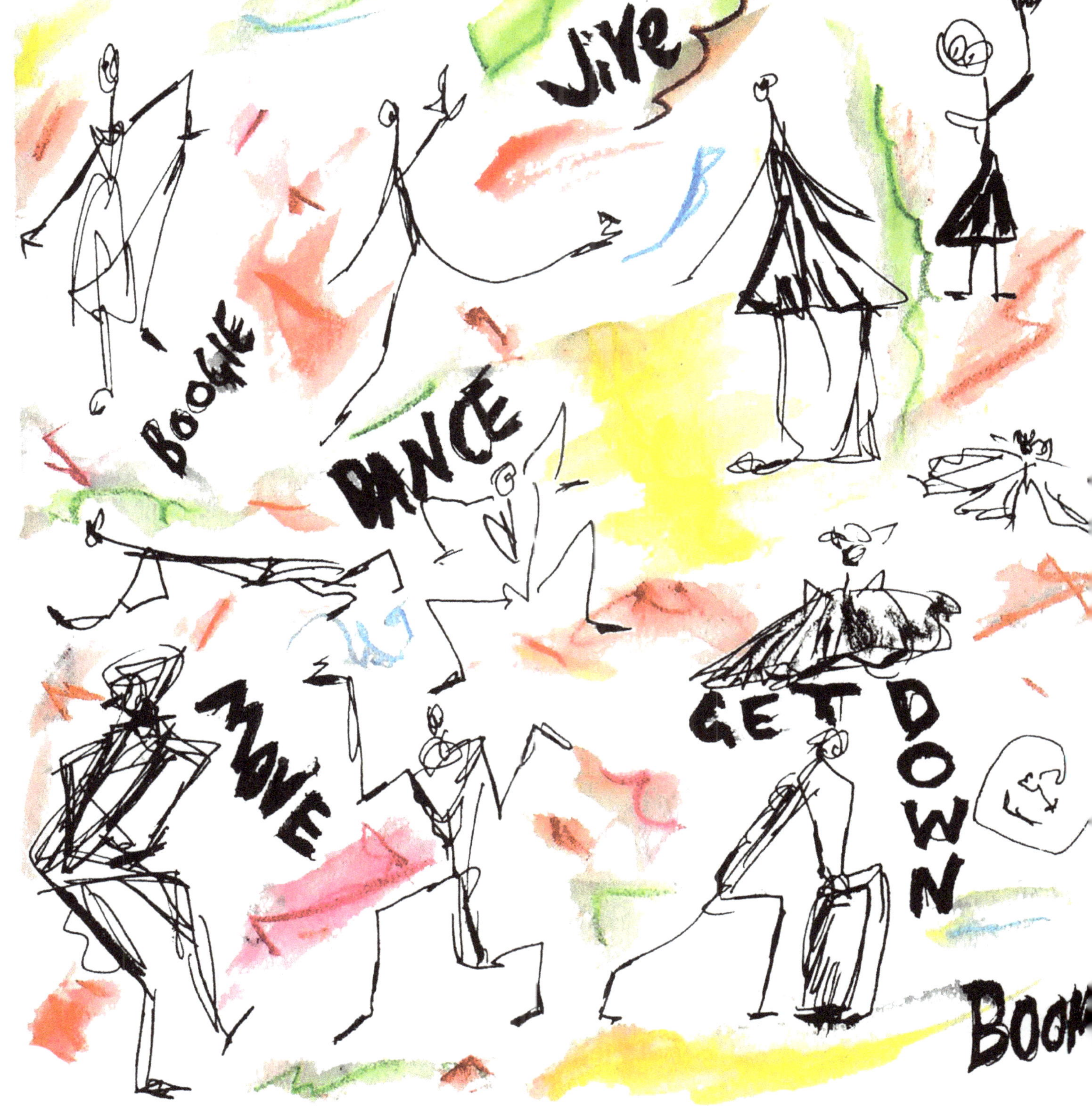

JIVE
BOOGIE
DANCE
MOVE
GET DOWN
BOO

First published by NoooBooks, 2019
Tweed Heads, NSW, Australia.

Doodle with Intent.
Series, Book 1
Copyright:
By Dude LI© 2019
NoooBooks© 2019



Printed and bound by your closest POD to reduce waste and Carbon footprint.

The paper this book is printed on is FSC® certified  (Forest Stewardship Council®).
FSC promotes environmentally responsible, socially beneficial and economically viable management of the world's forests.
A catalogue record for this book is available from the National Library of Australia.

ISBN:978-1-925991-50-5

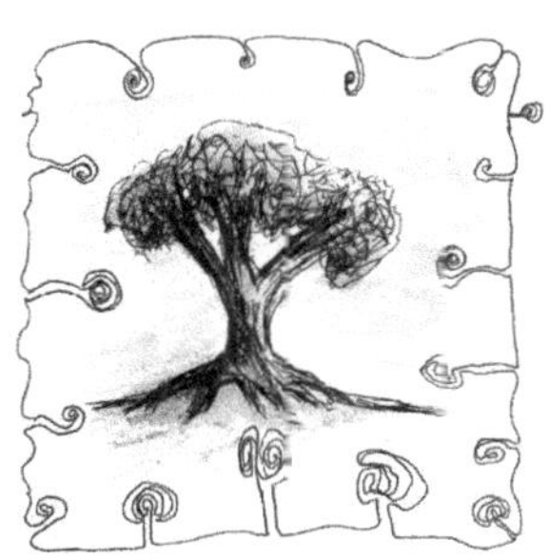

# Doodle with Intent
## by Dude LI.

Moogbooks

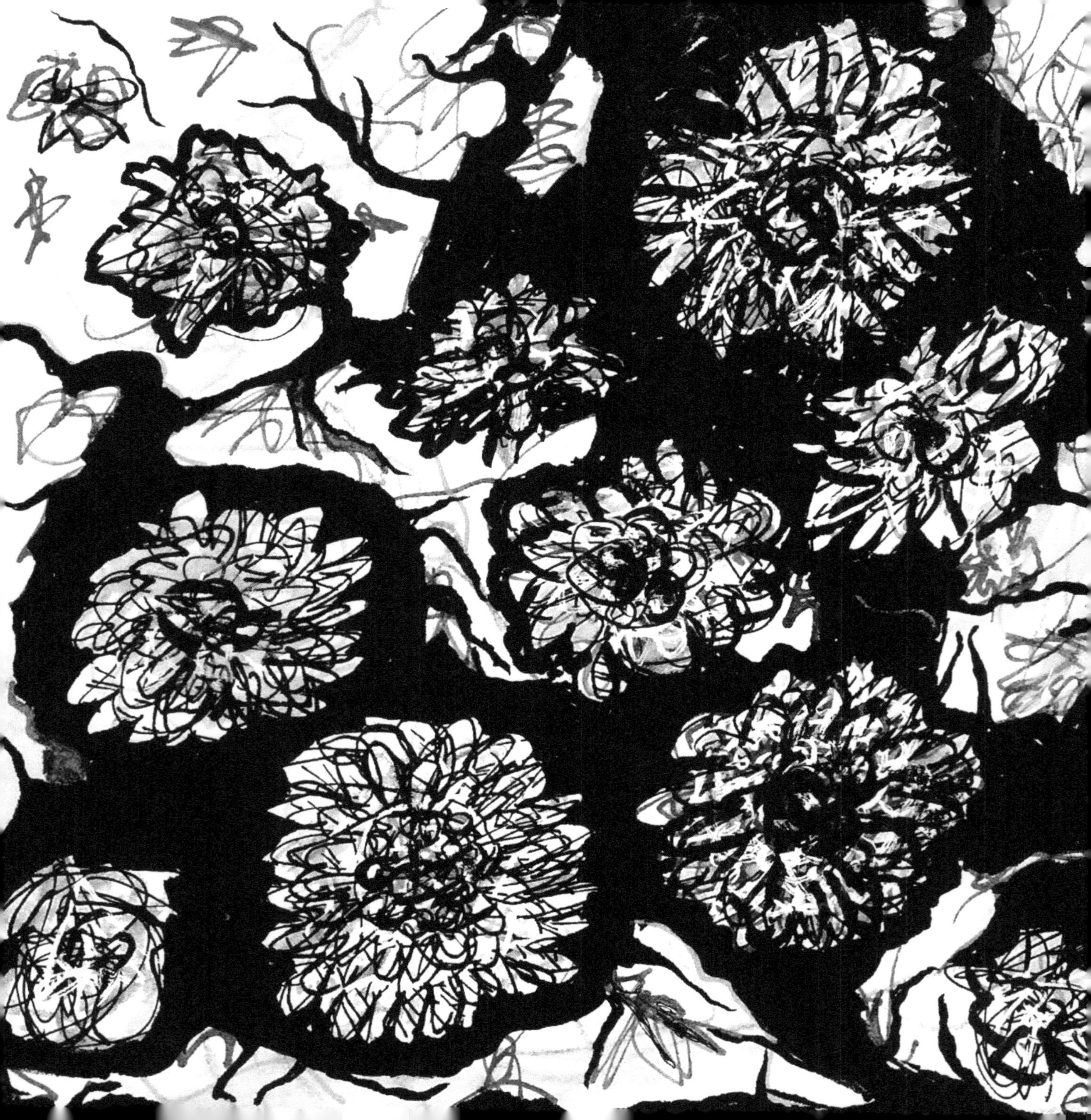

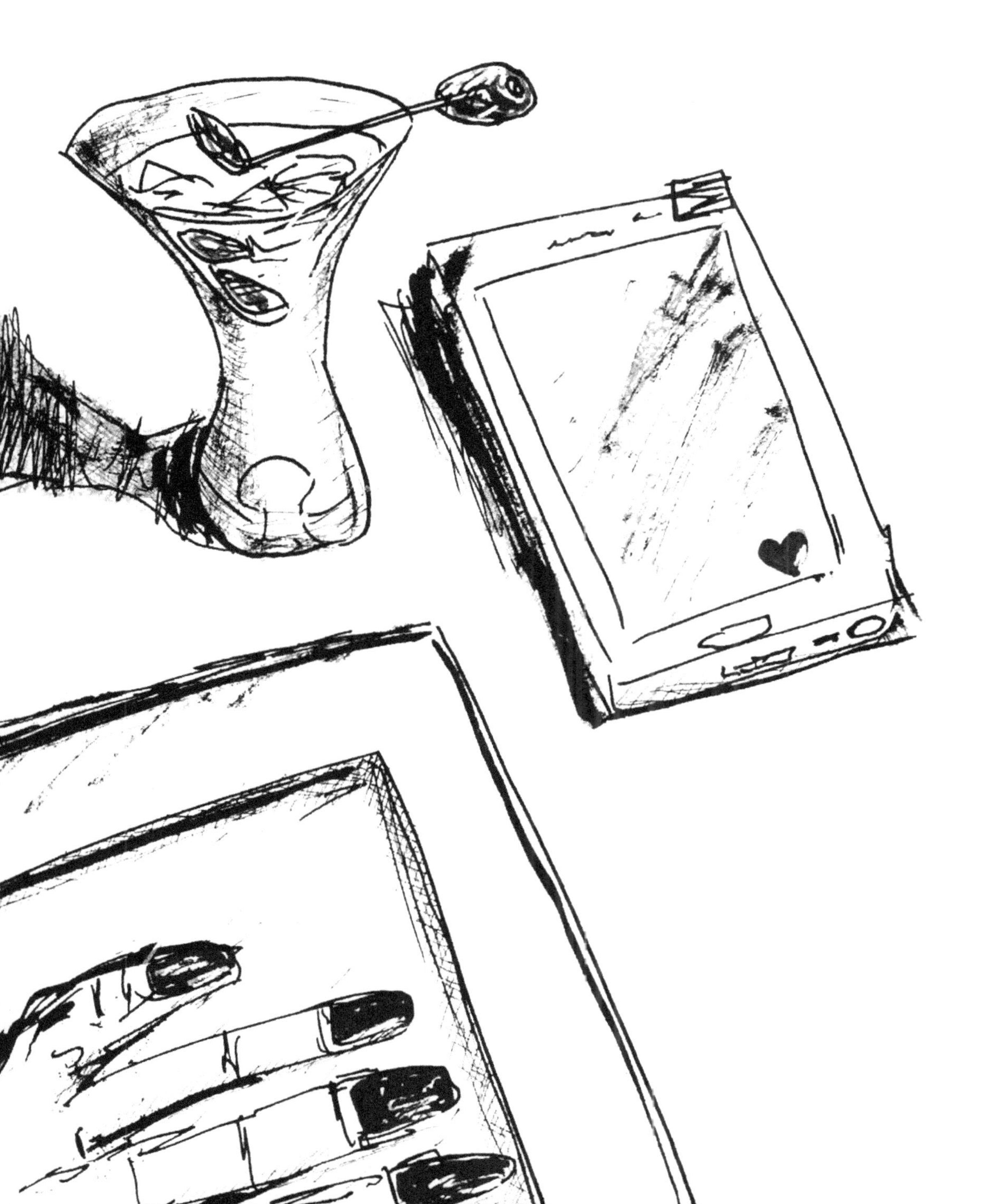

You
Are
going to
die
so make
NOW
count...

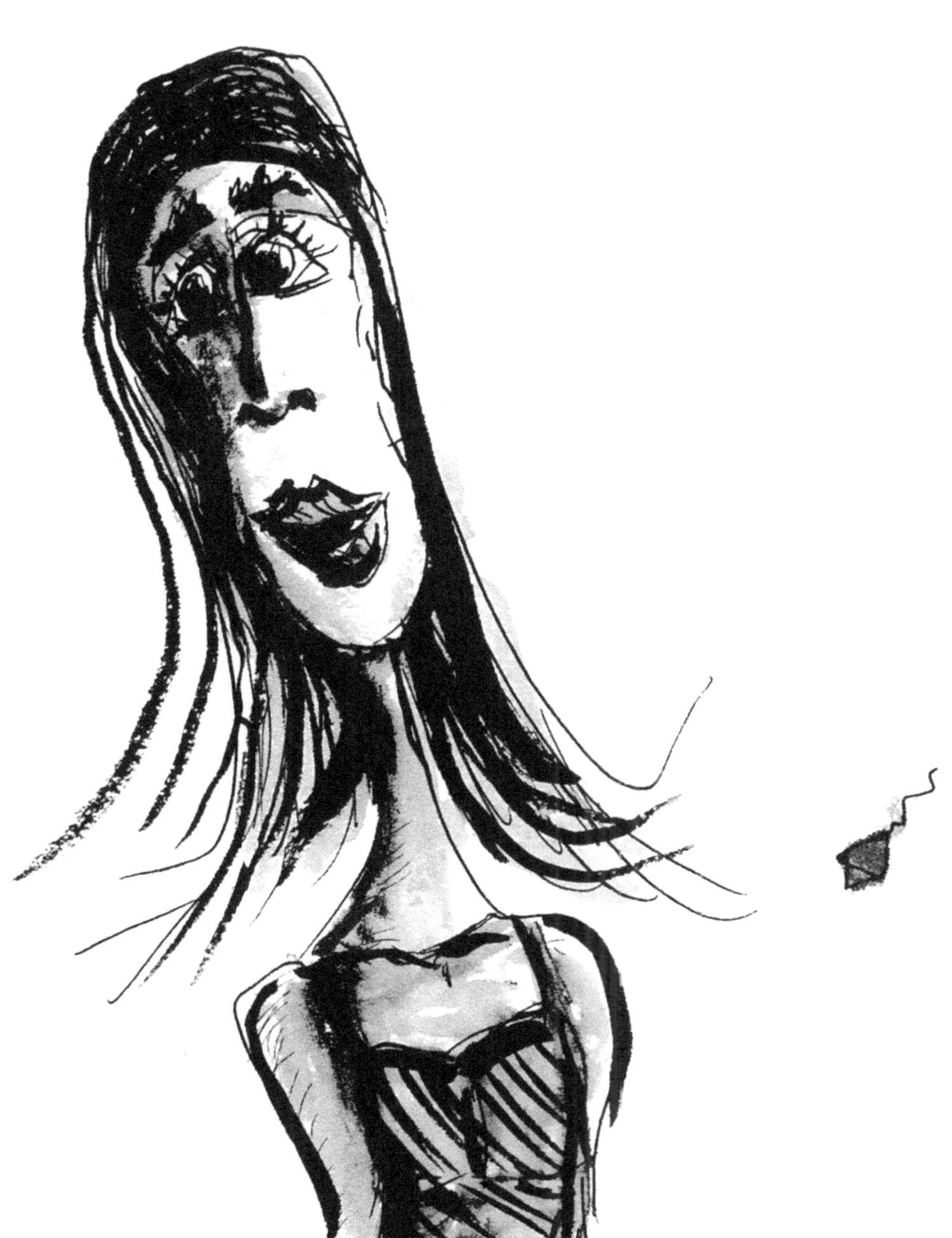

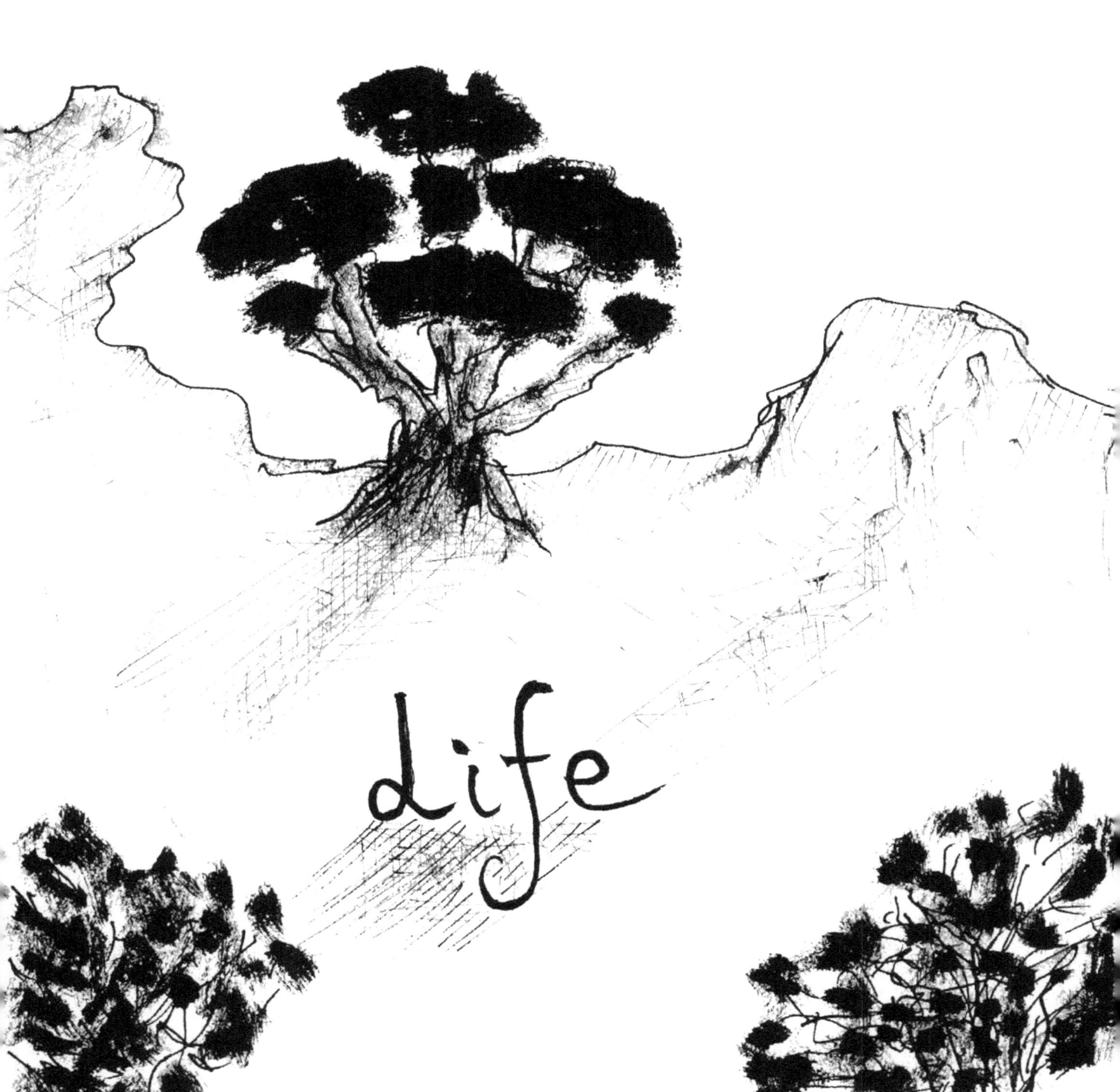
life

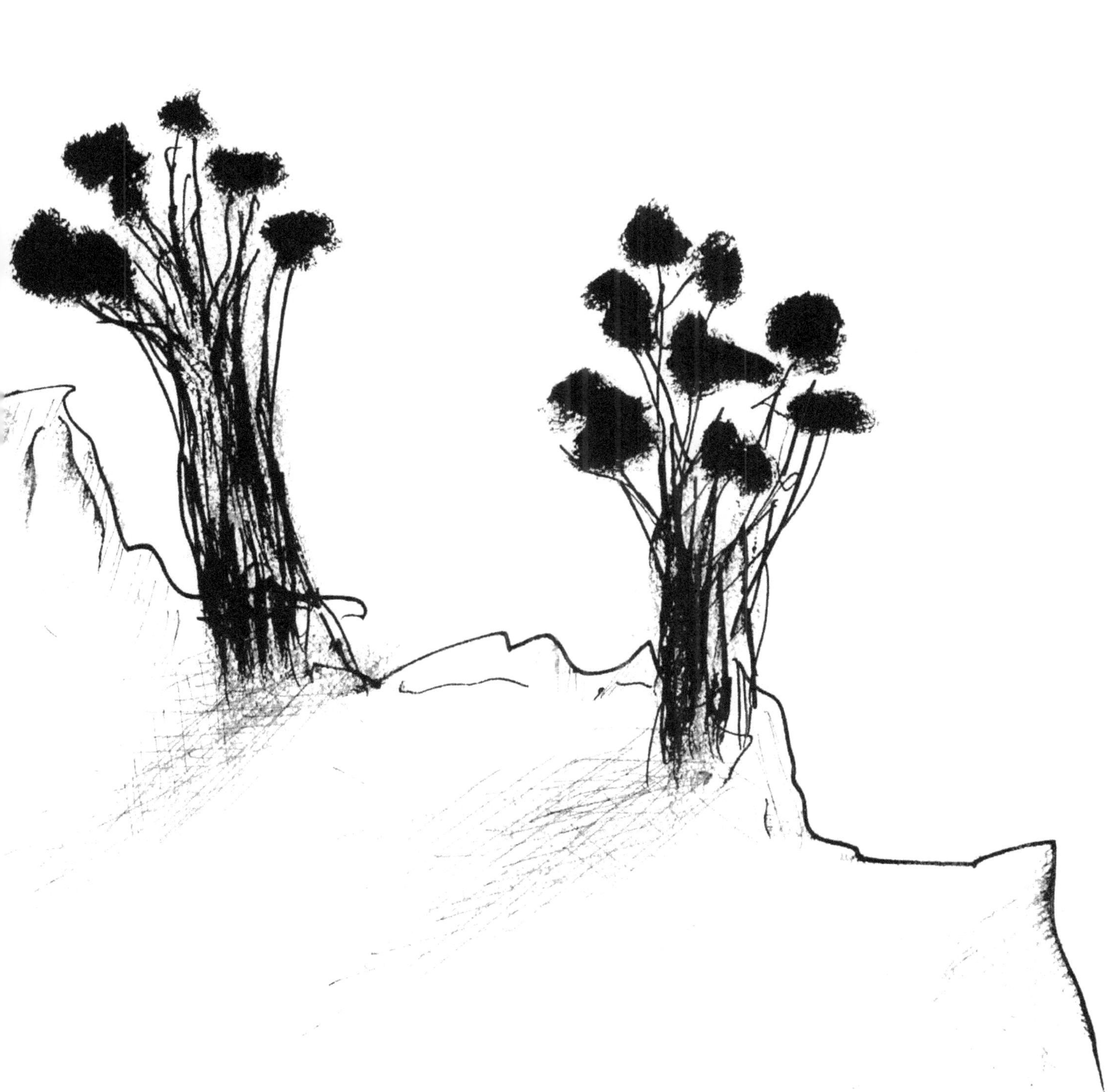

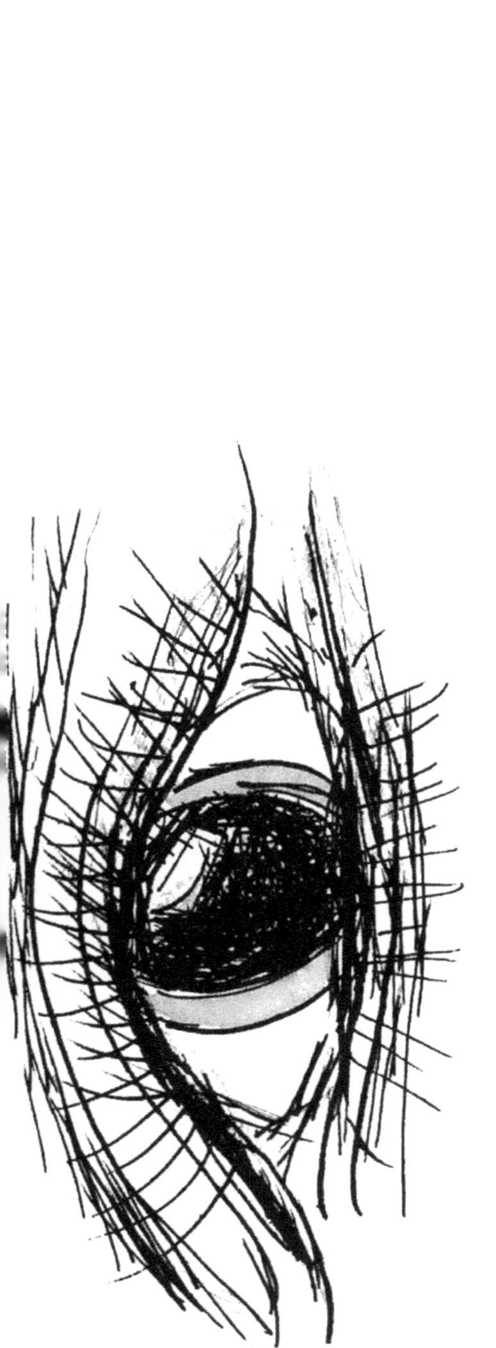

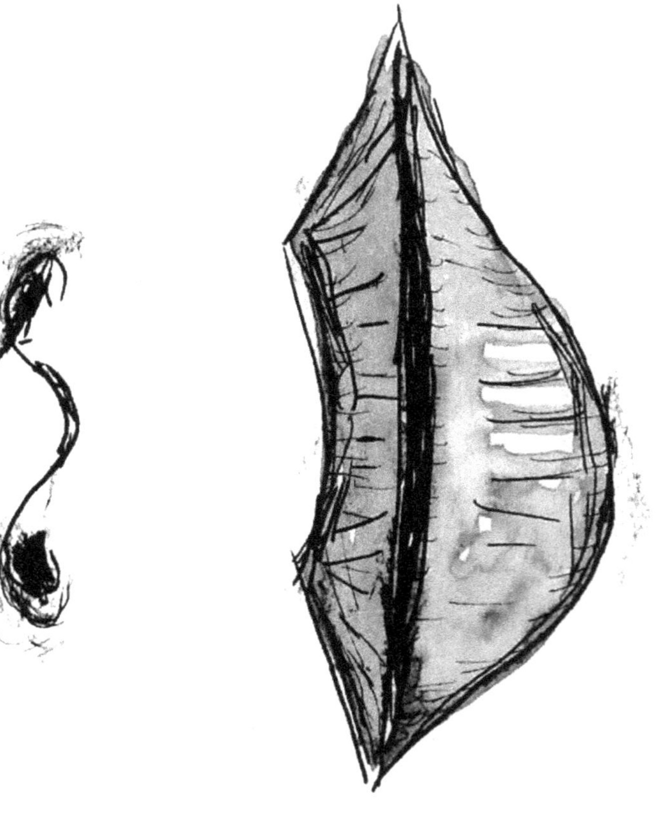

Mind

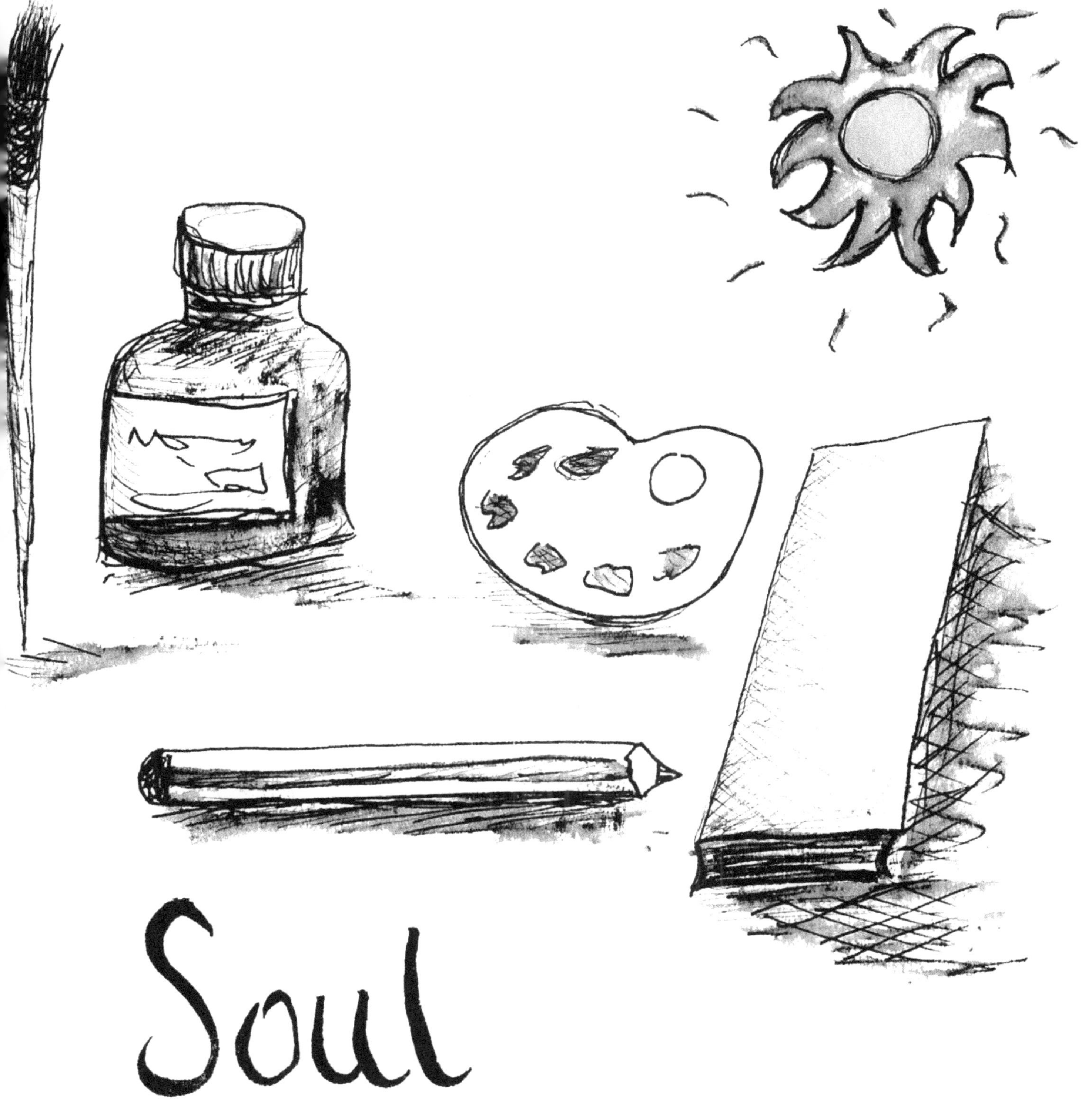

Soul

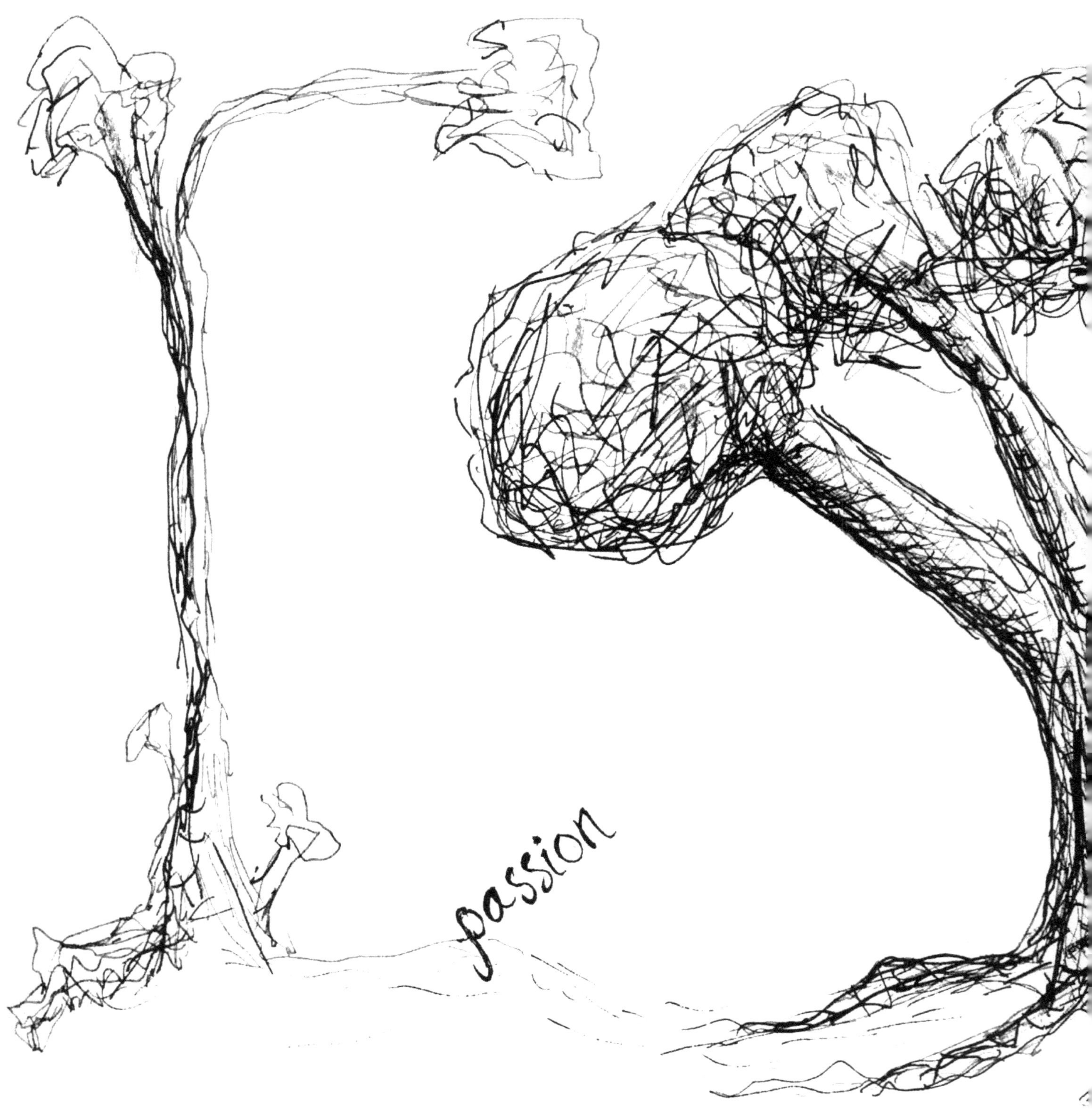
passion

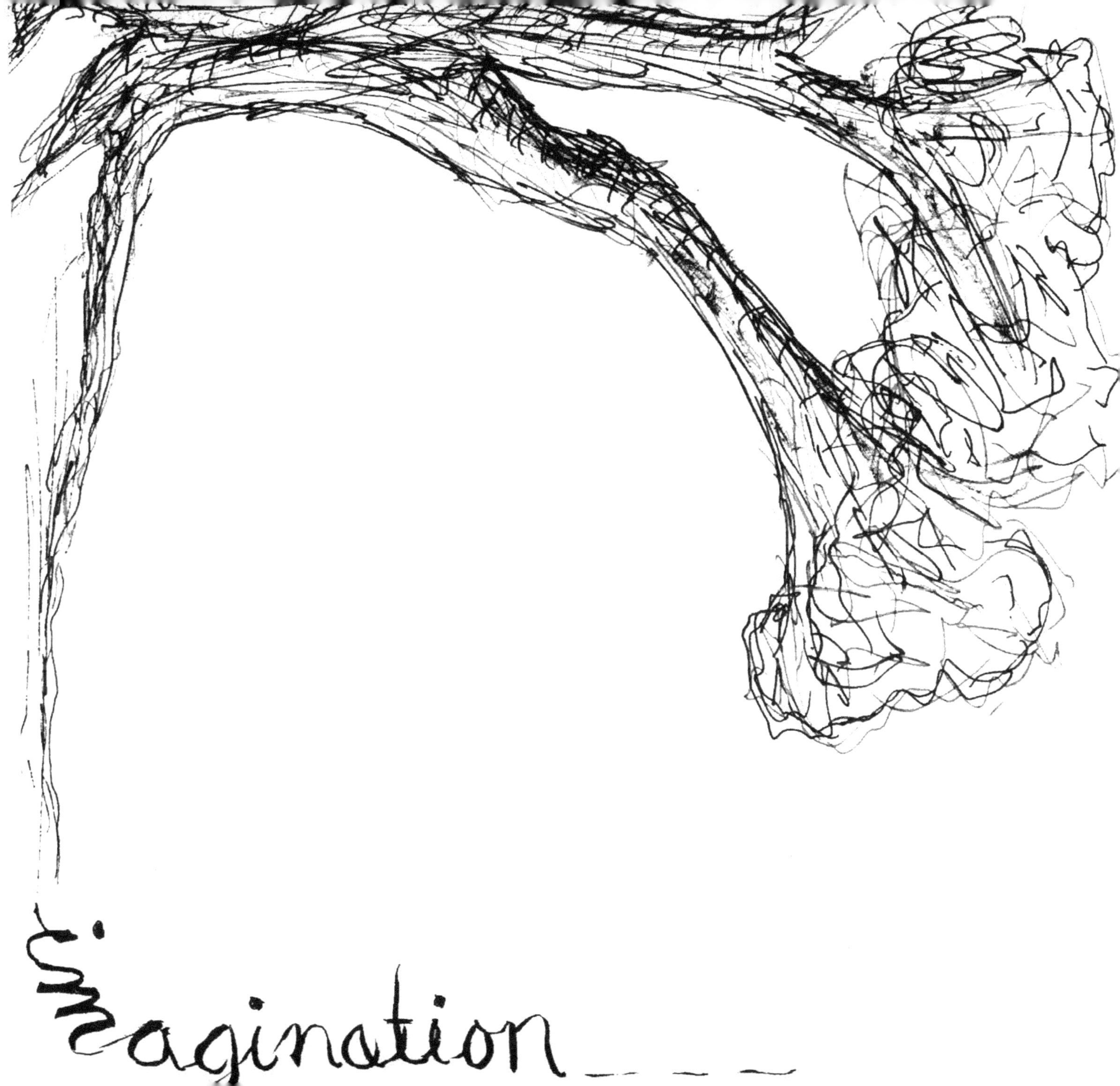
imagination

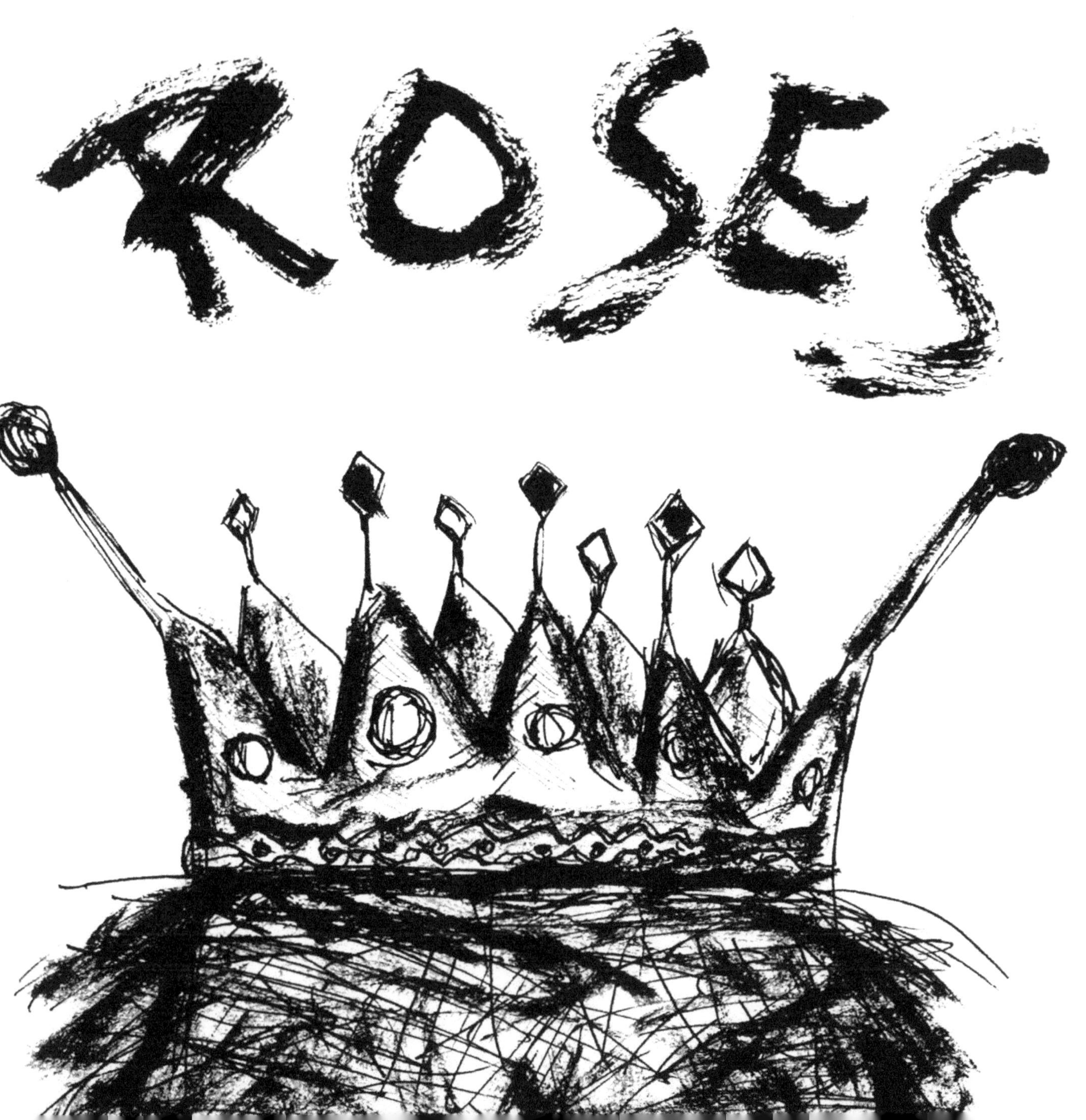

ROSES

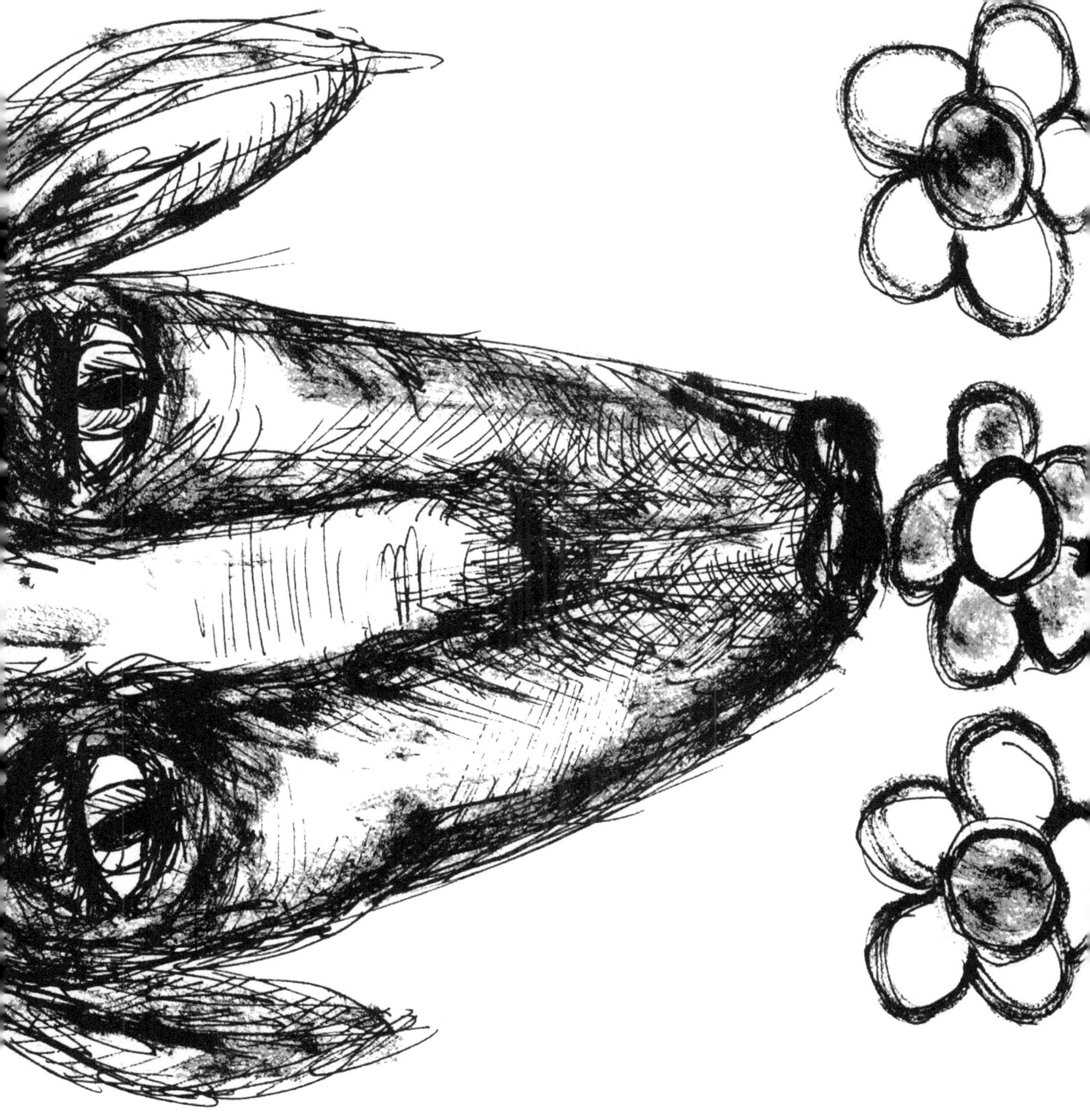

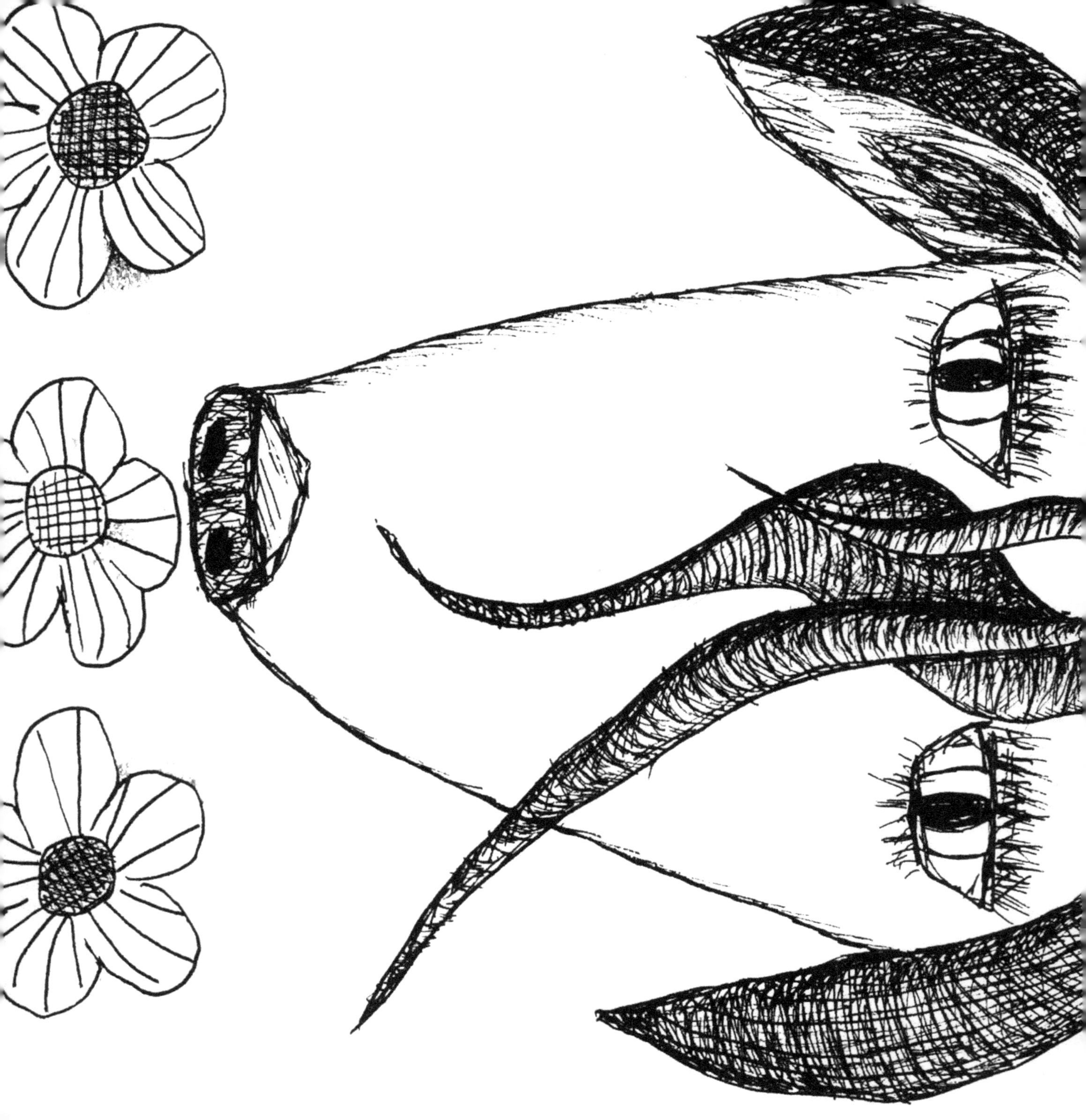

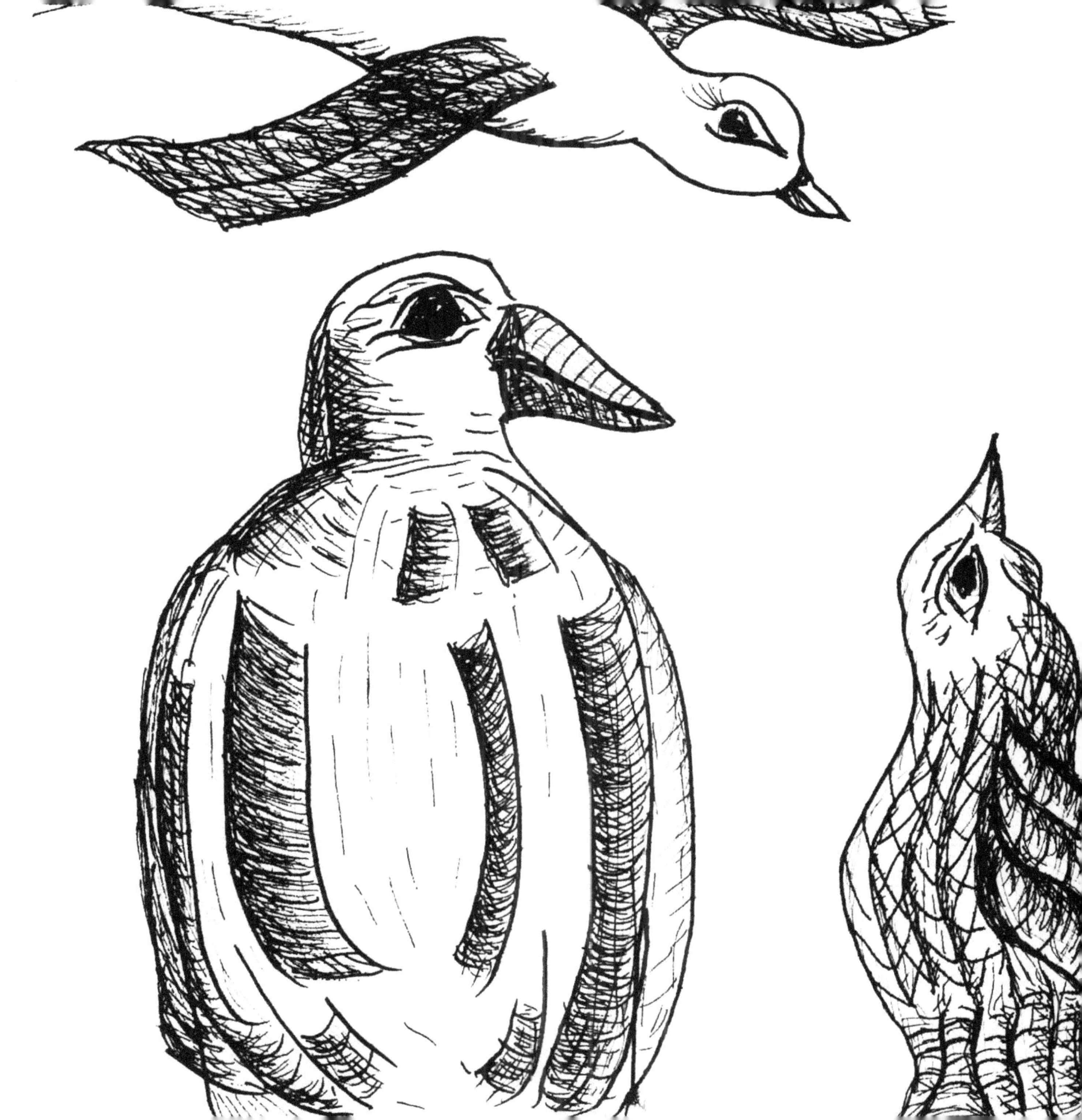

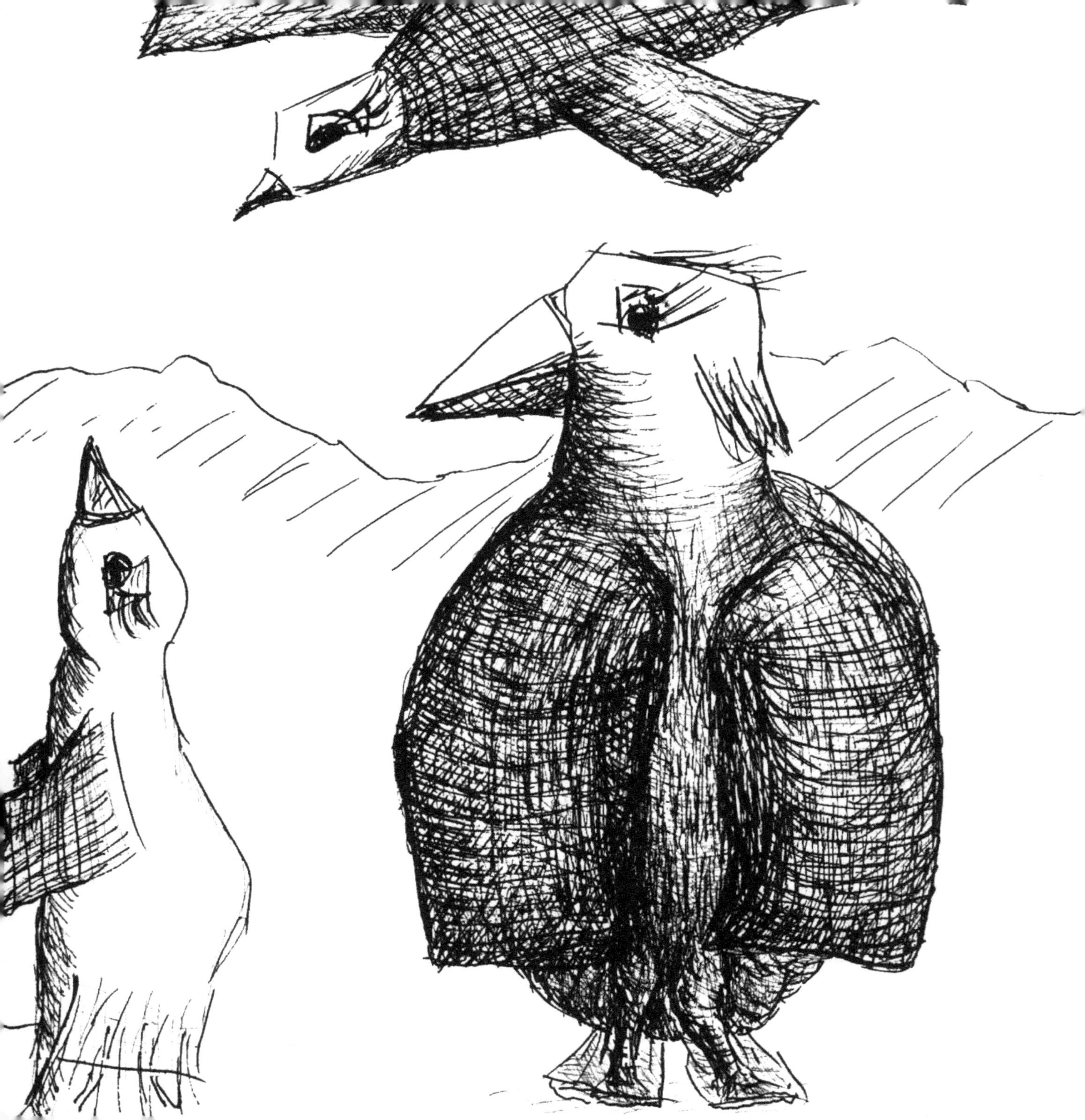

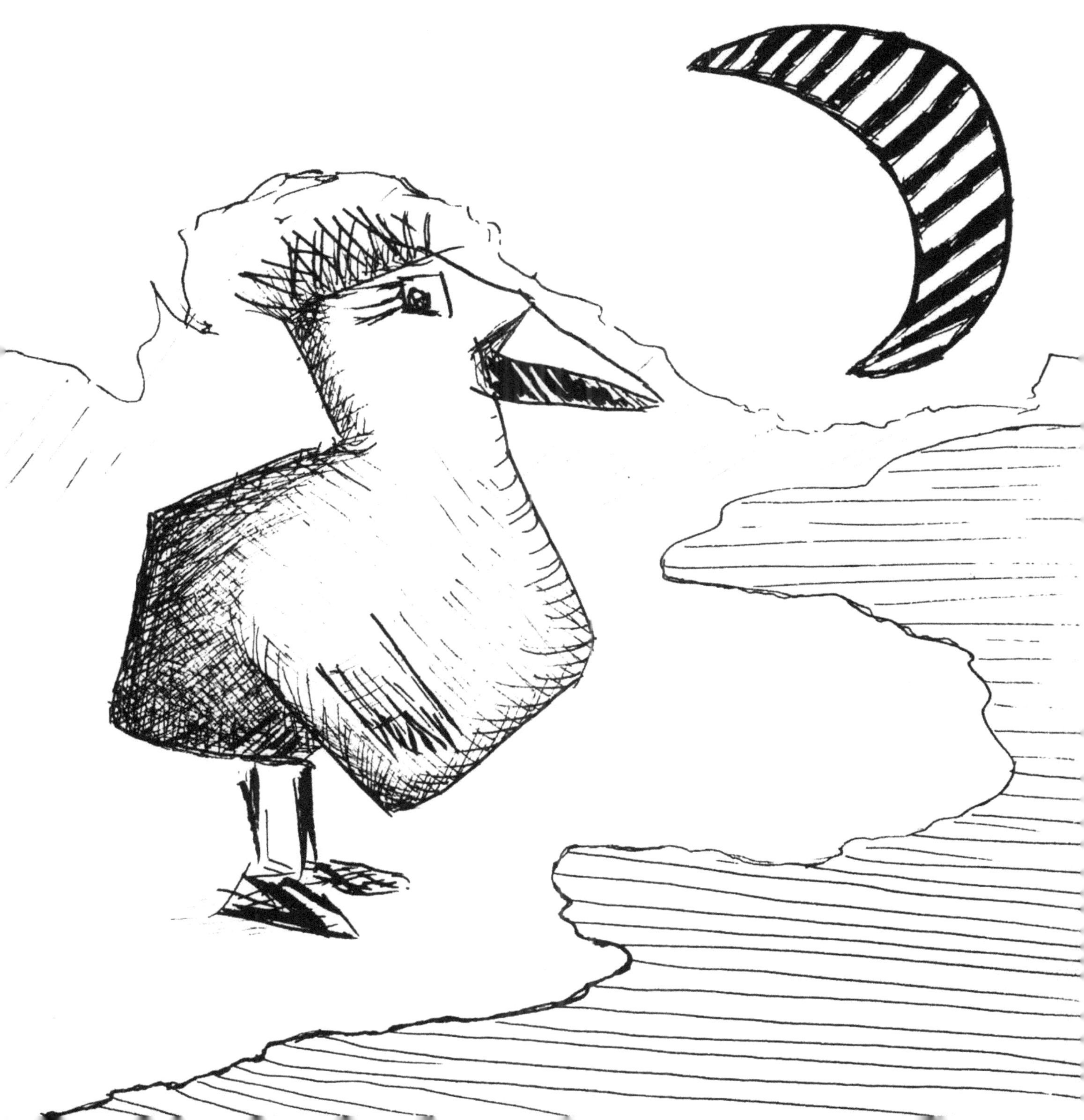

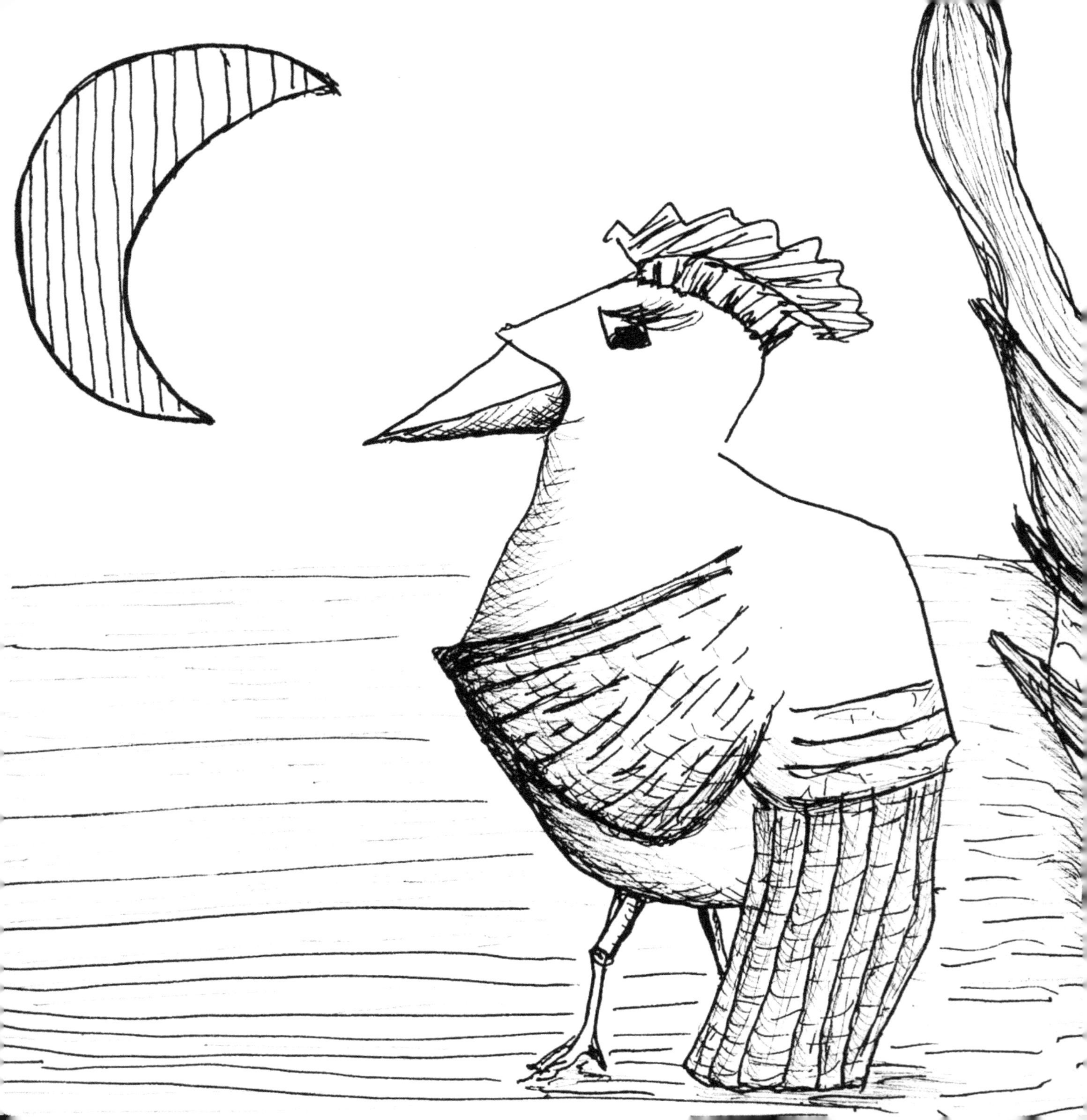

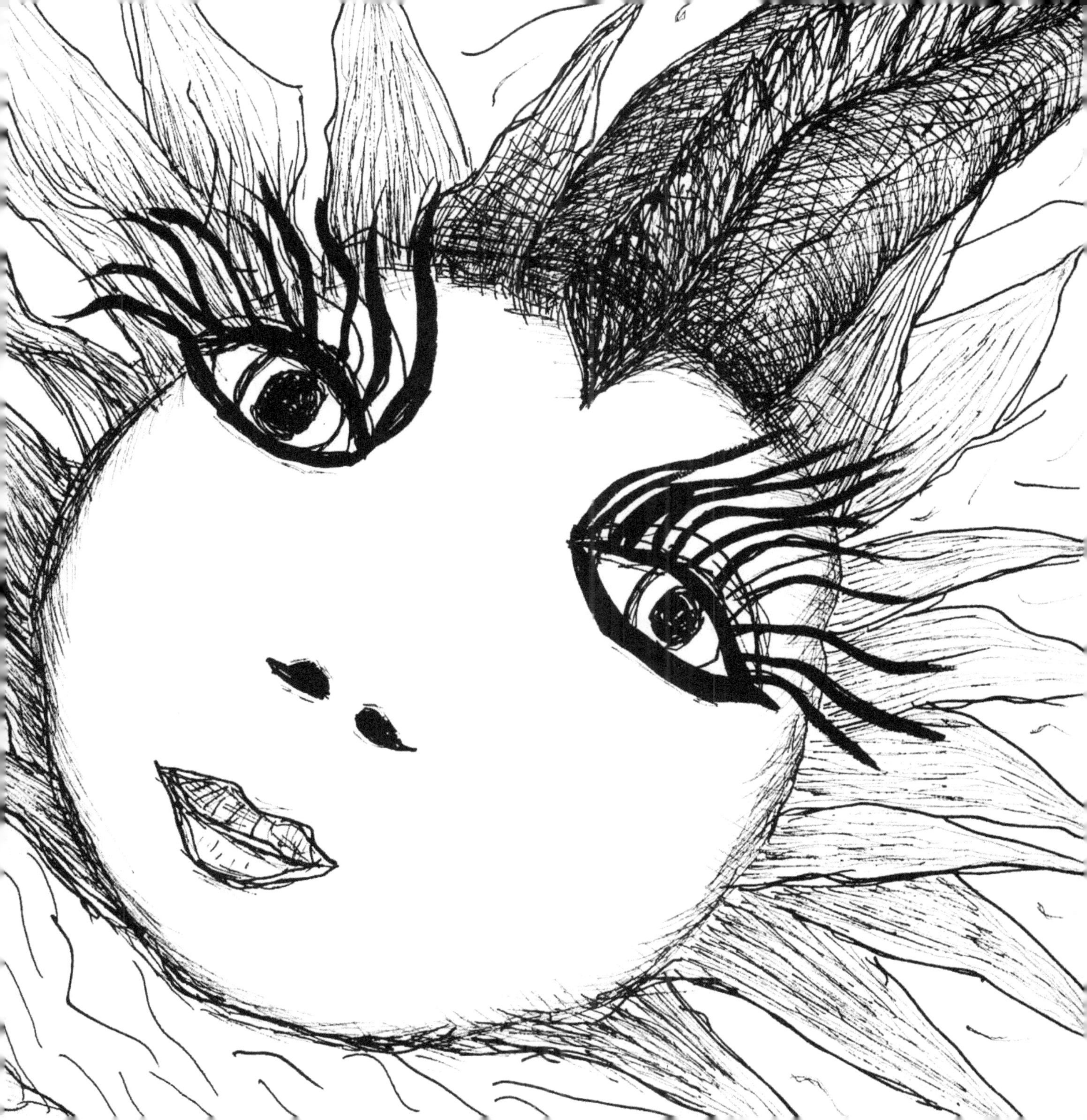

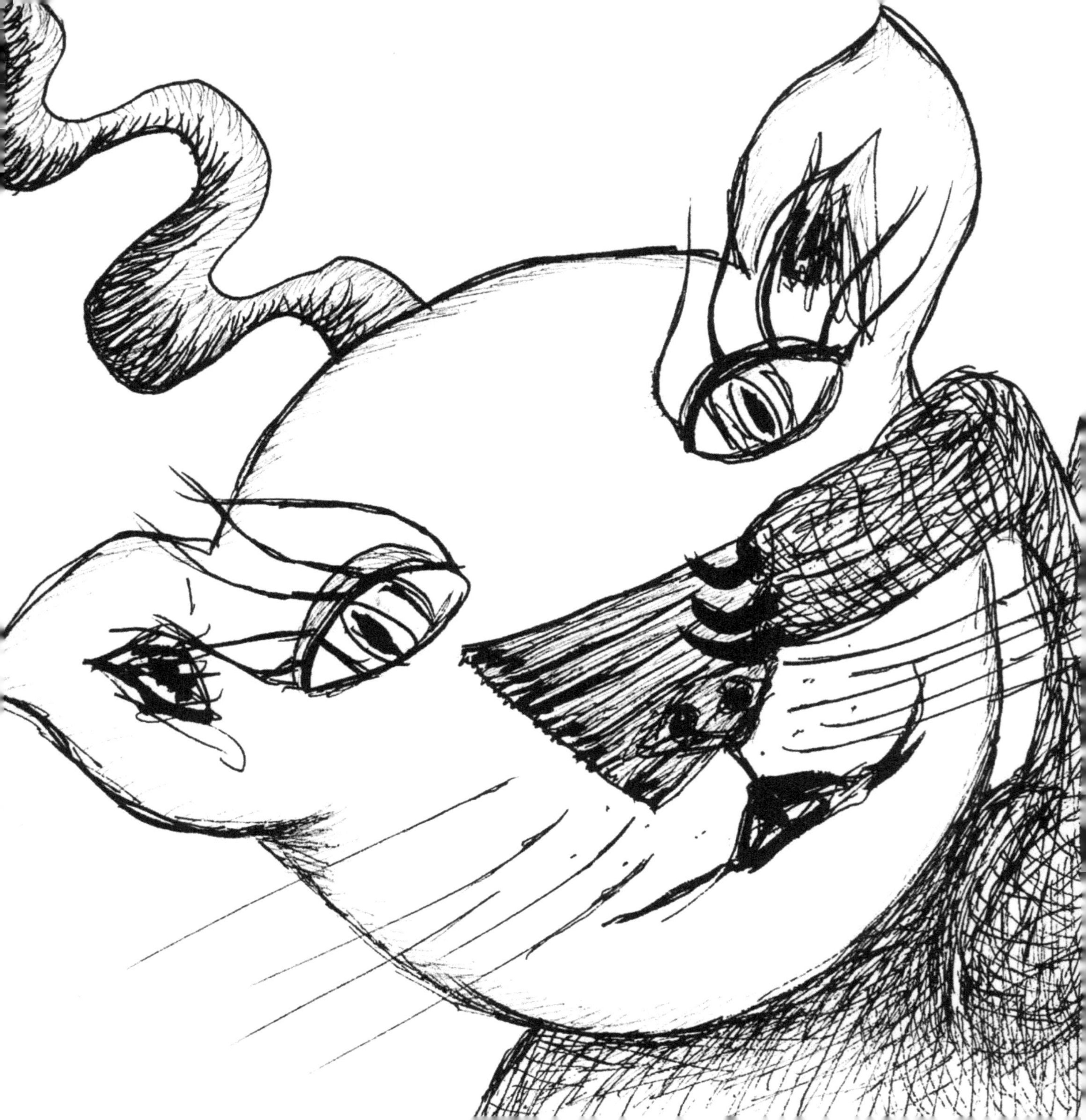

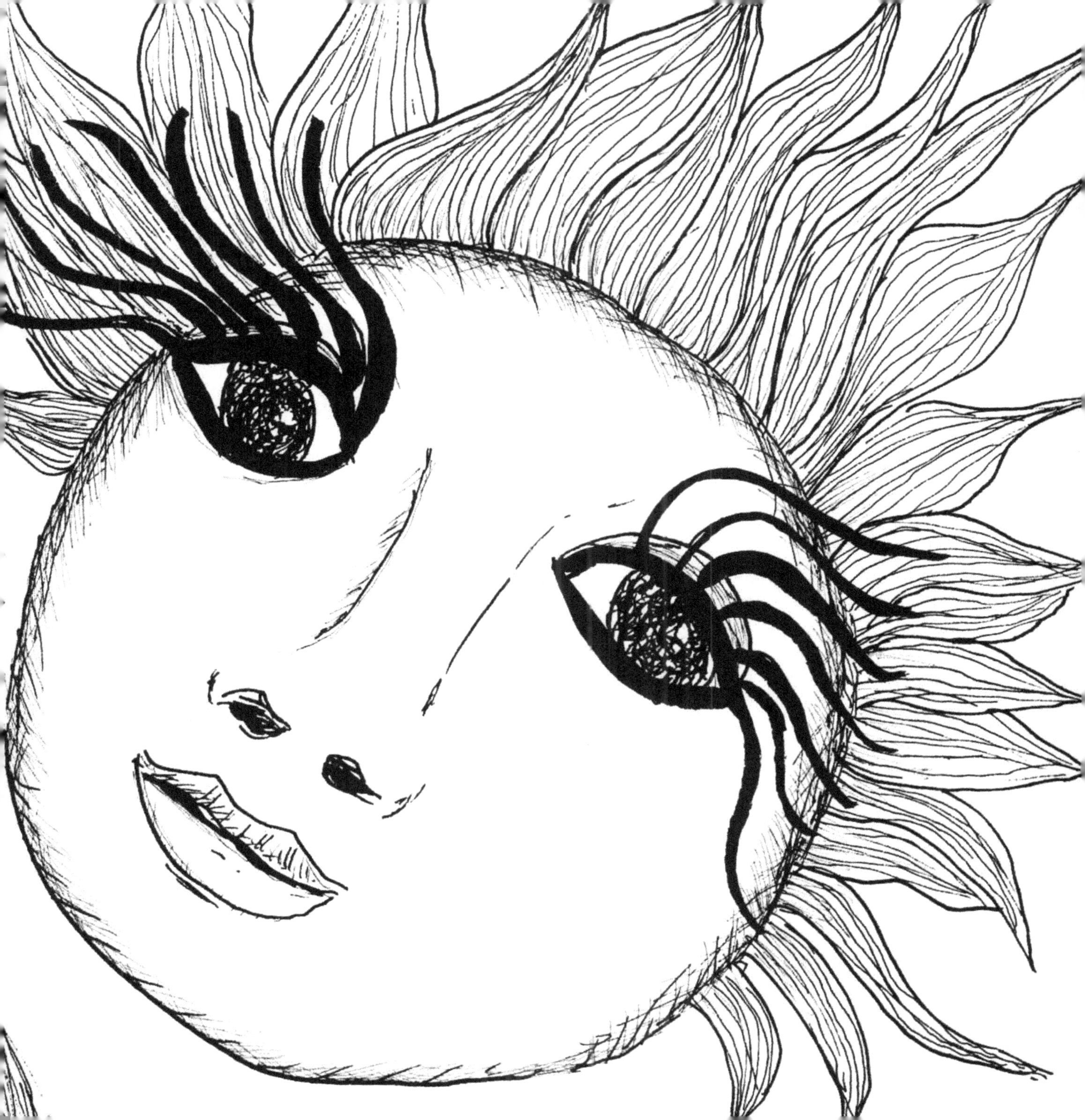

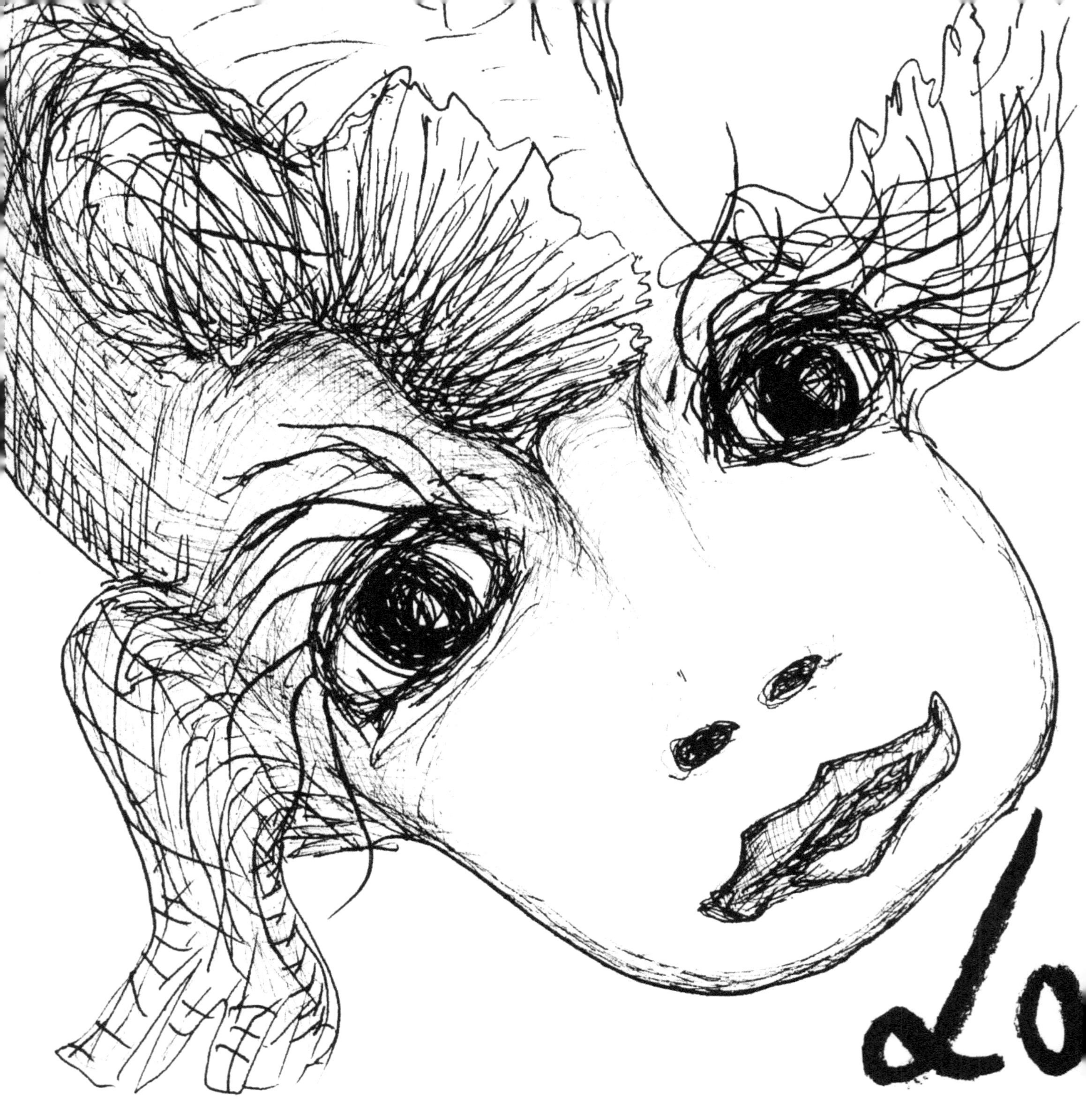

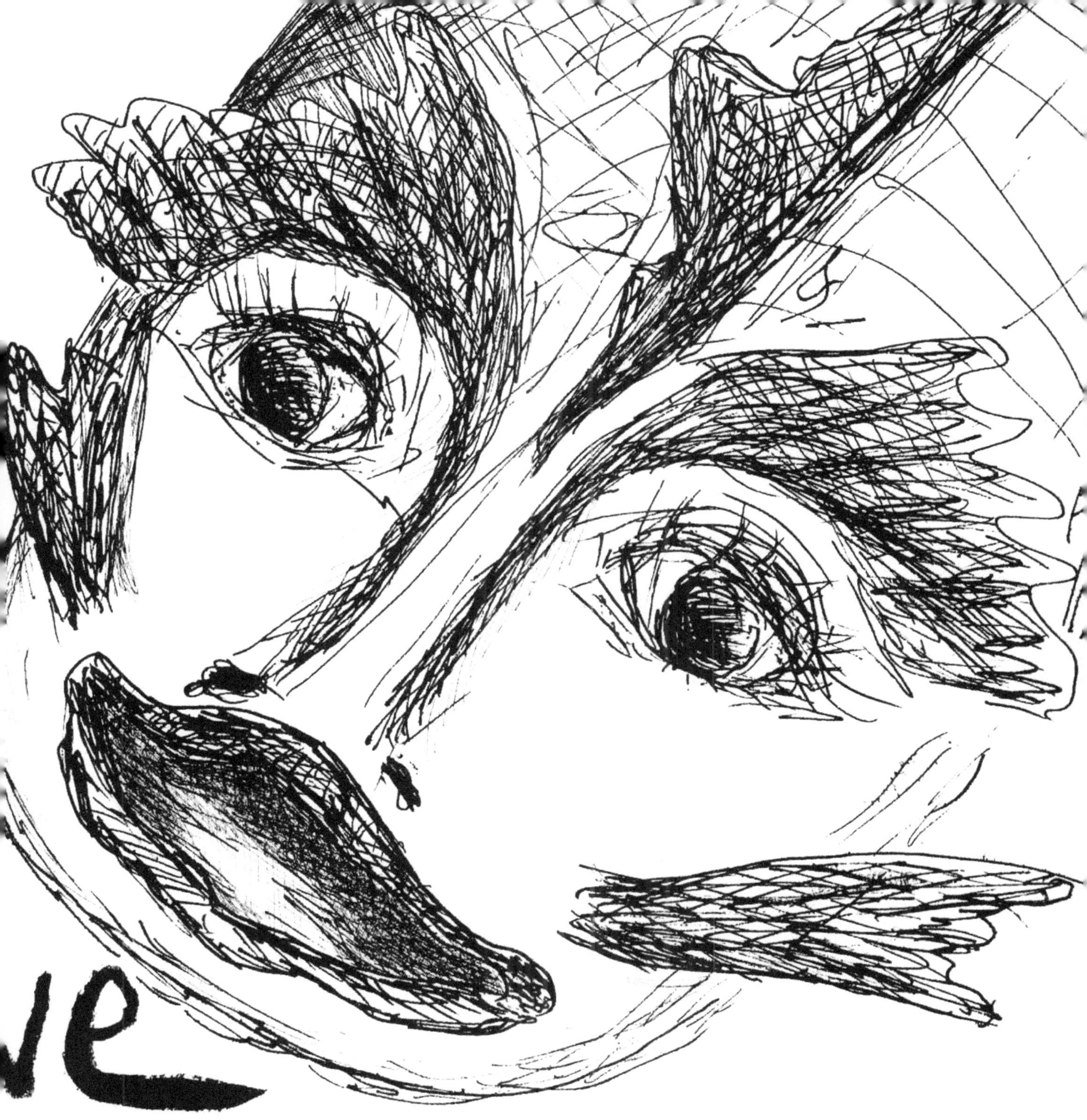

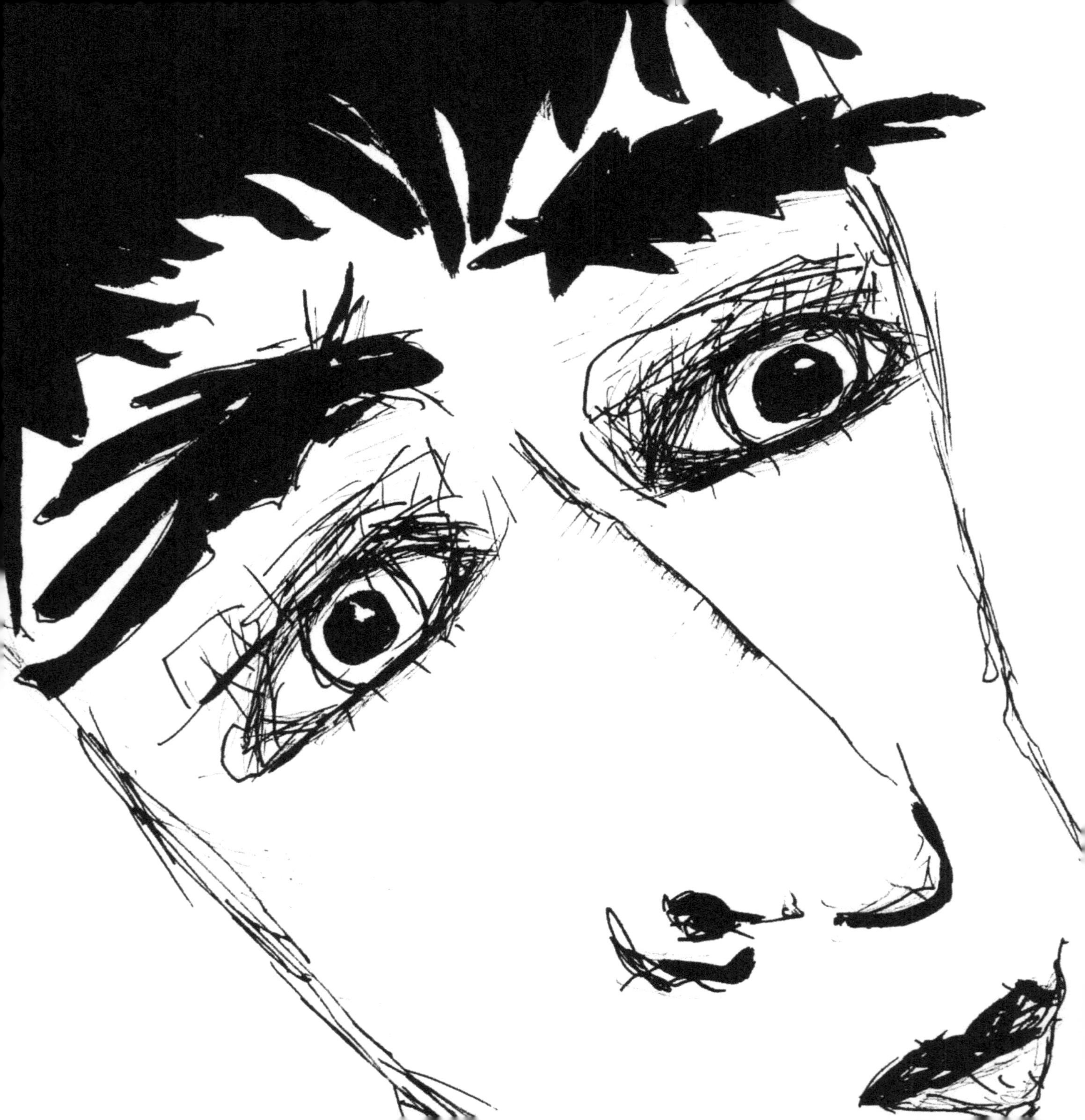

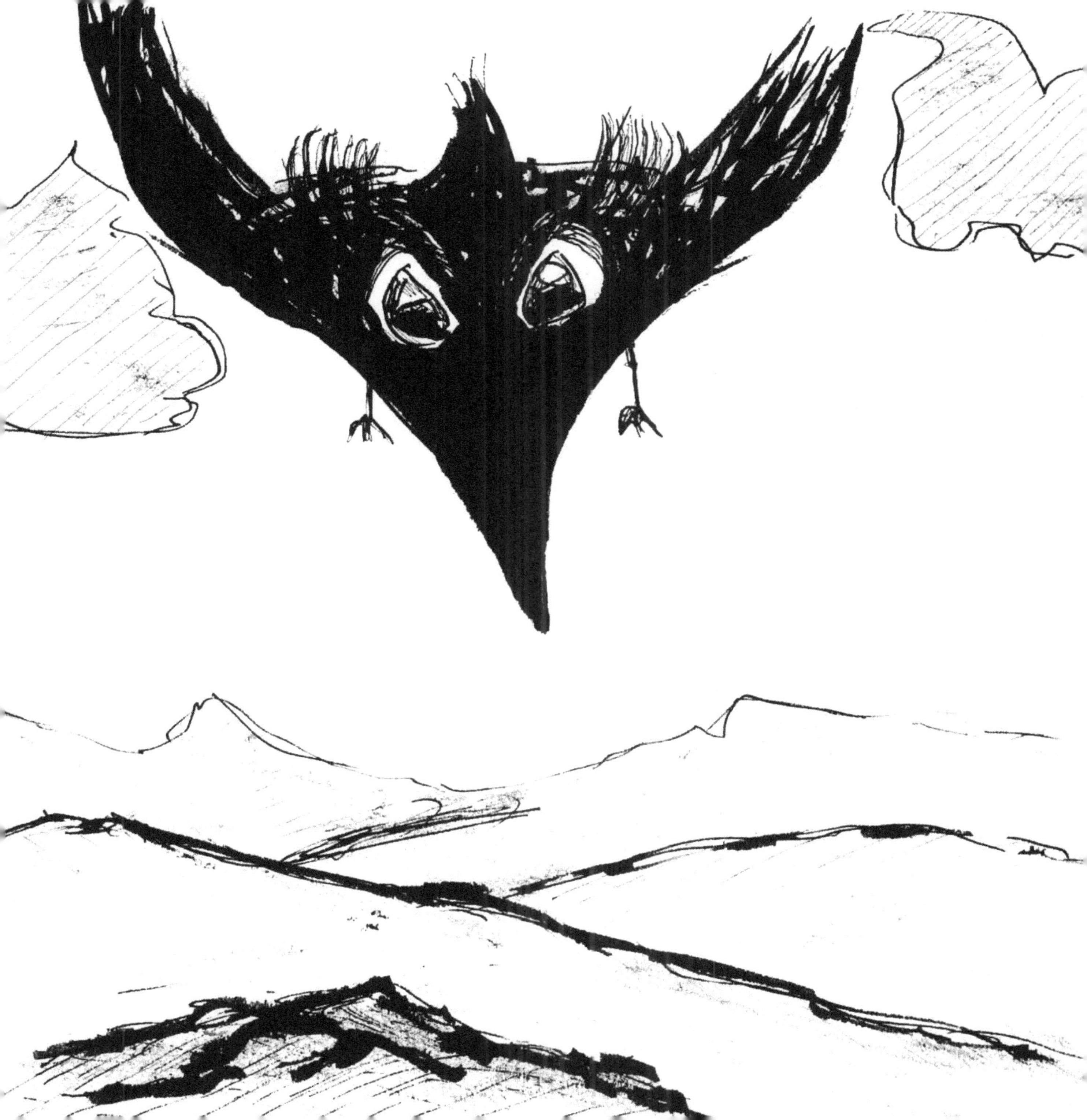

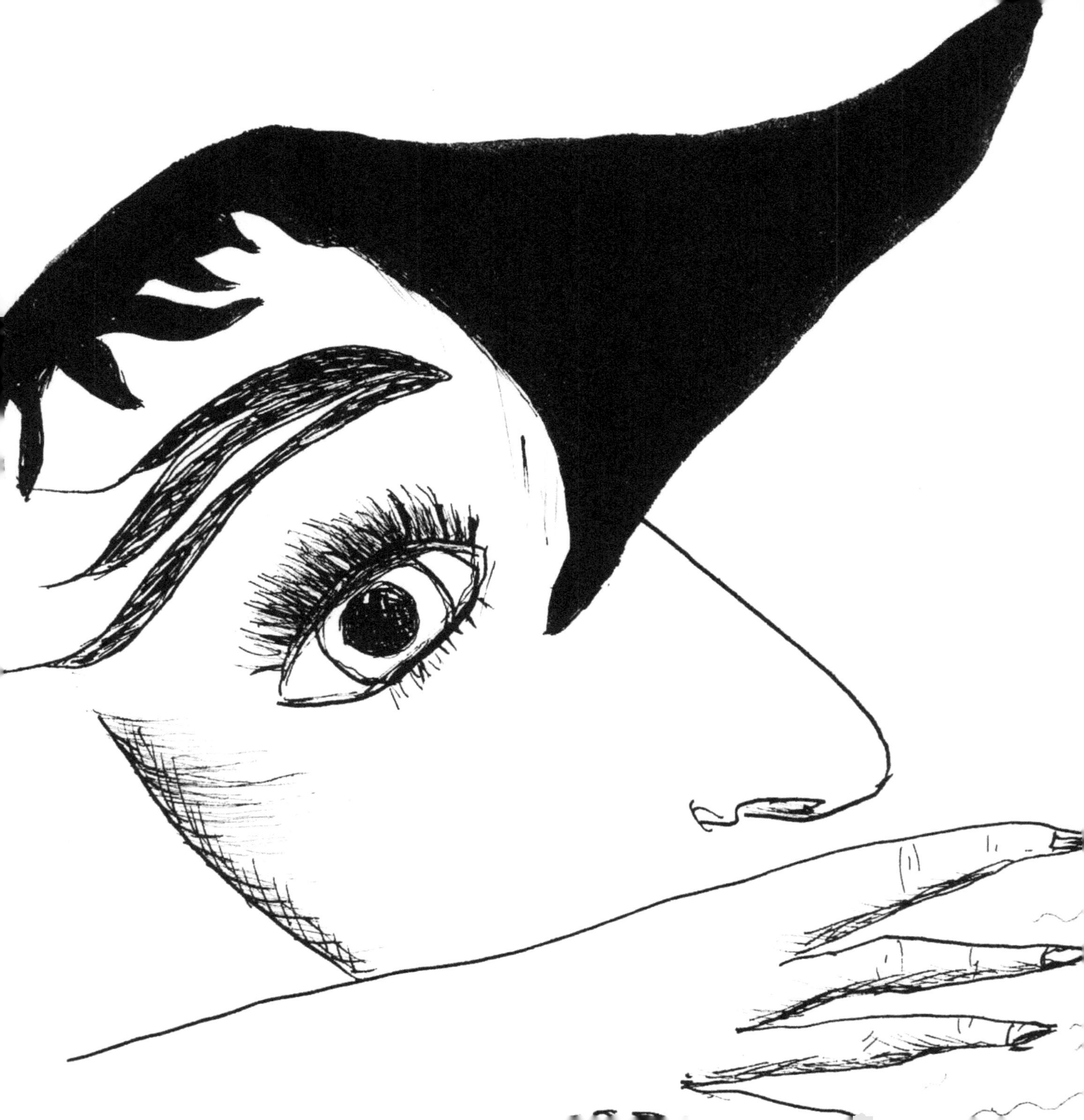

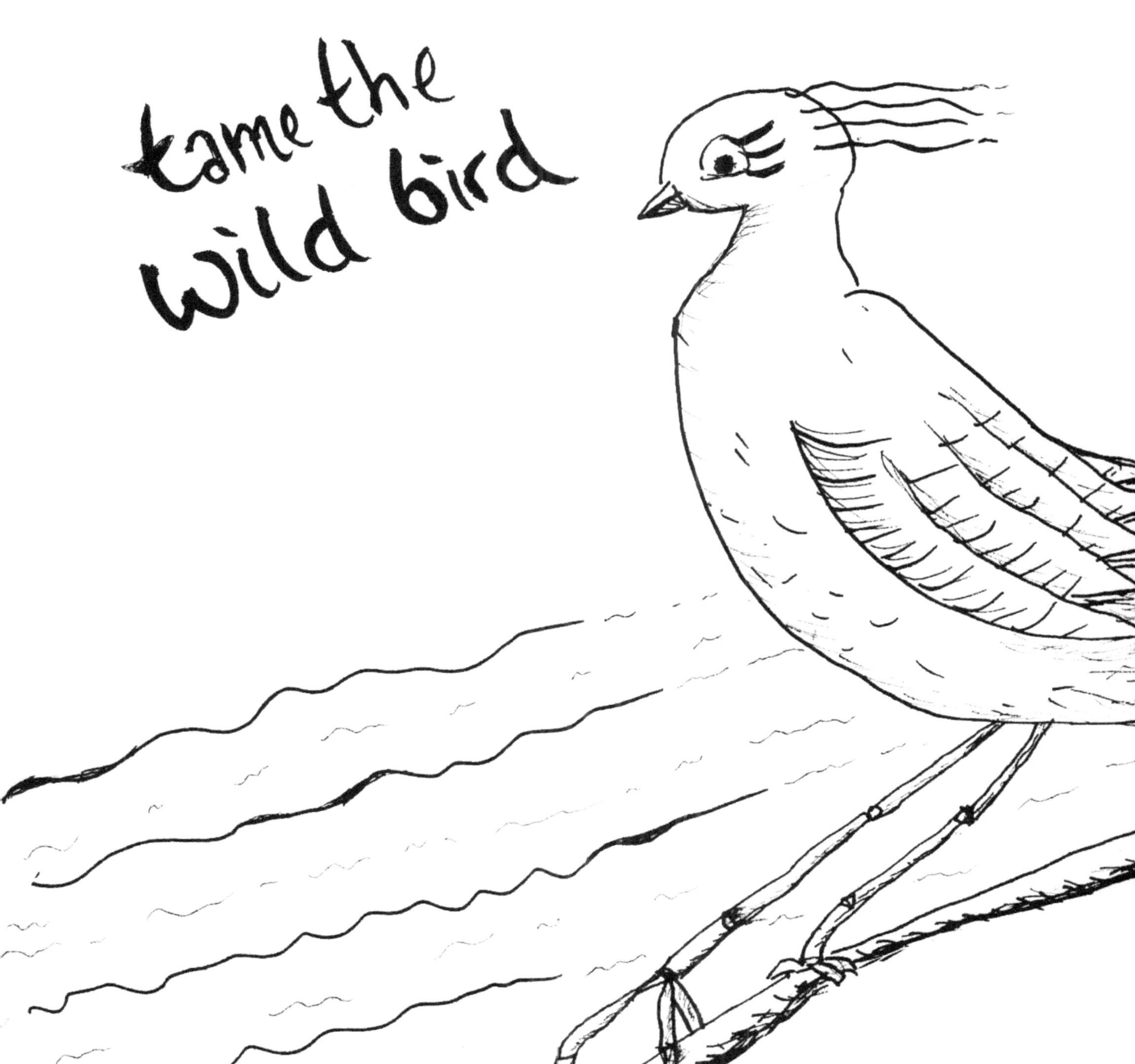
tame the
wild bird

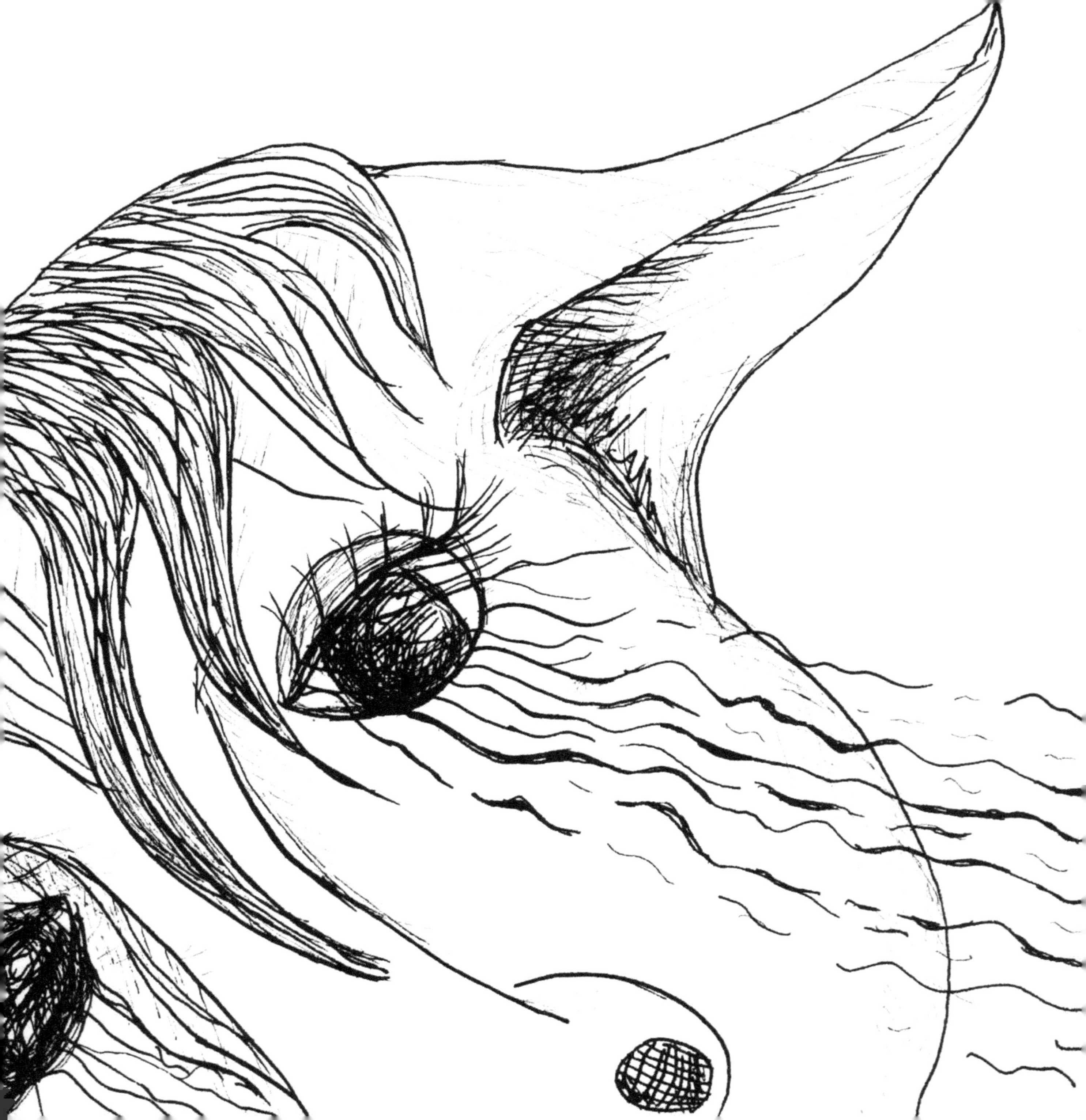

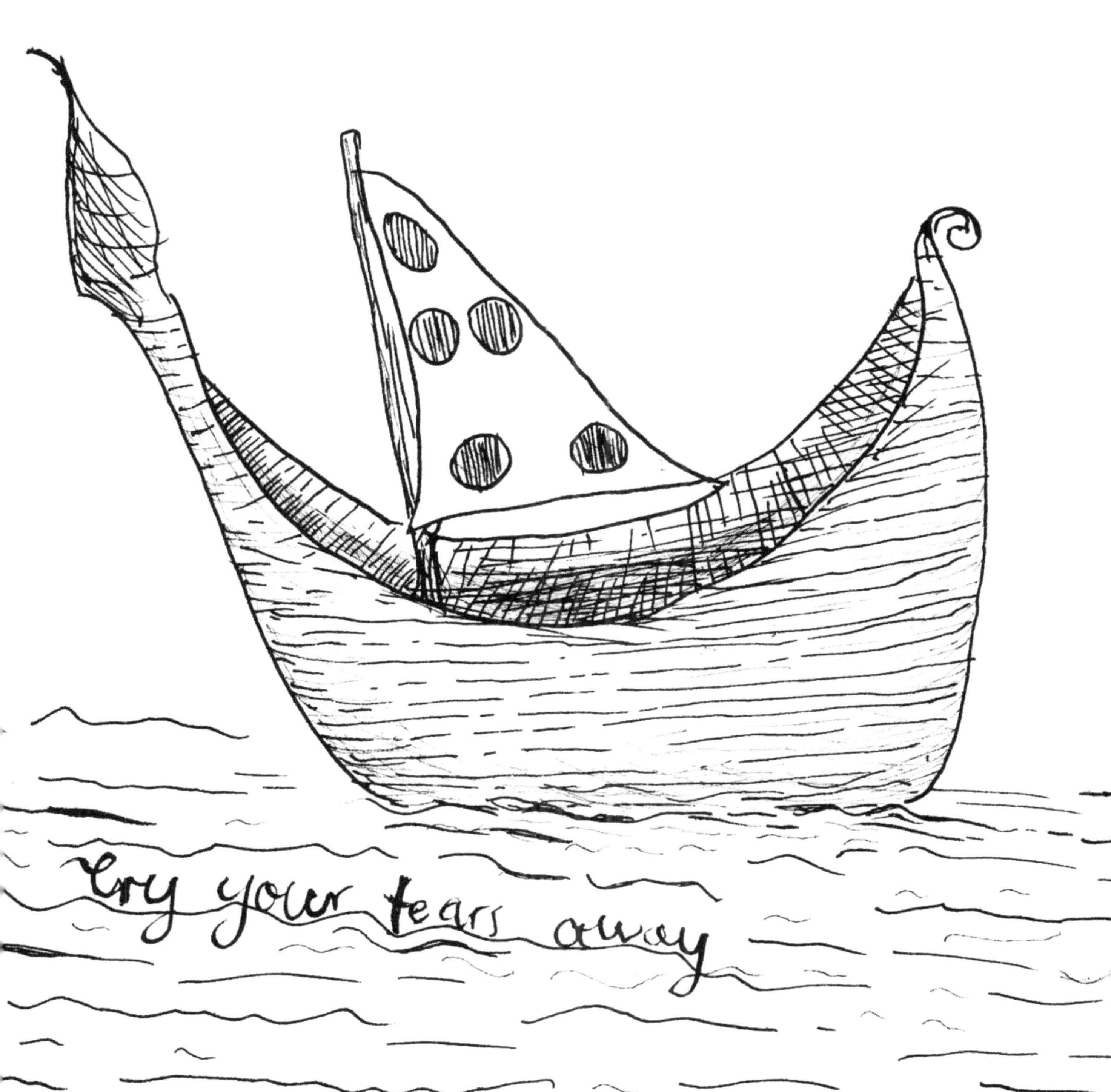

cry your tears away

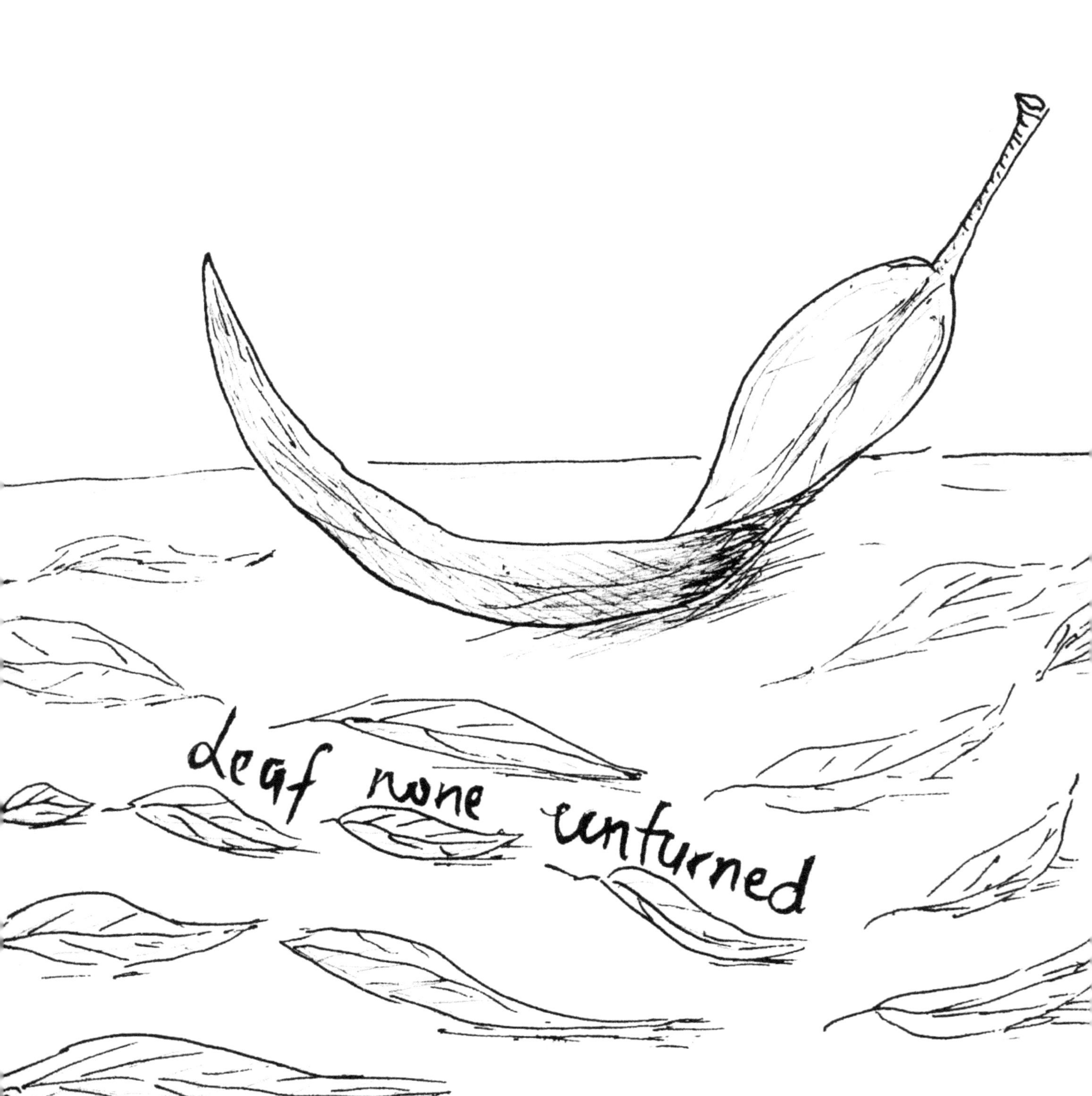
leaf none unturned

call off the ocean

the ocean   ocean   tide

sand, sun, ocean, salt, tides

tide comes in

comes in tide goes out

the oceans the tide goes out, tide

Sea the tides

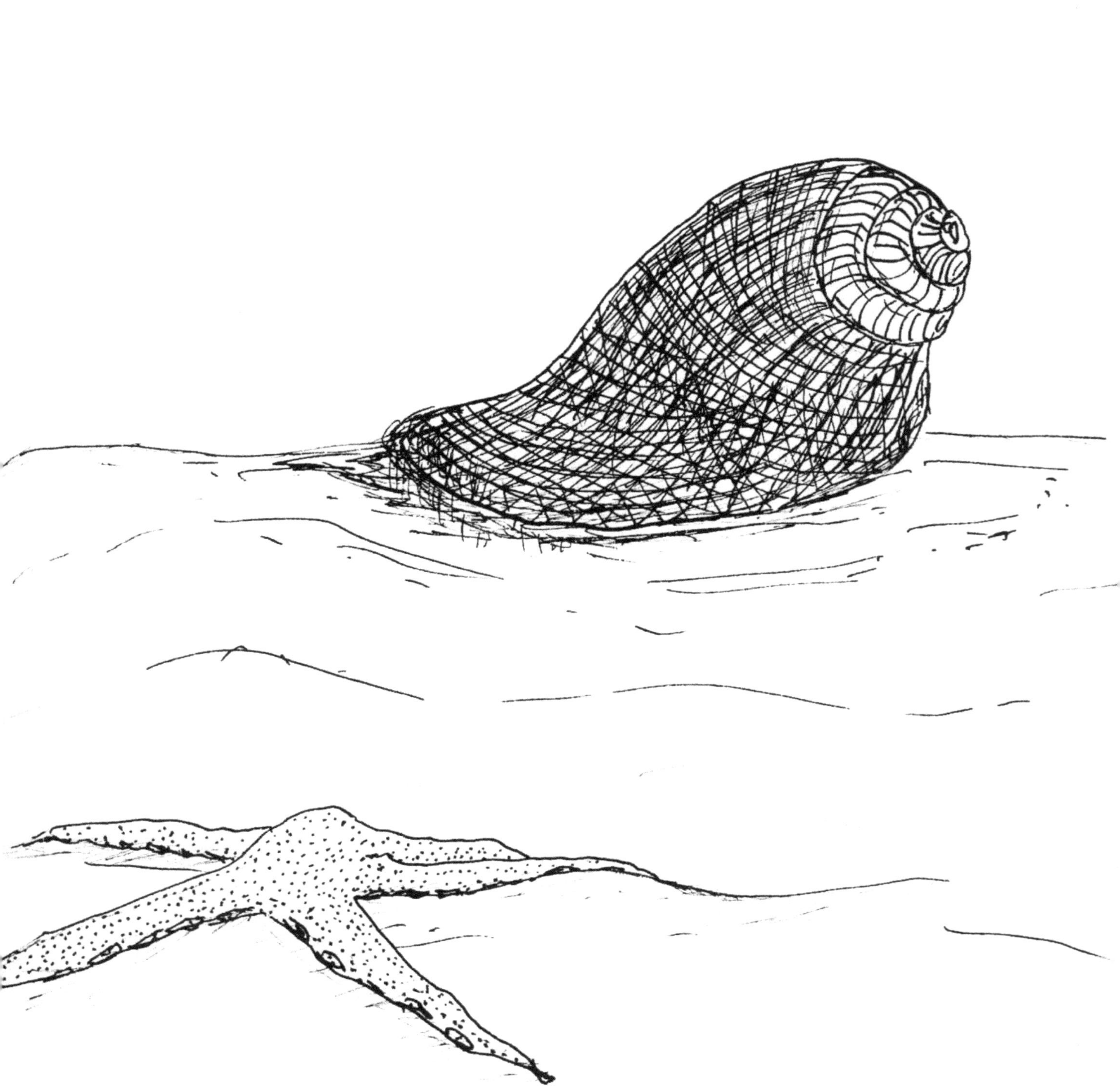

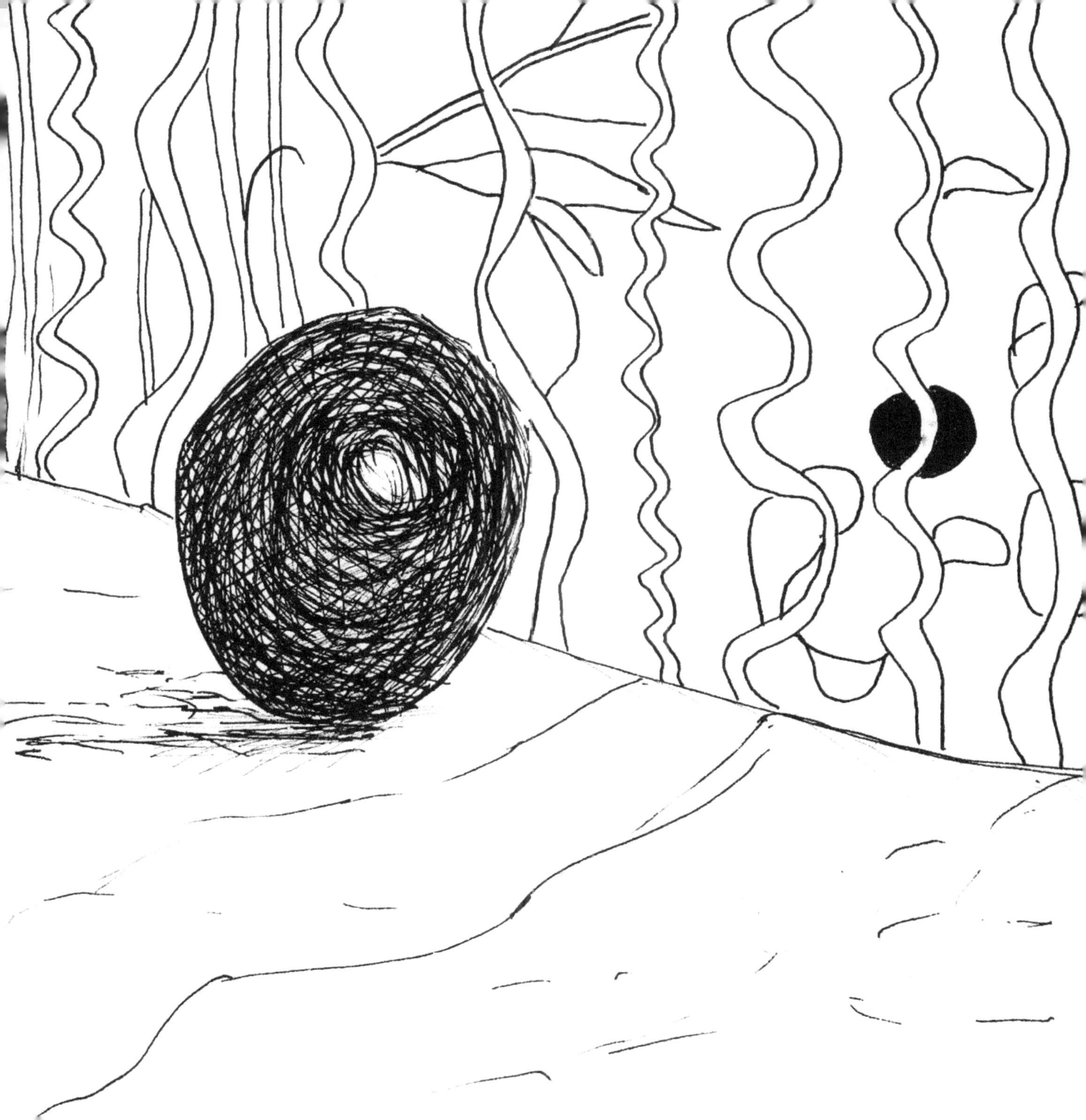

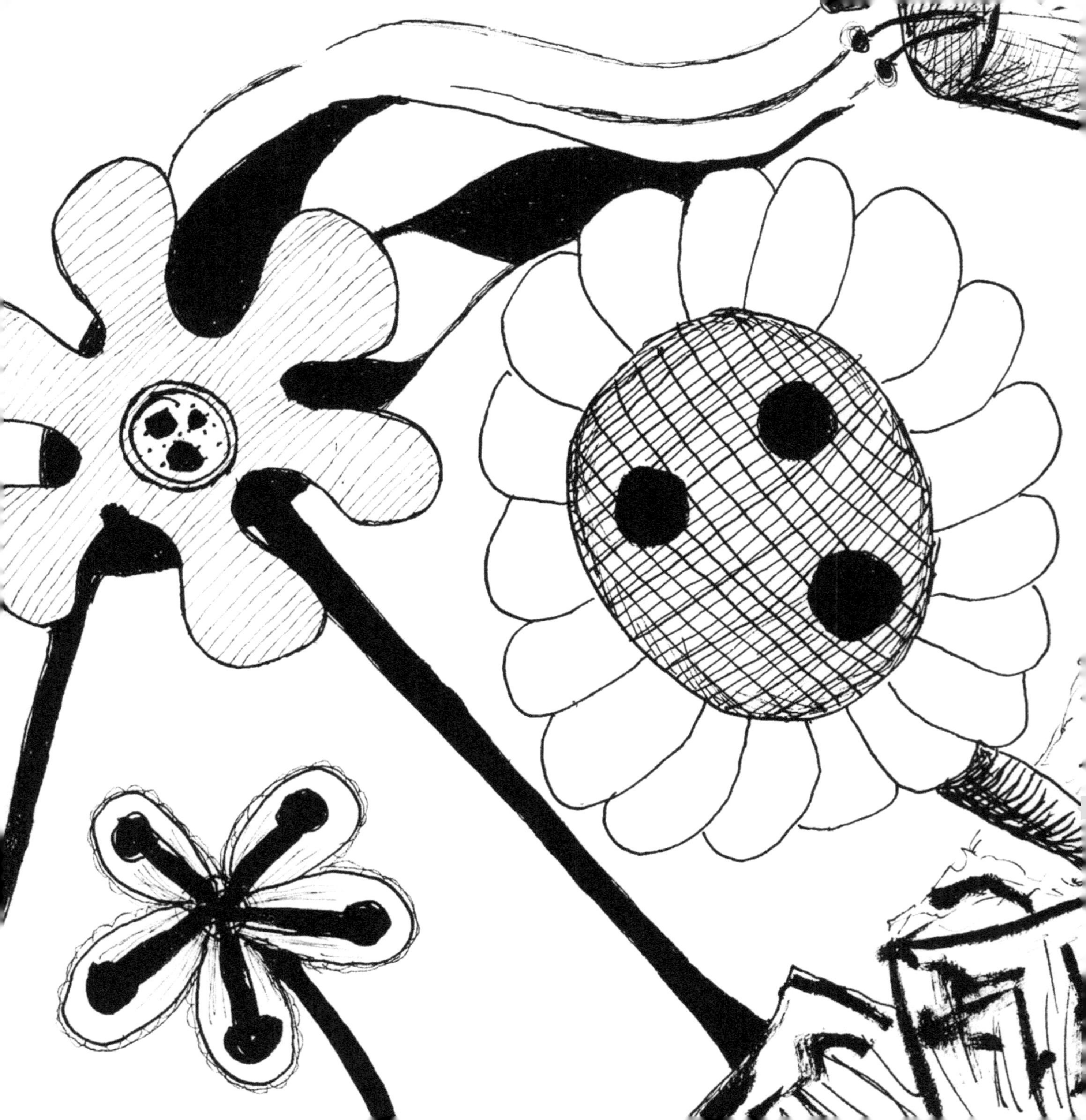

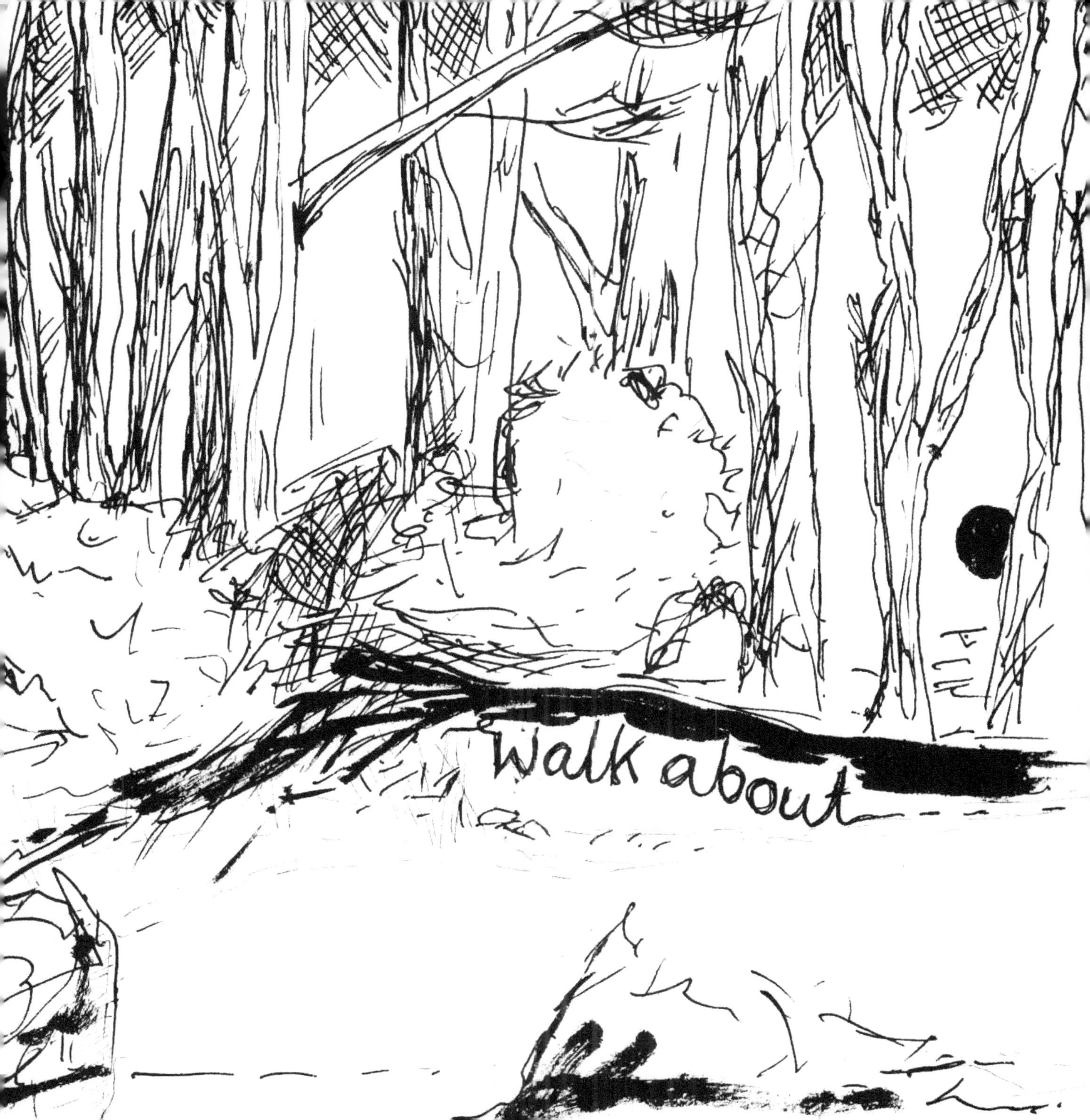
walk about

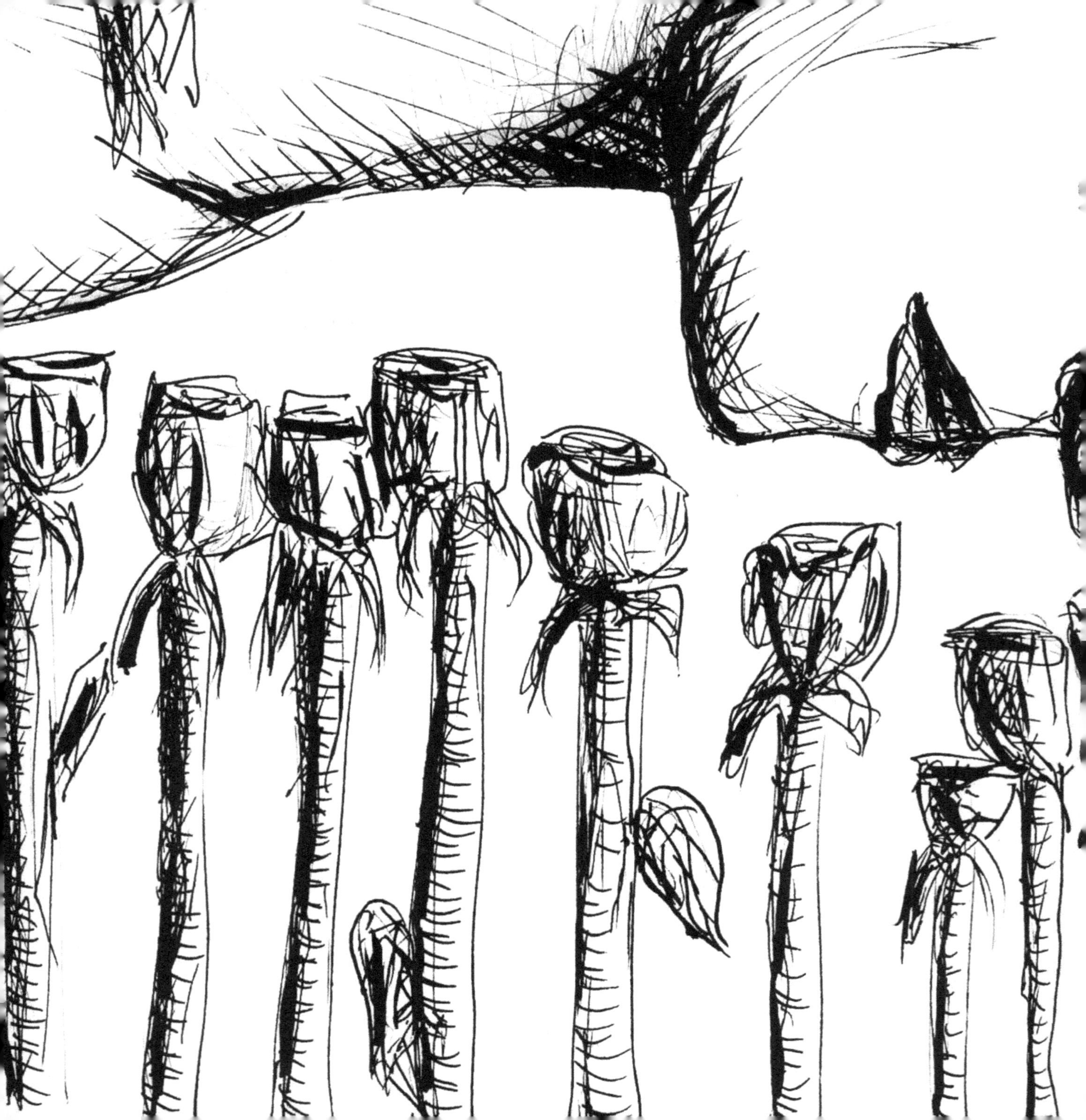

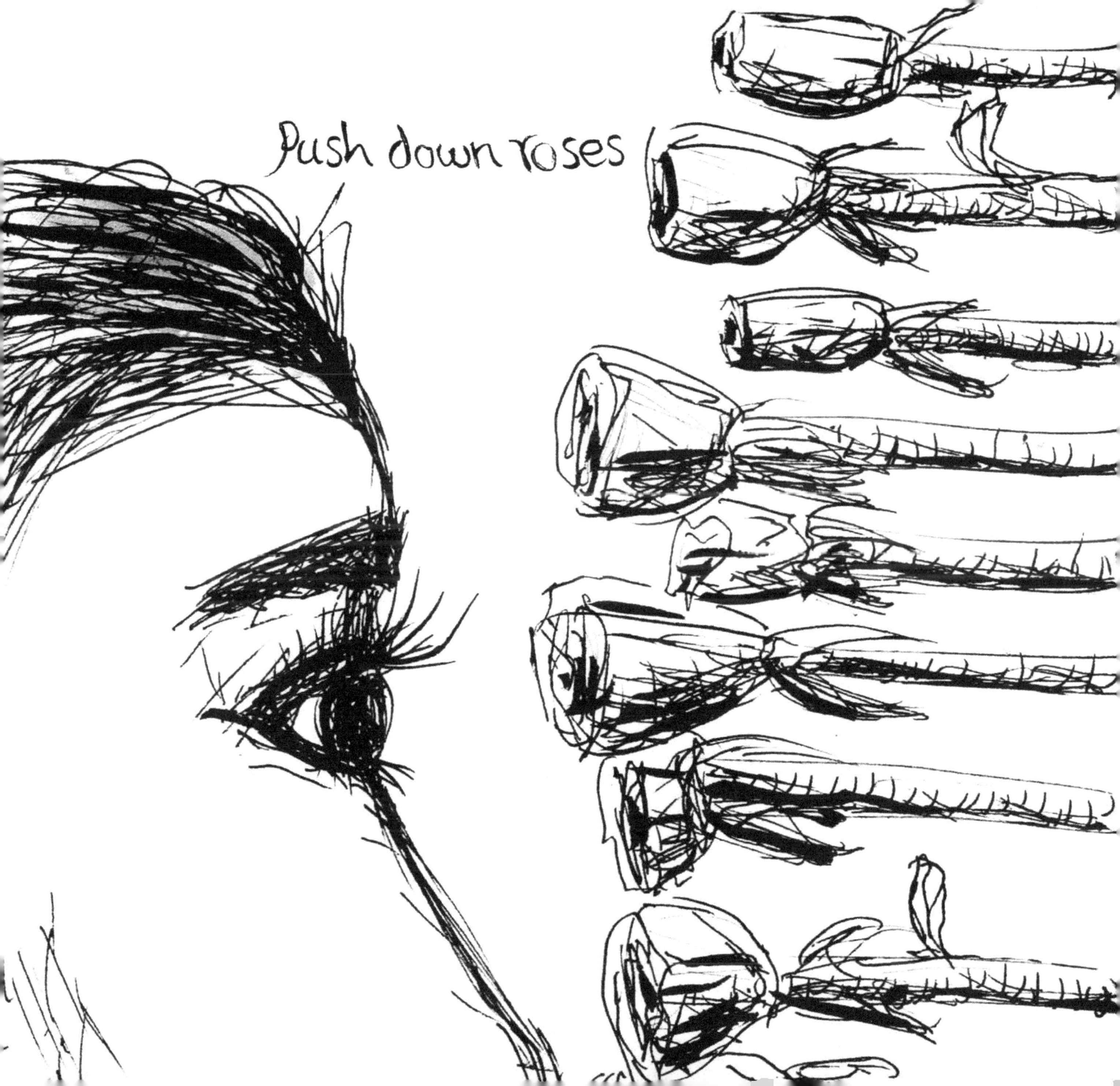
Push down roses

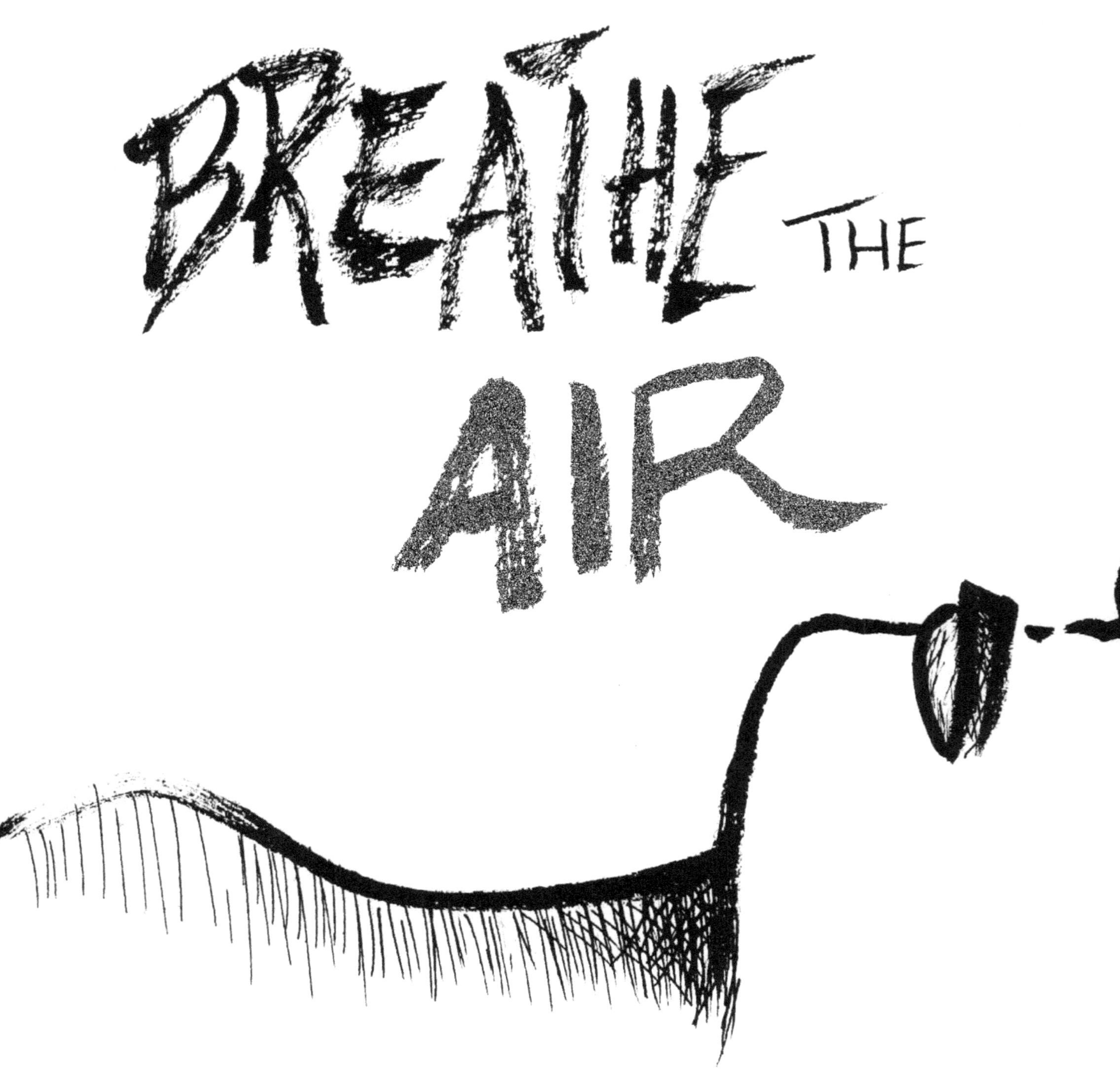
BREATHE THE AIR

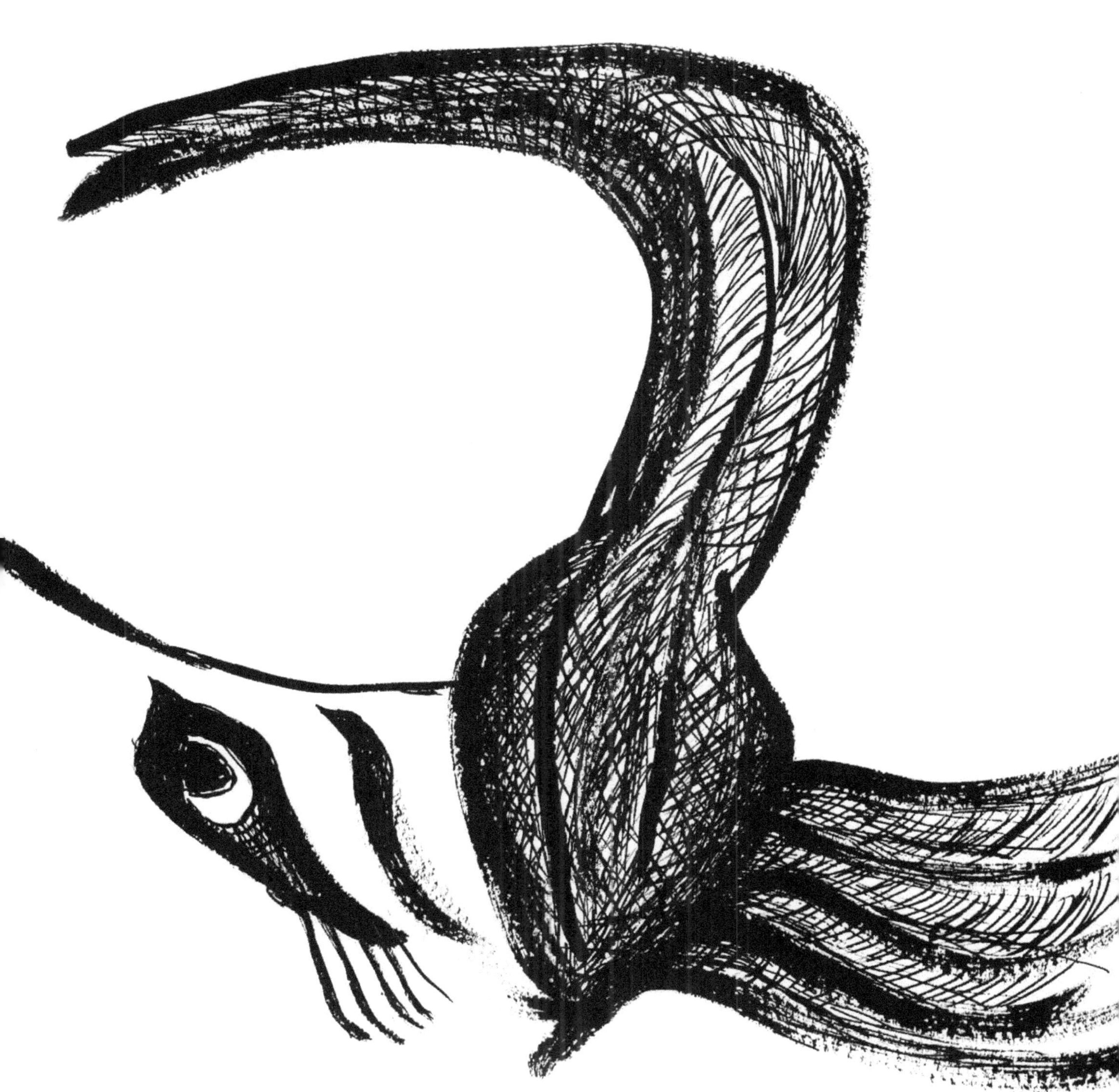

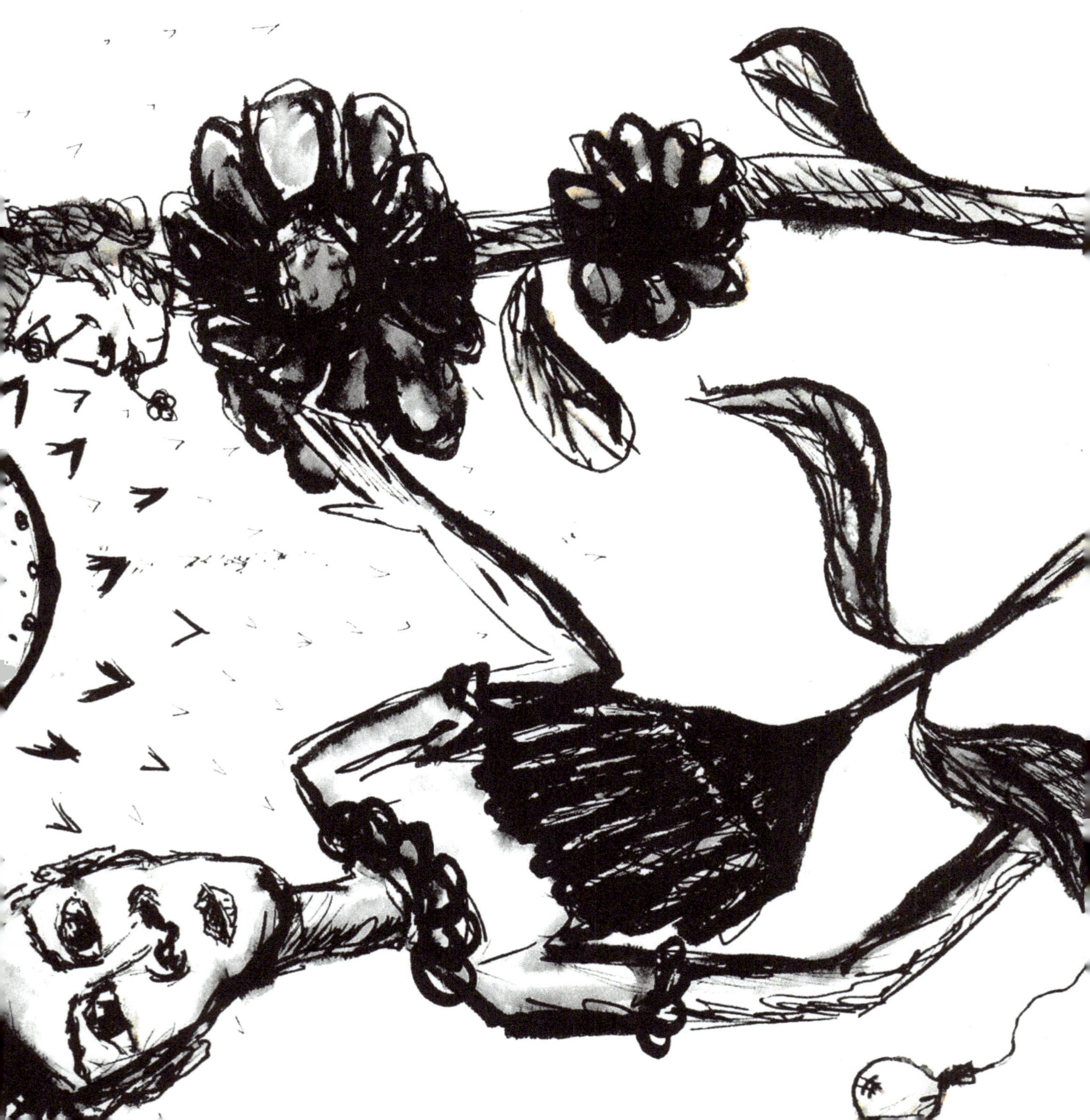

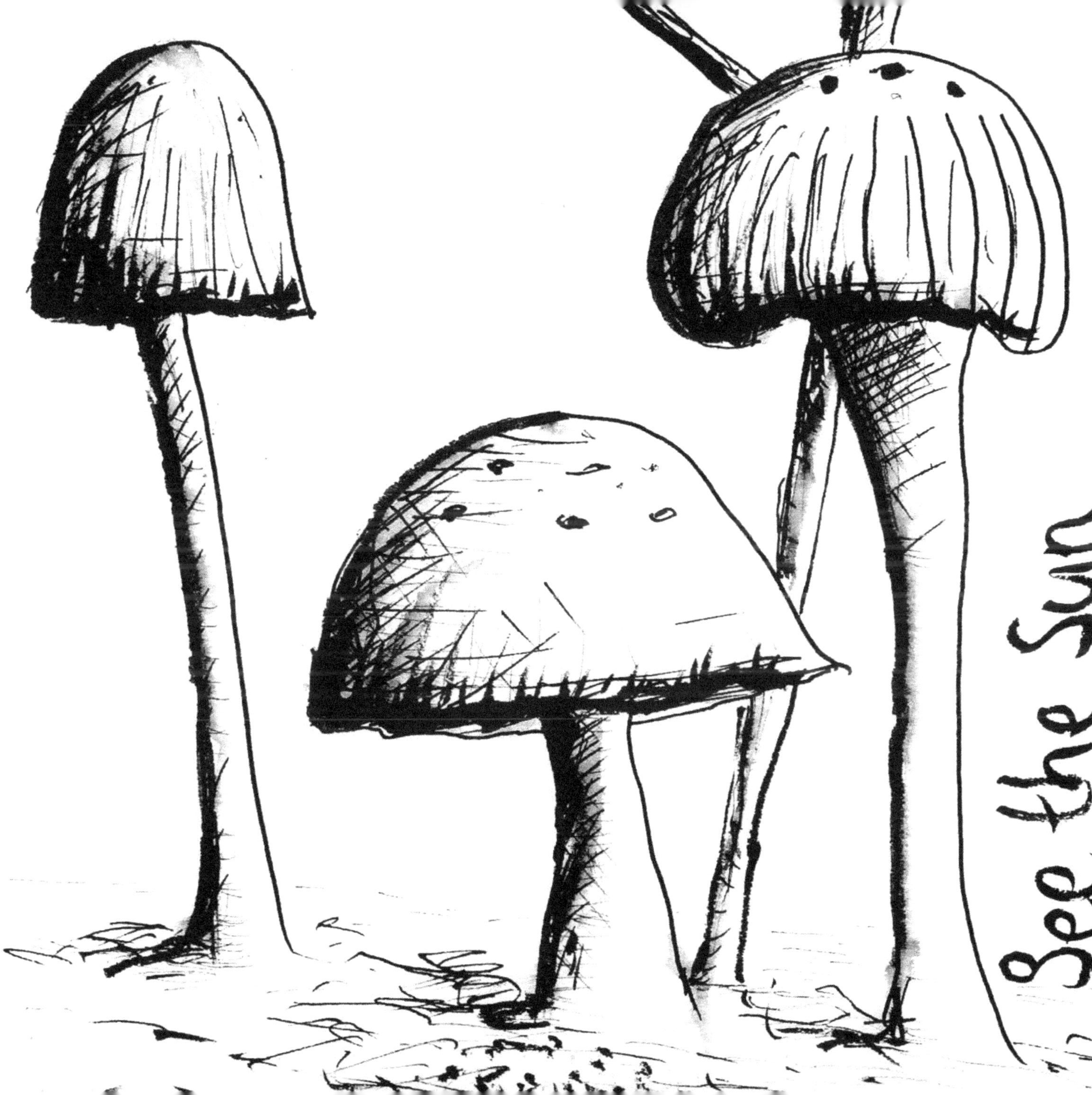
See the Sun

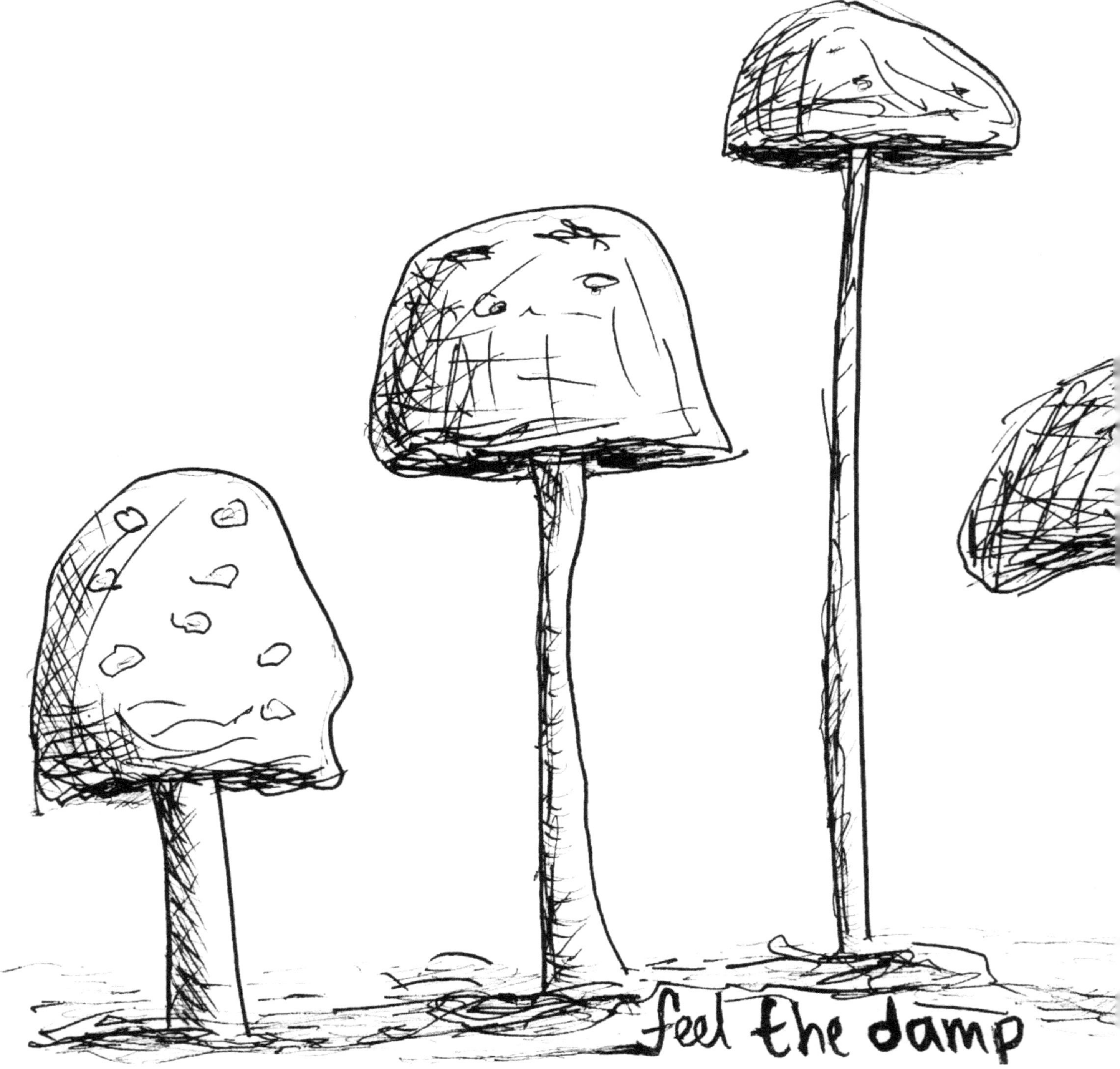
feel the damp

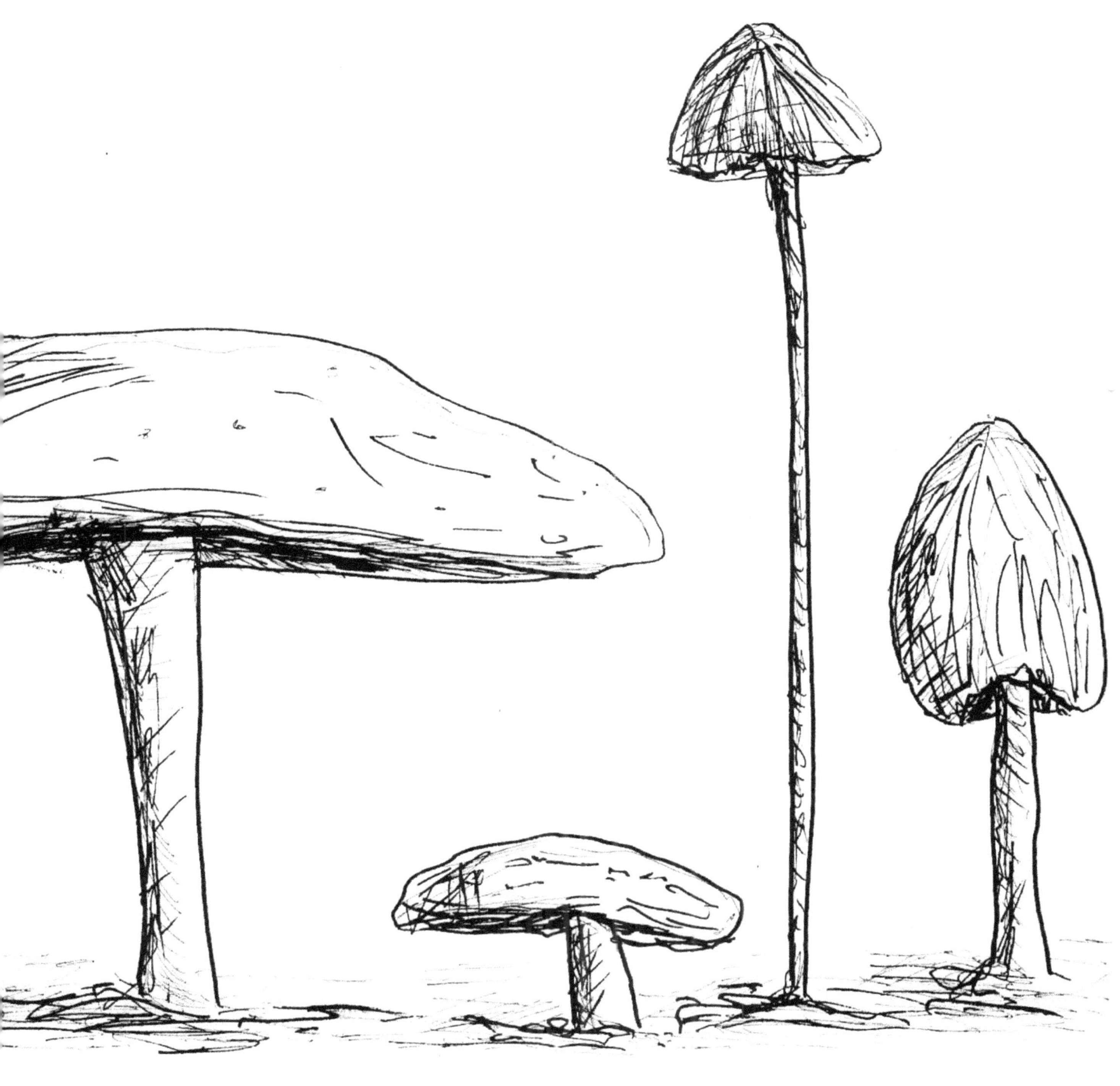

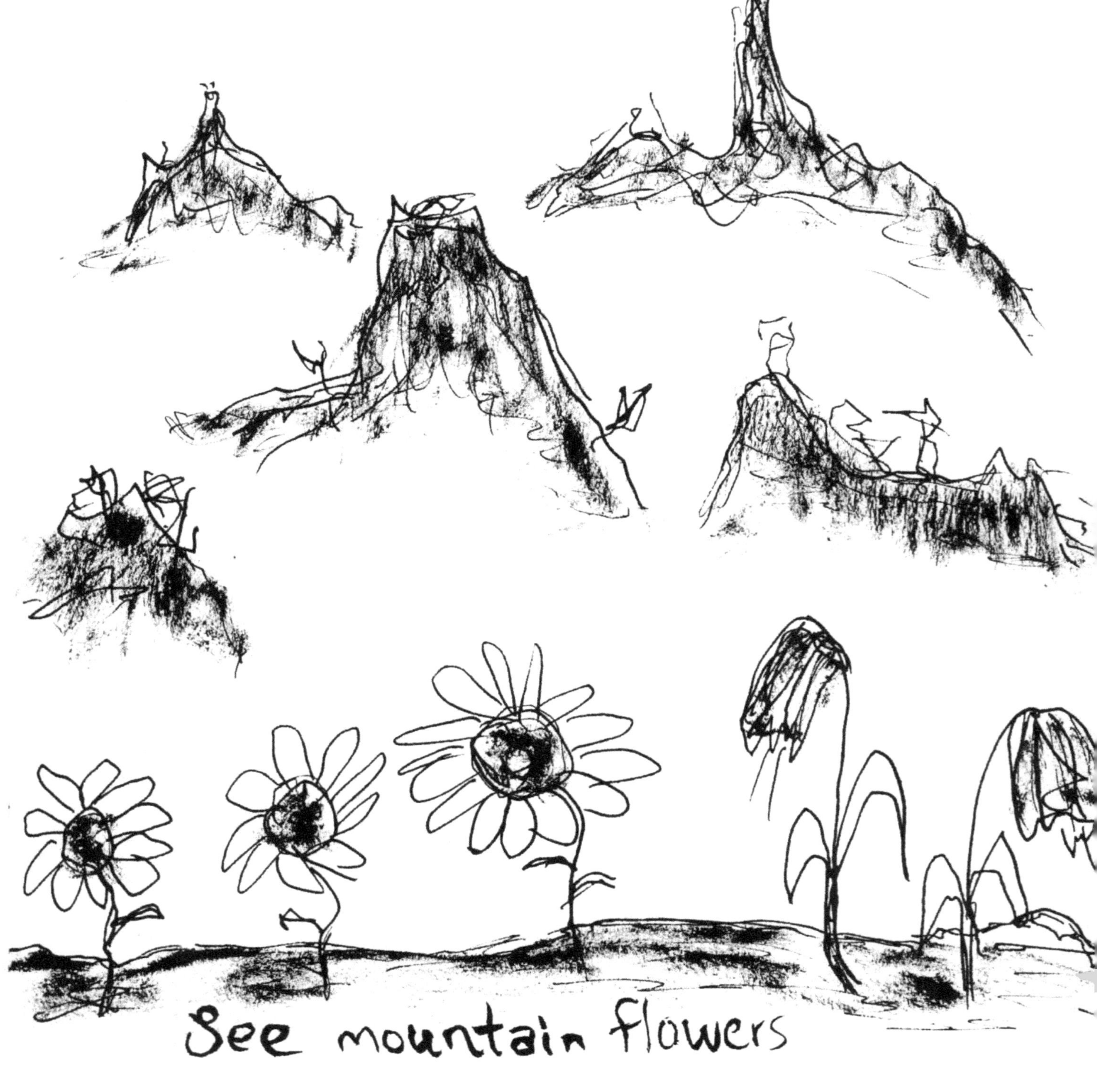
See mountain flowers

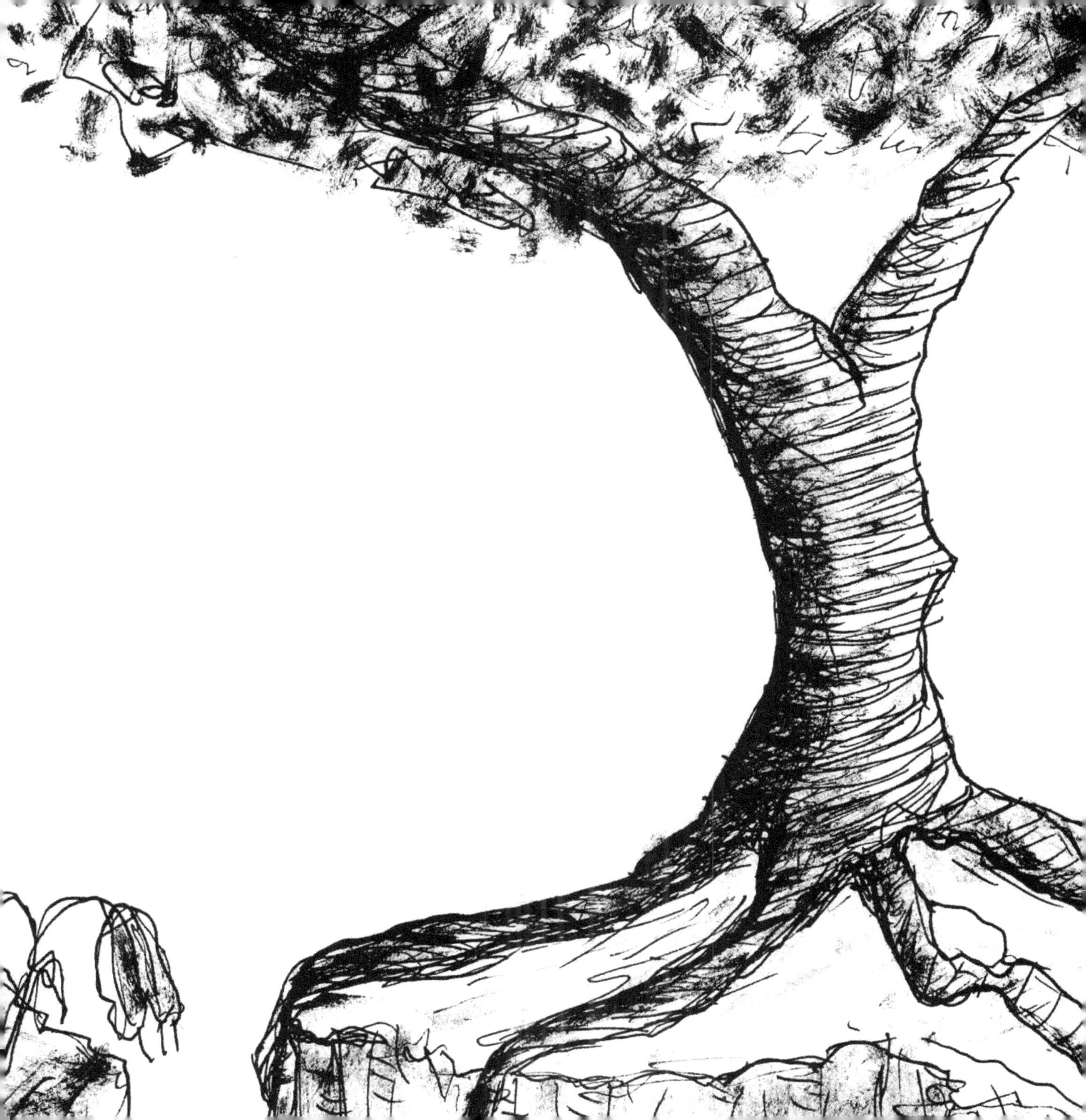

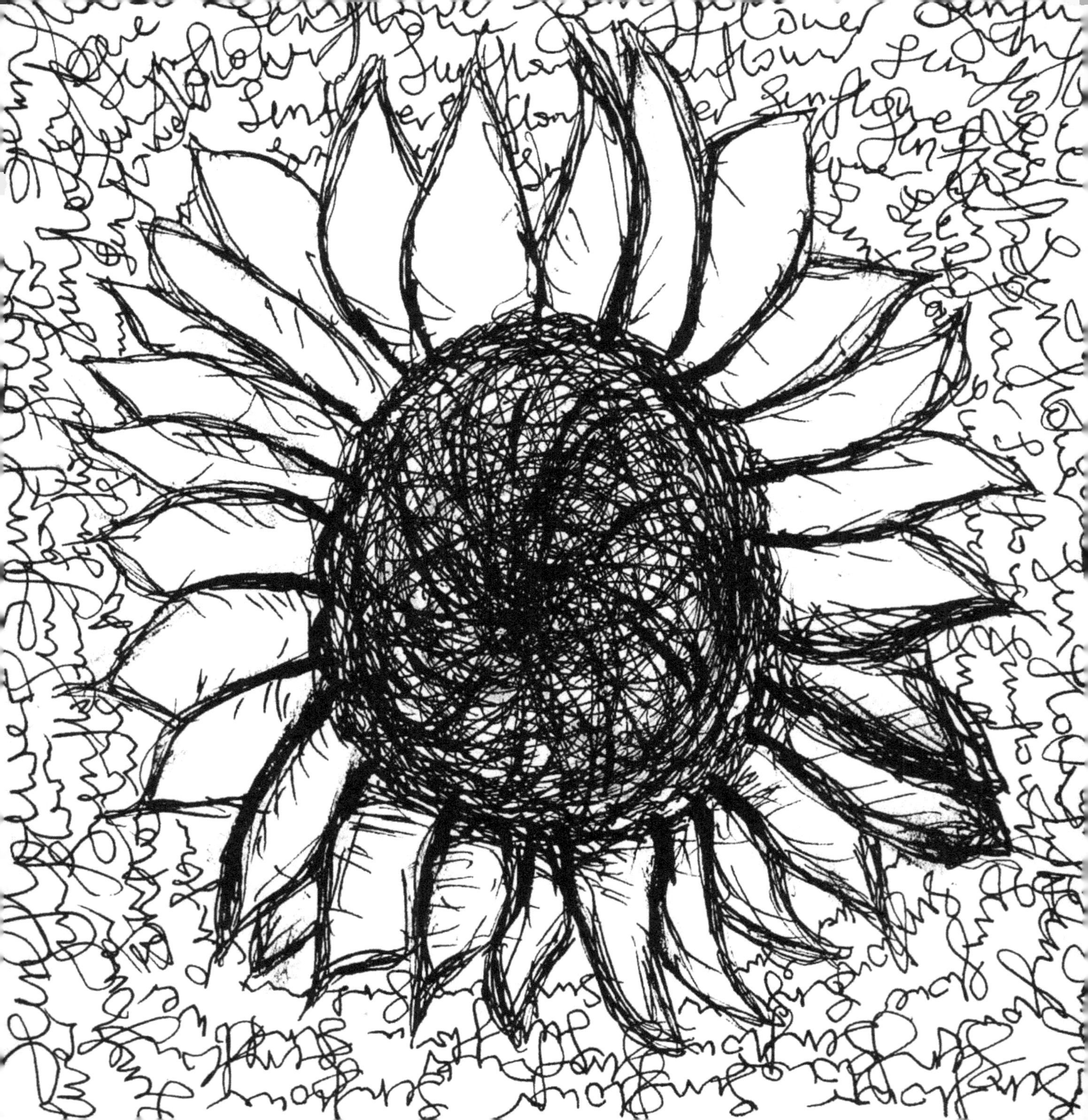

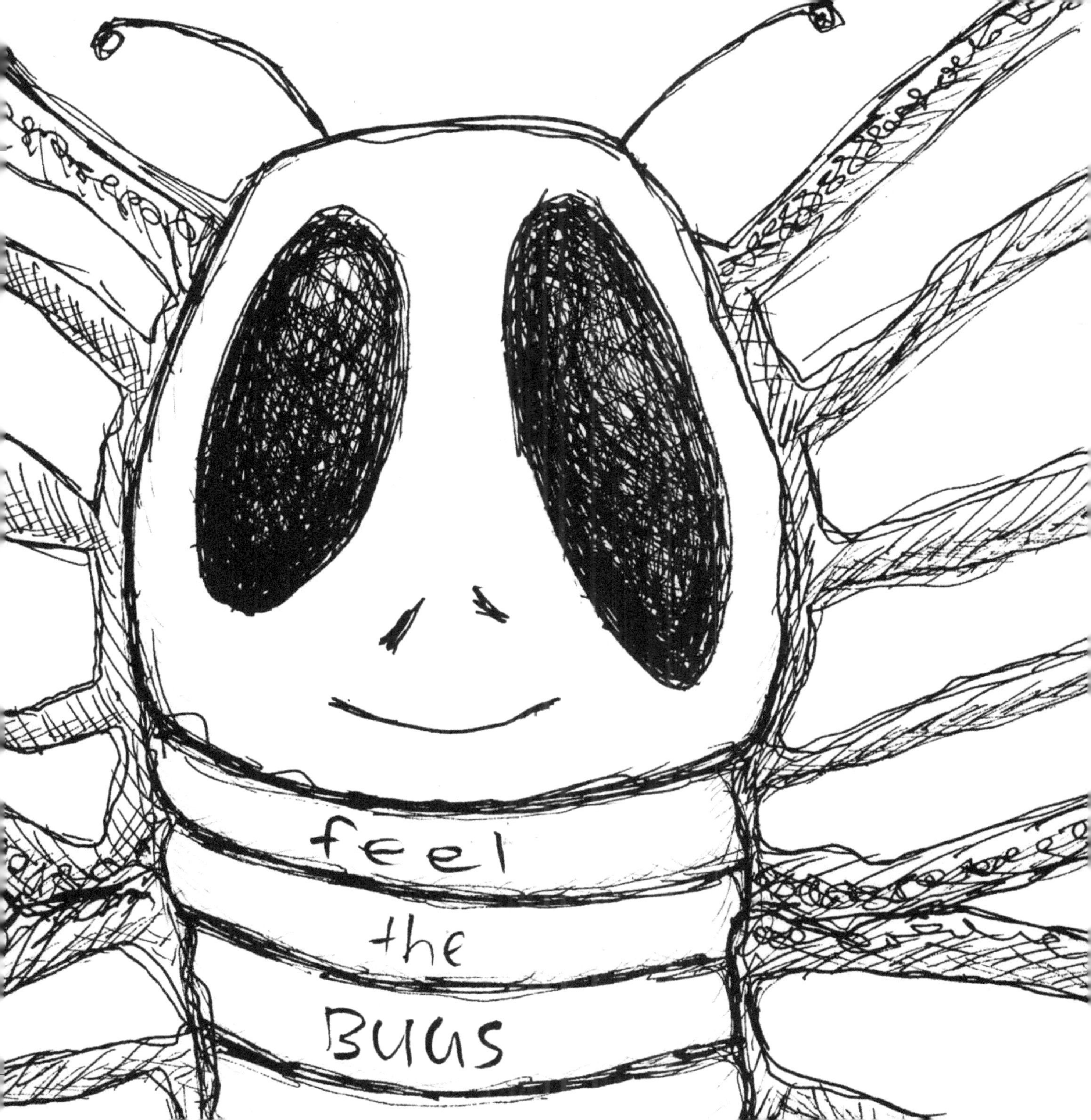

feel
the
BUGS

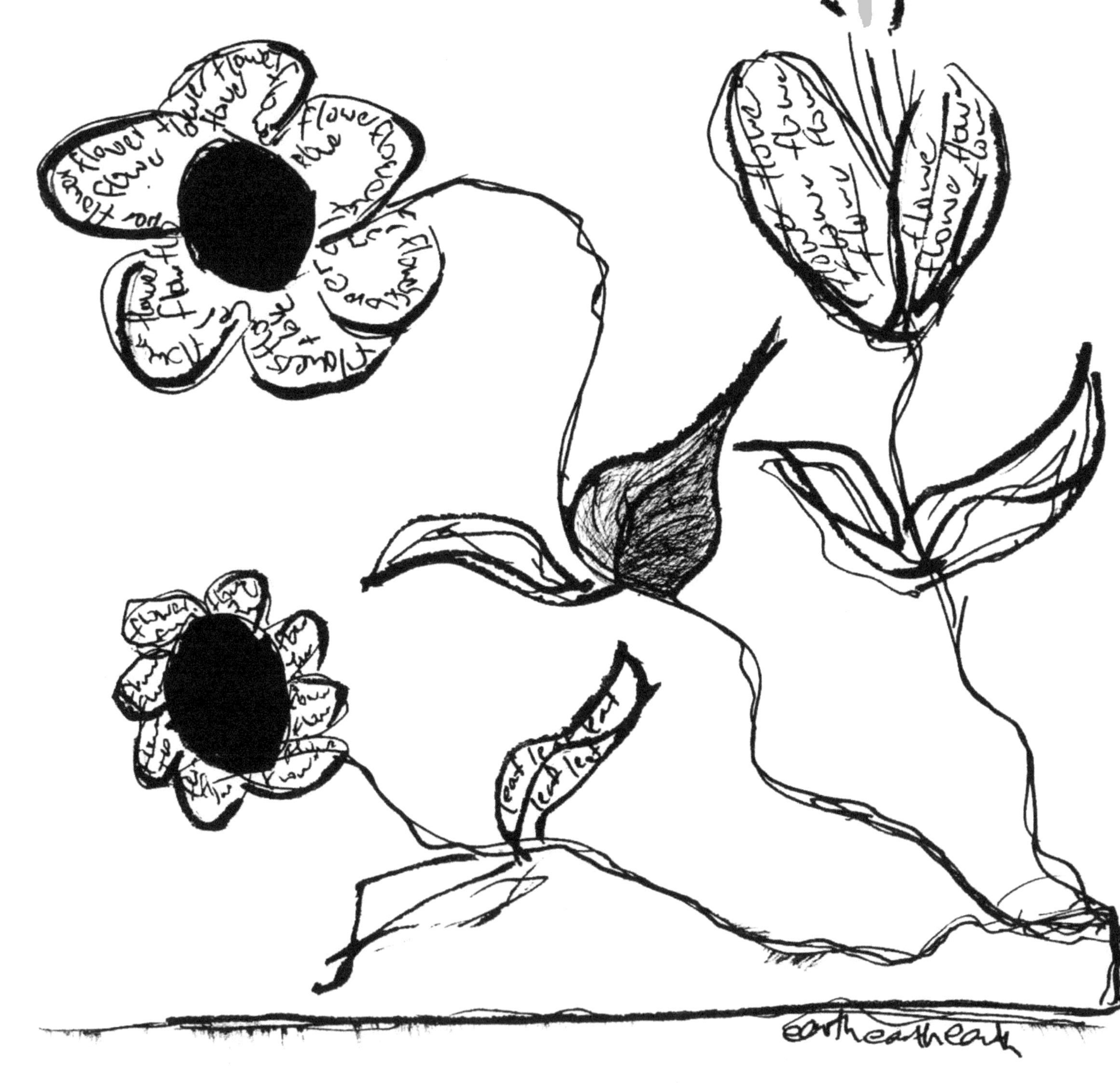

flower flower flower flower flower flower
flower flower flower flower flower flower
leaf leaf leaf leaf
earthearthearth

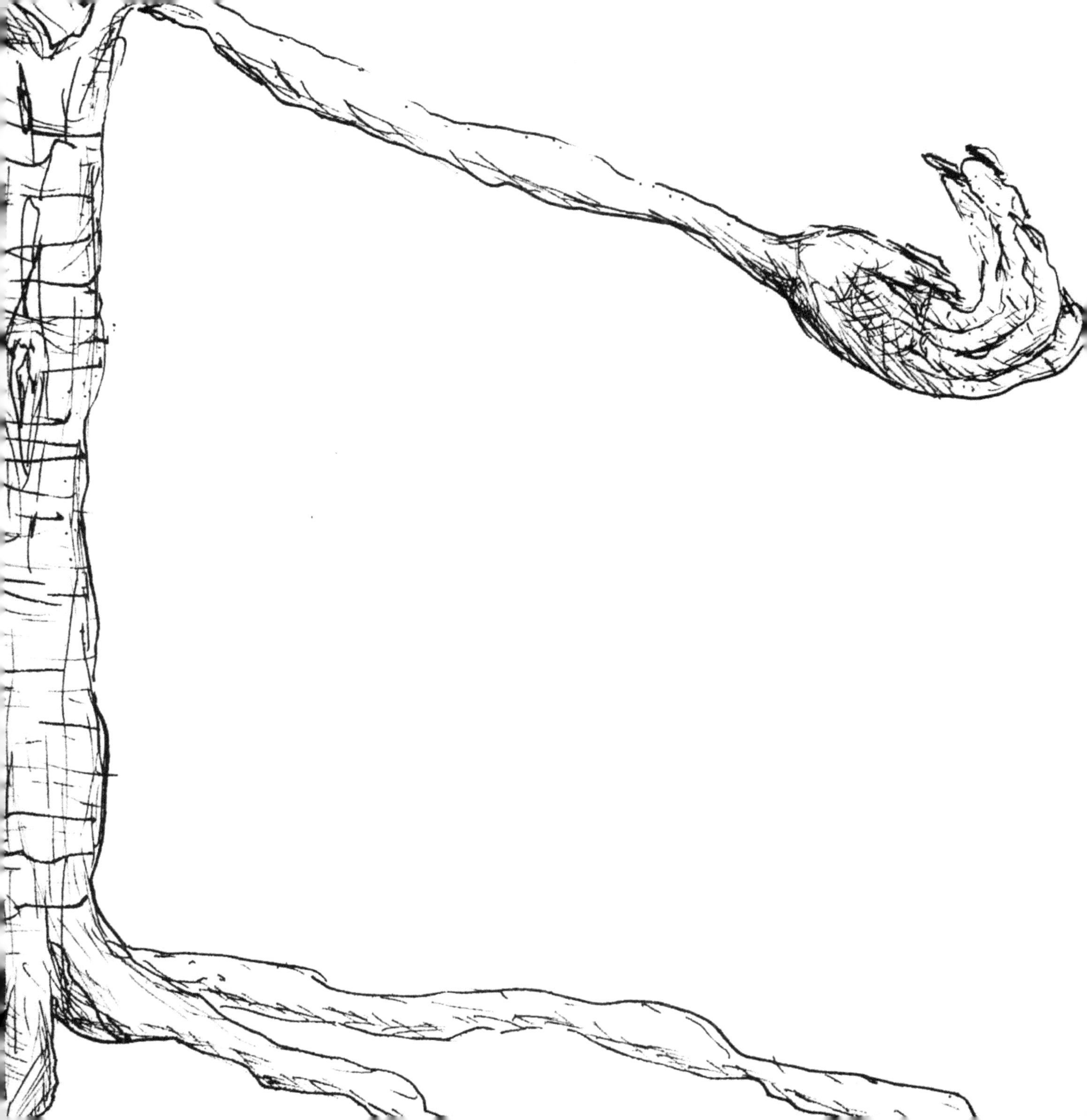

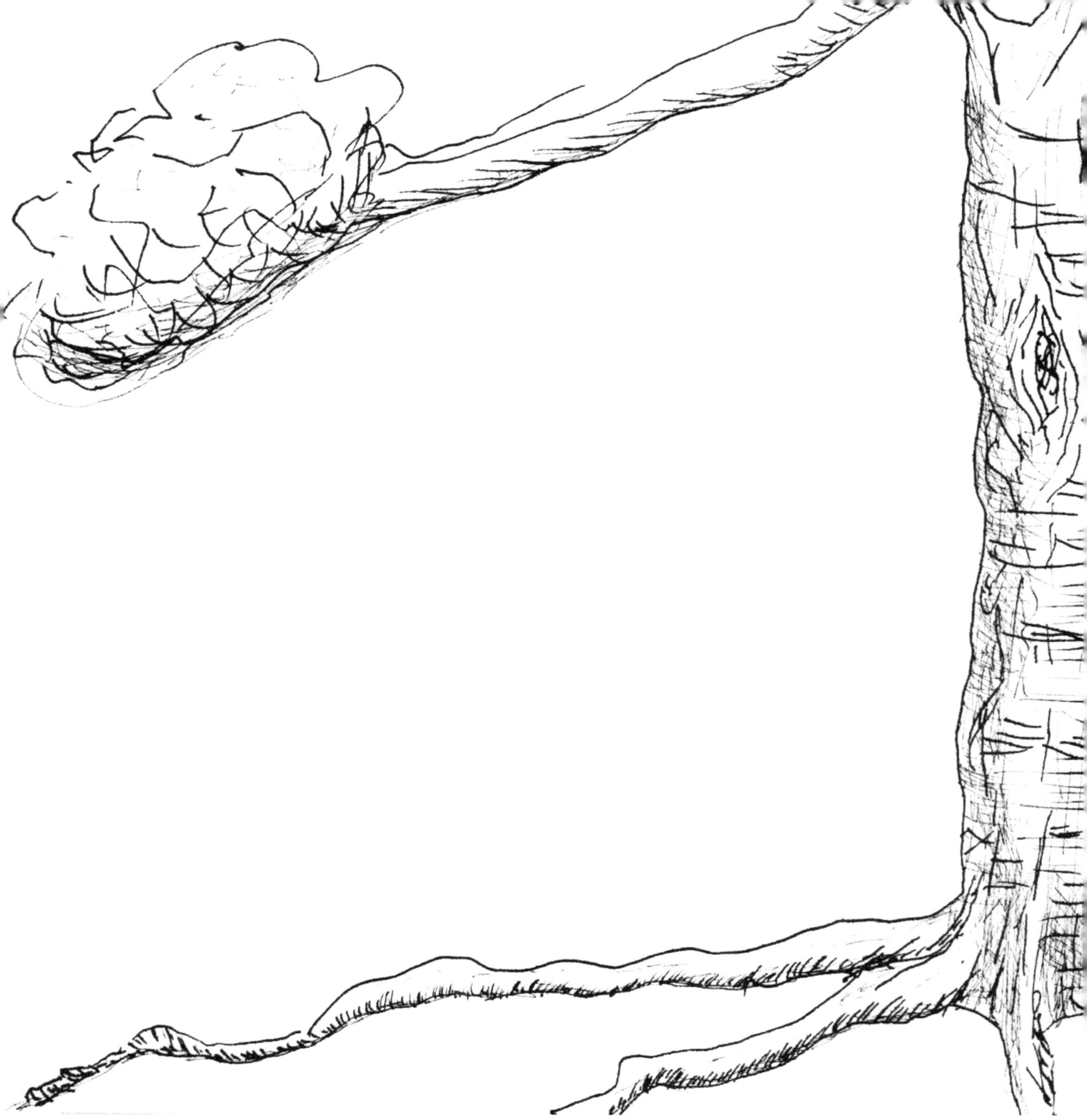

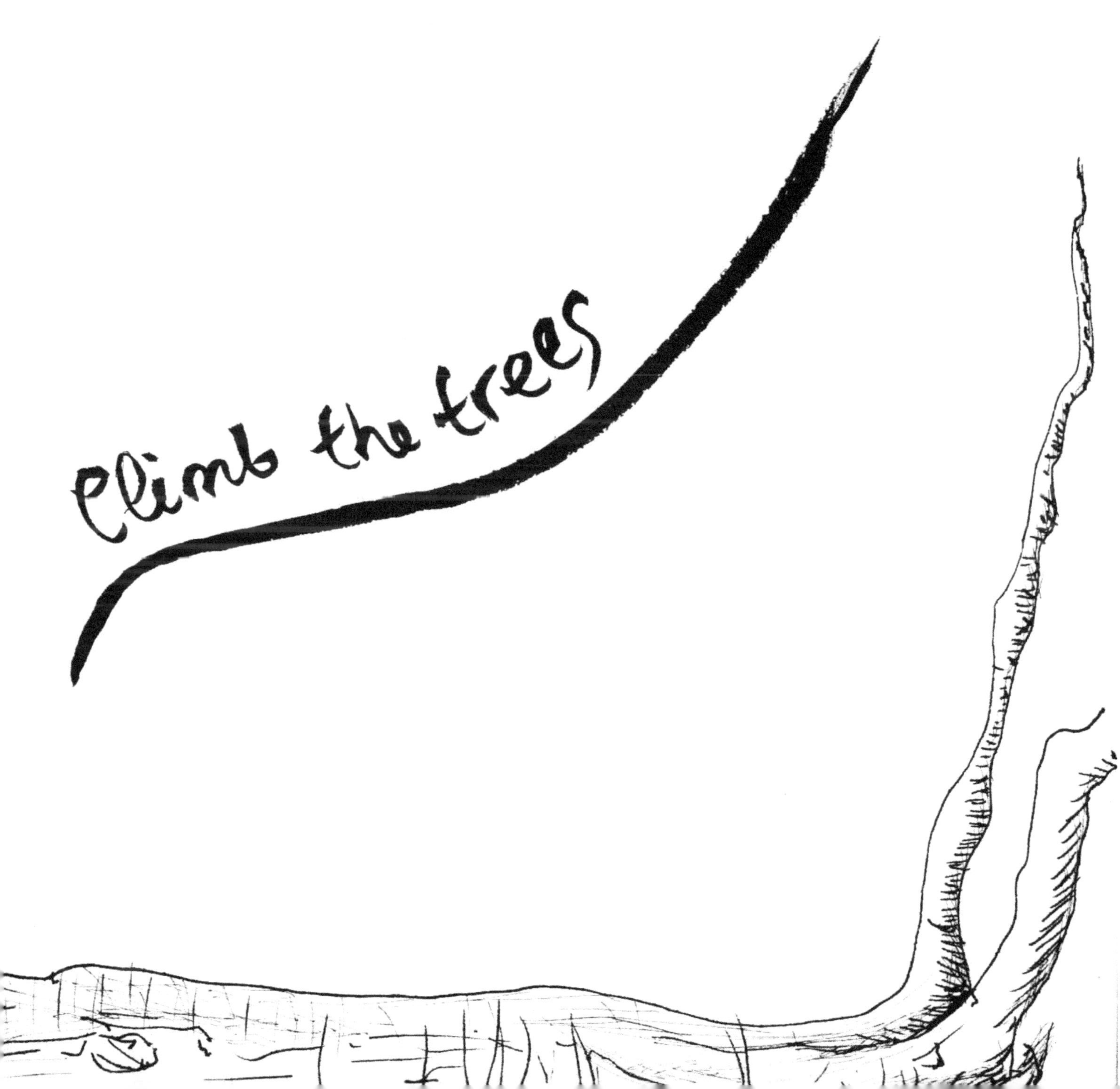
Climb the trees

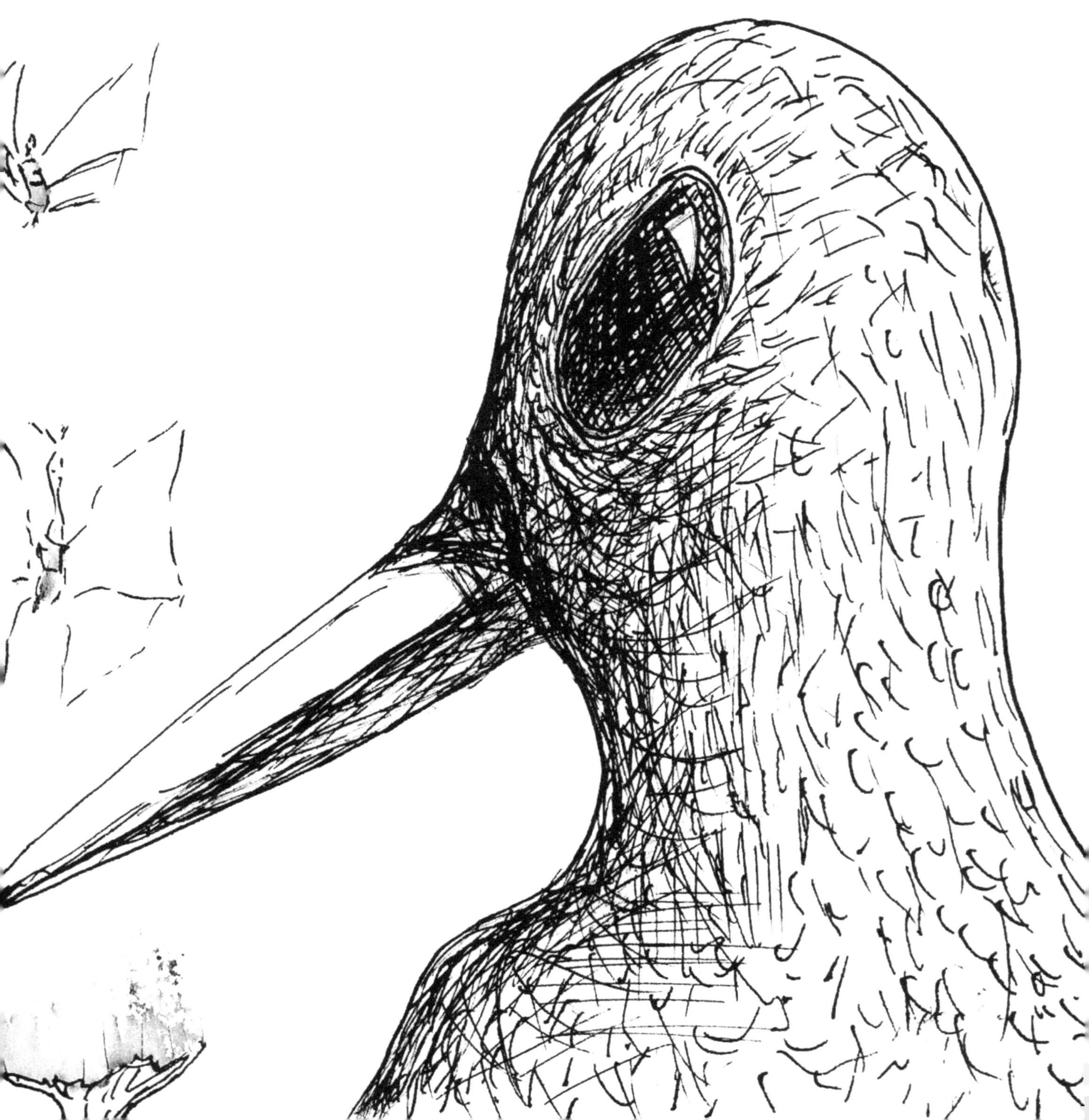

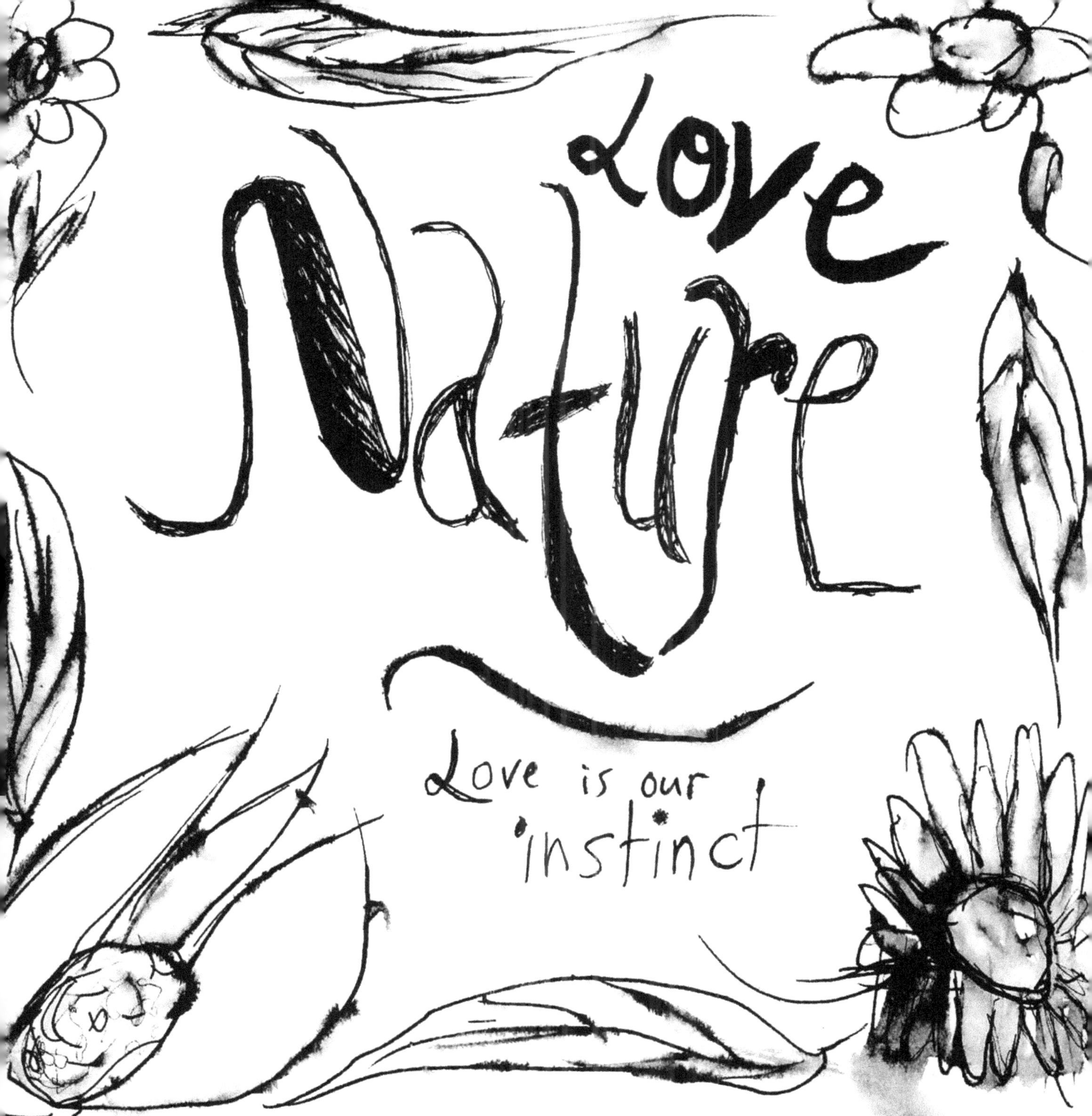
Love
Nature
Love is our
'instinct

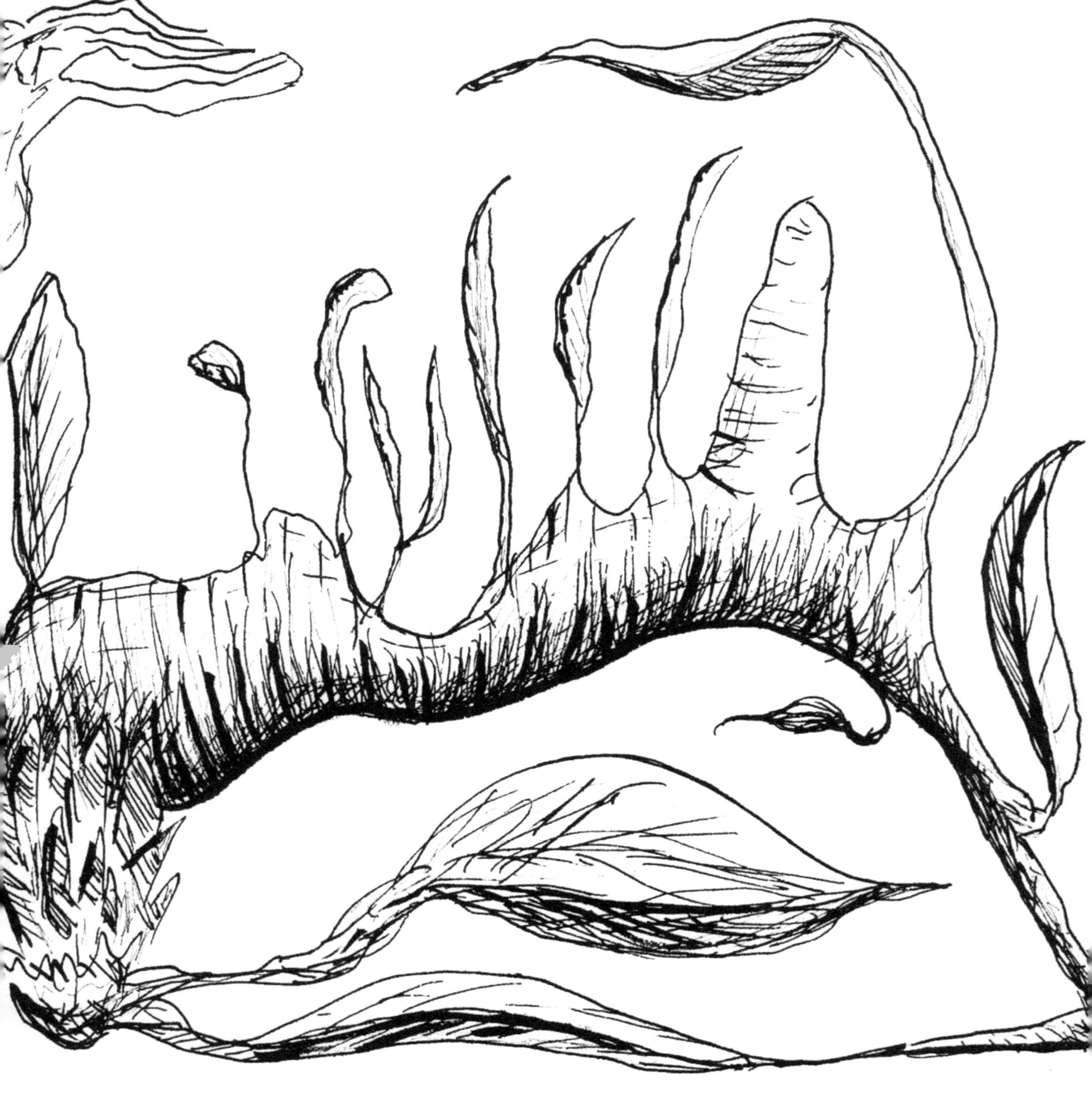

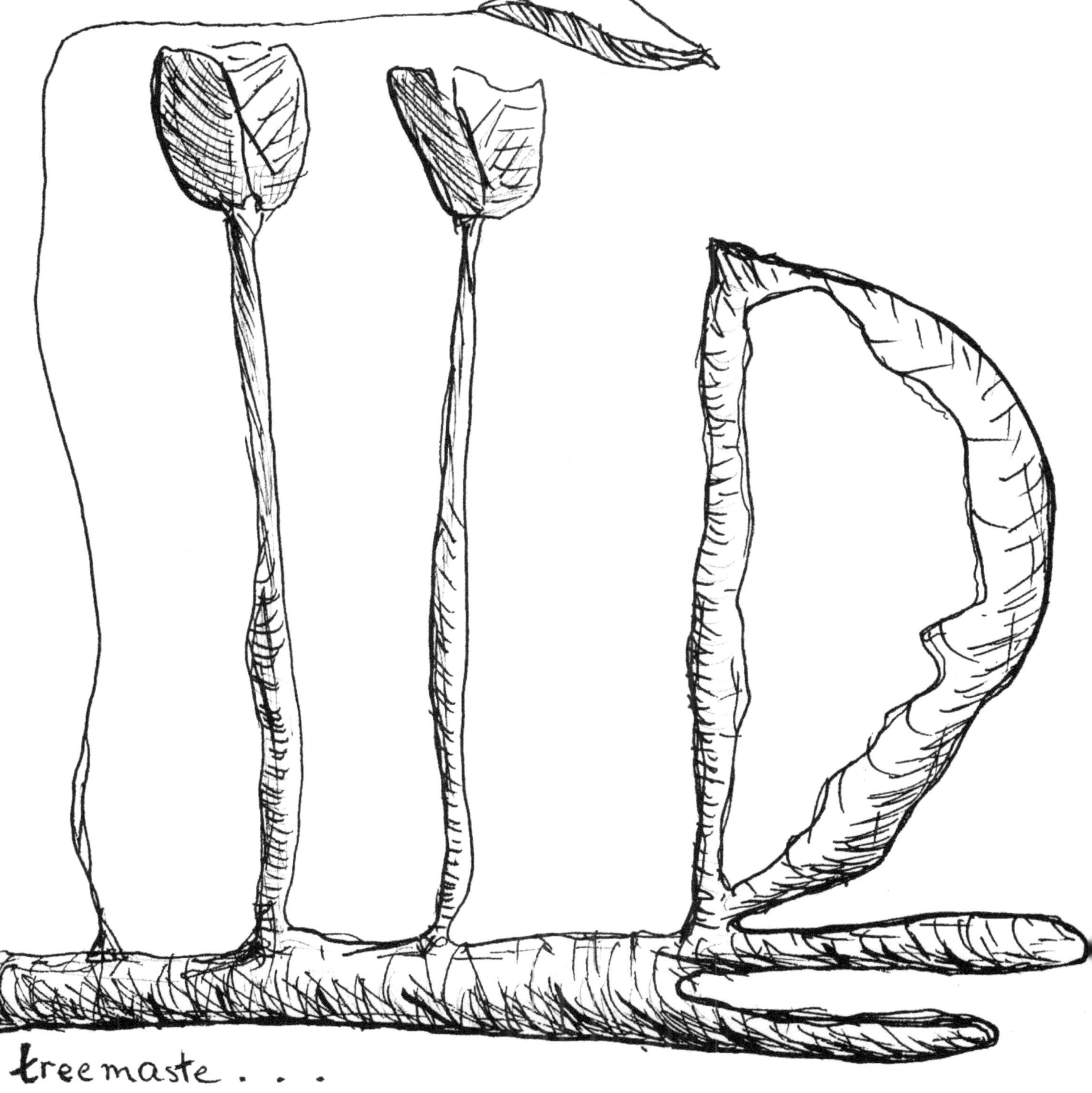

treemaste . . .

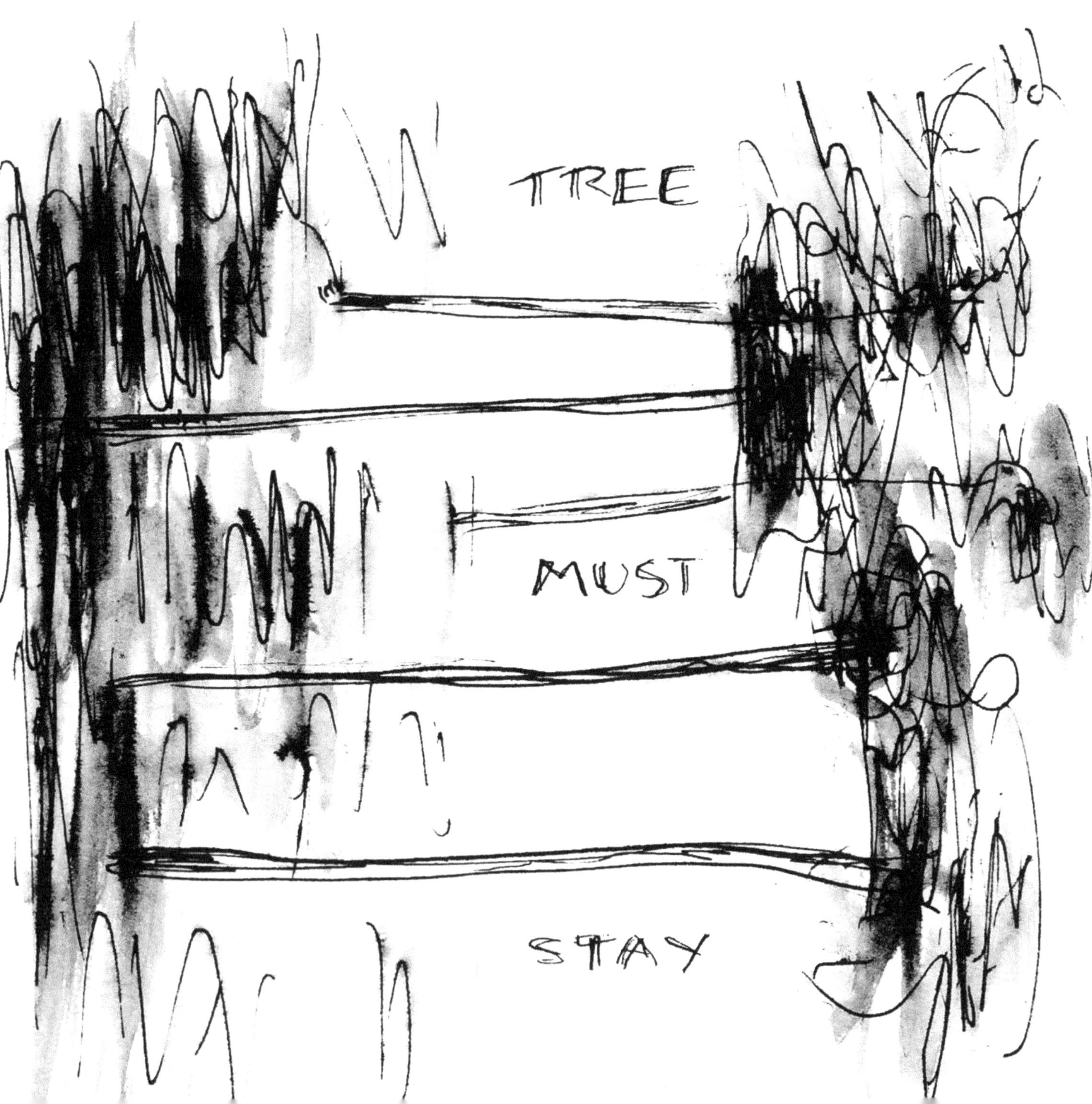

TREE
MUST
STAY

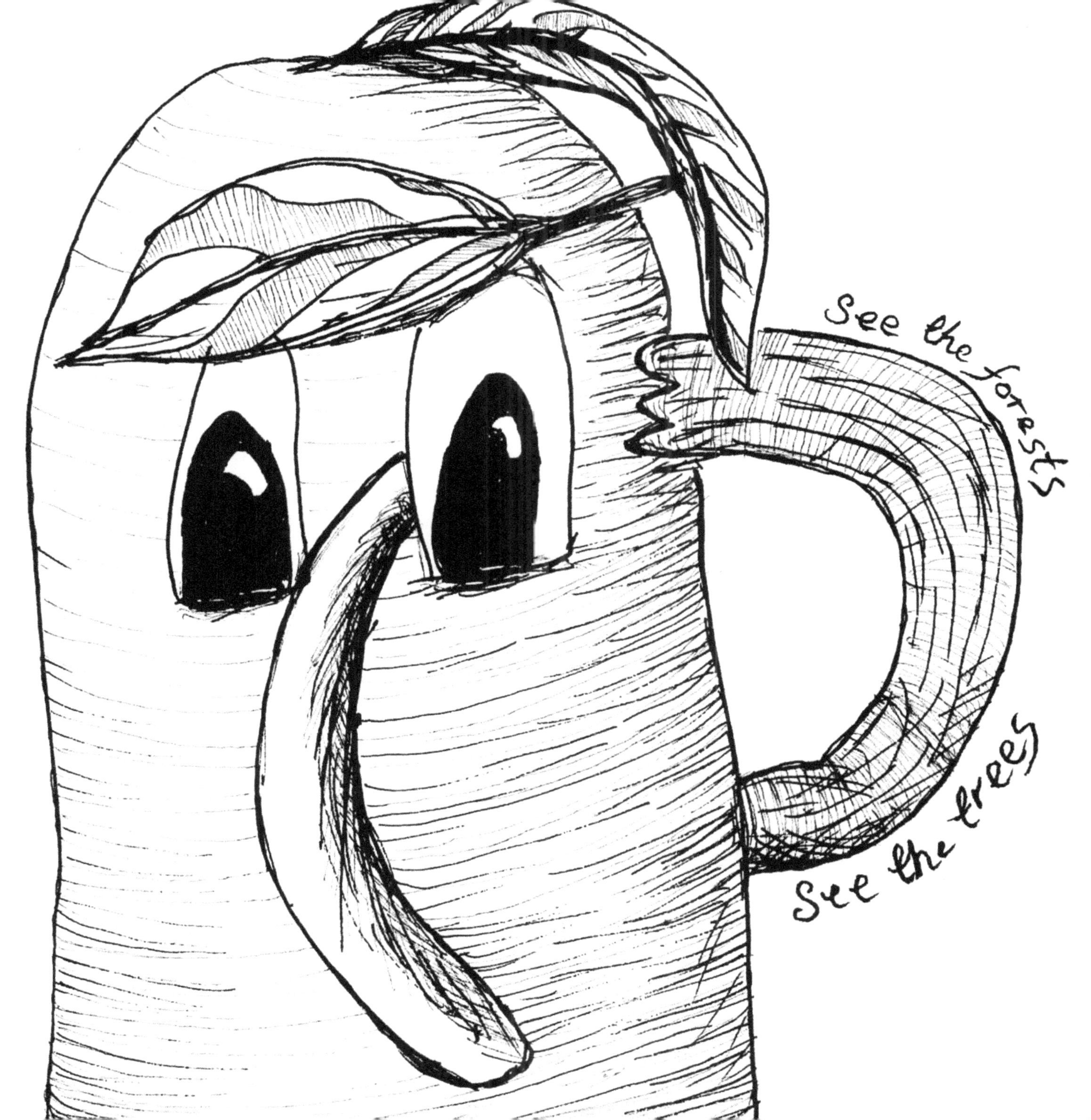

See the forests
See the trees

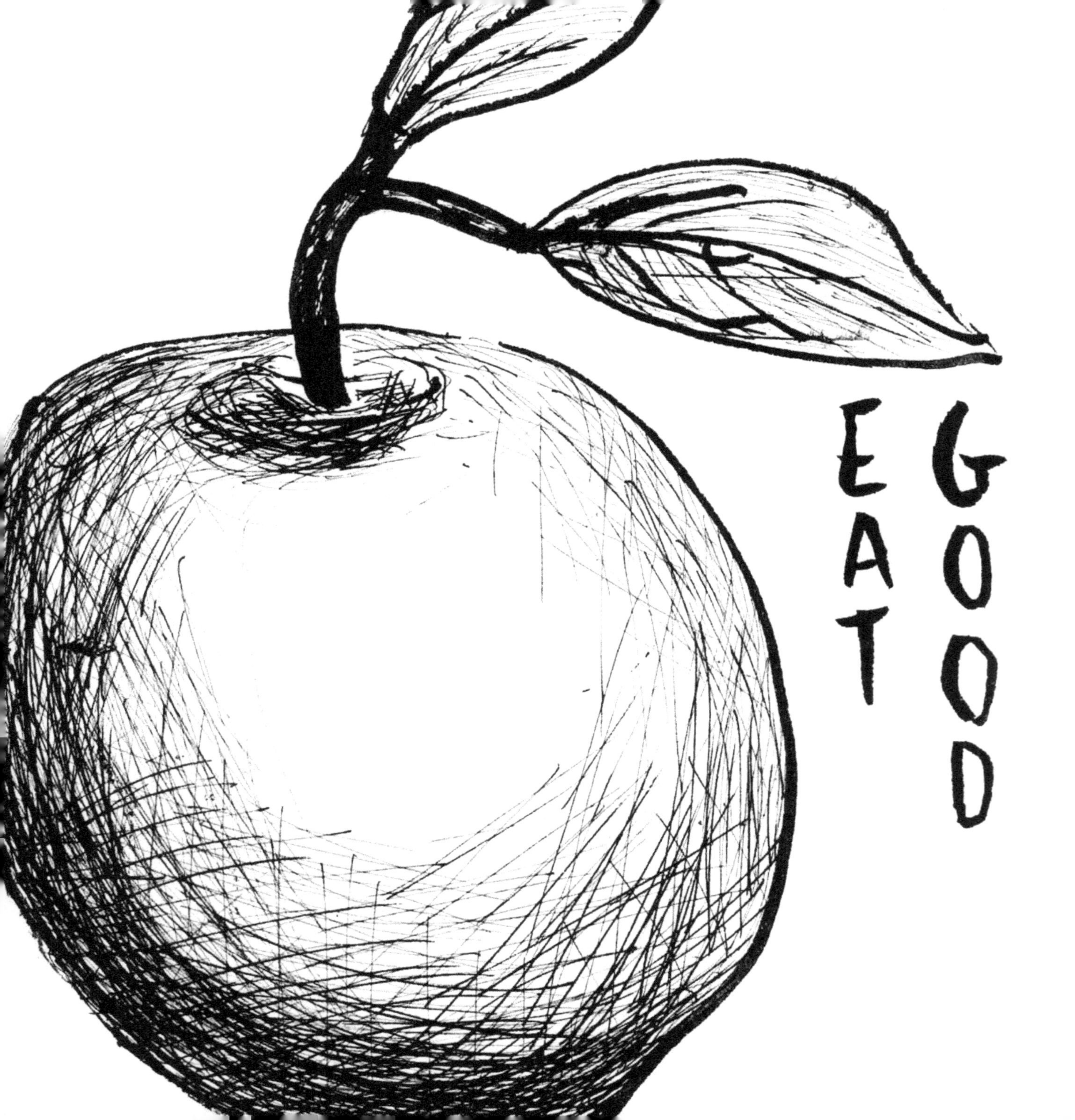

EAT
GOOD

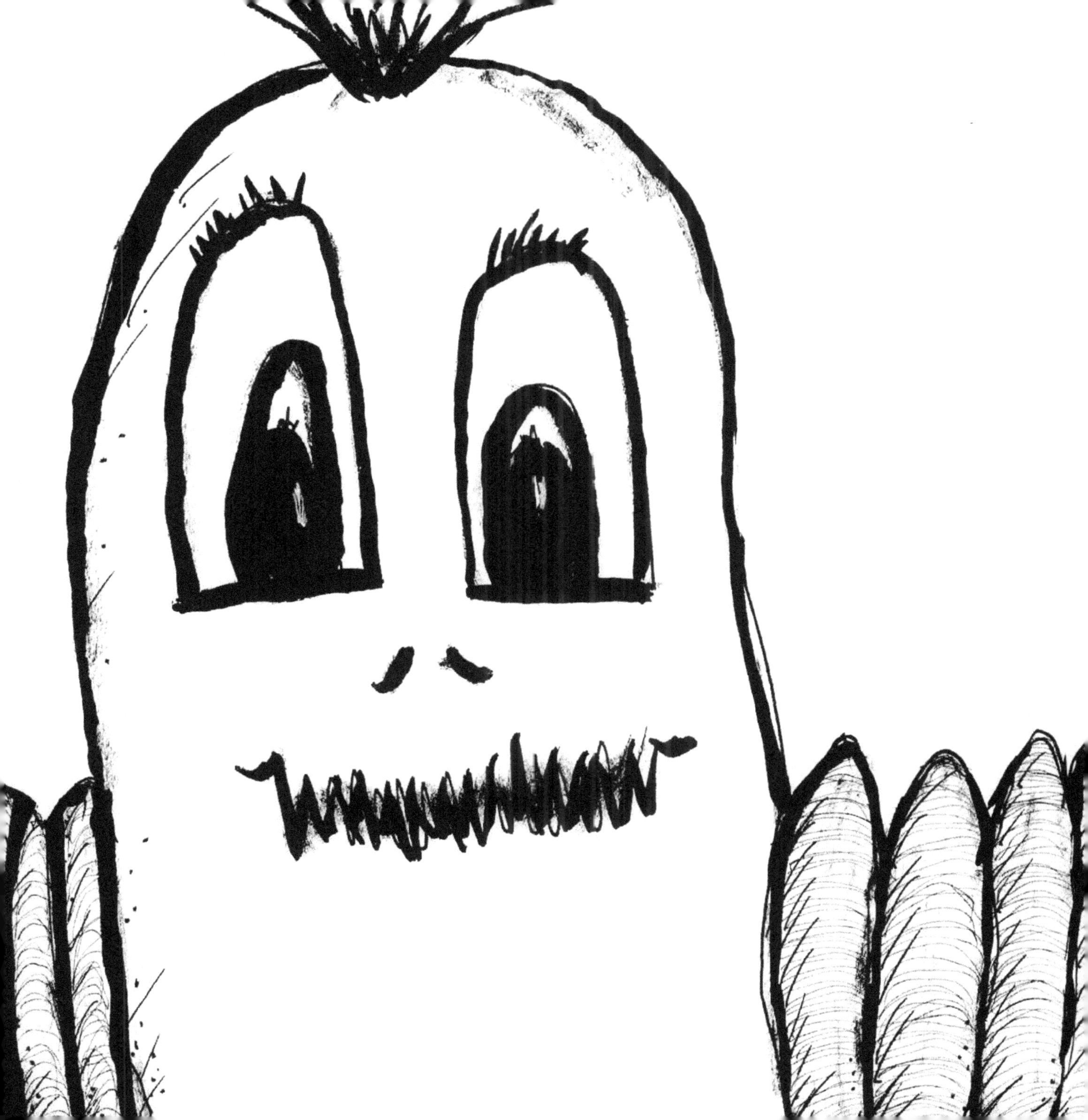

longtime

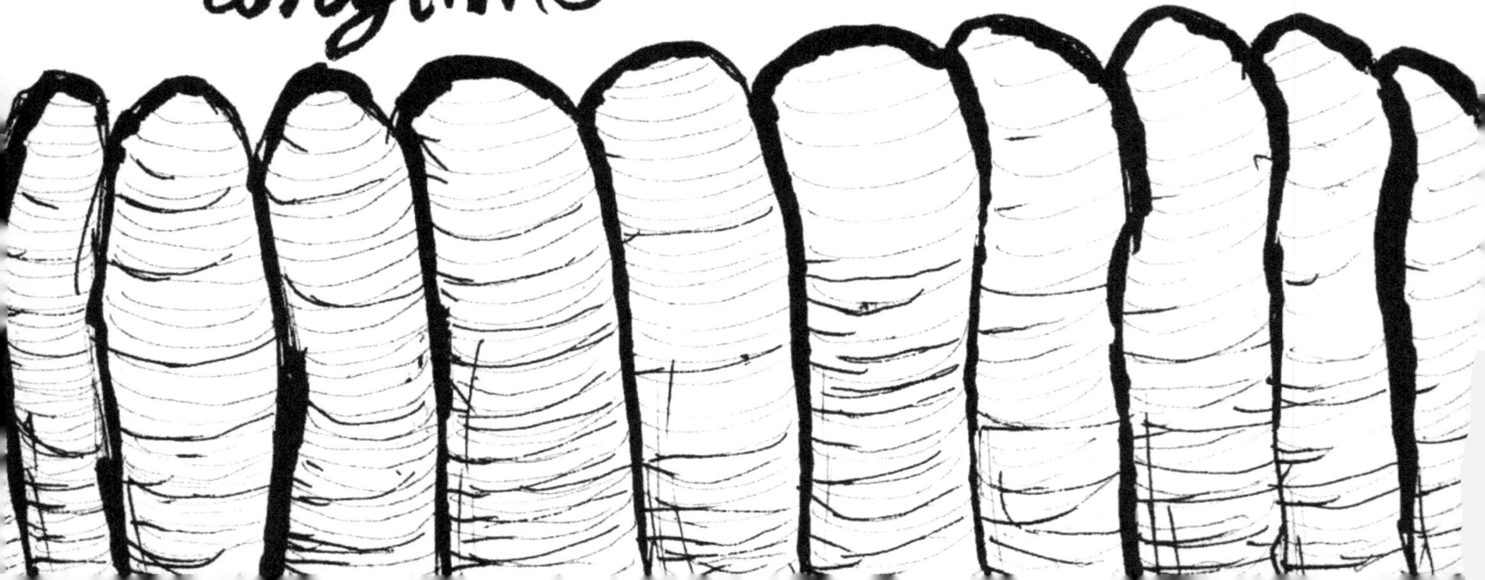

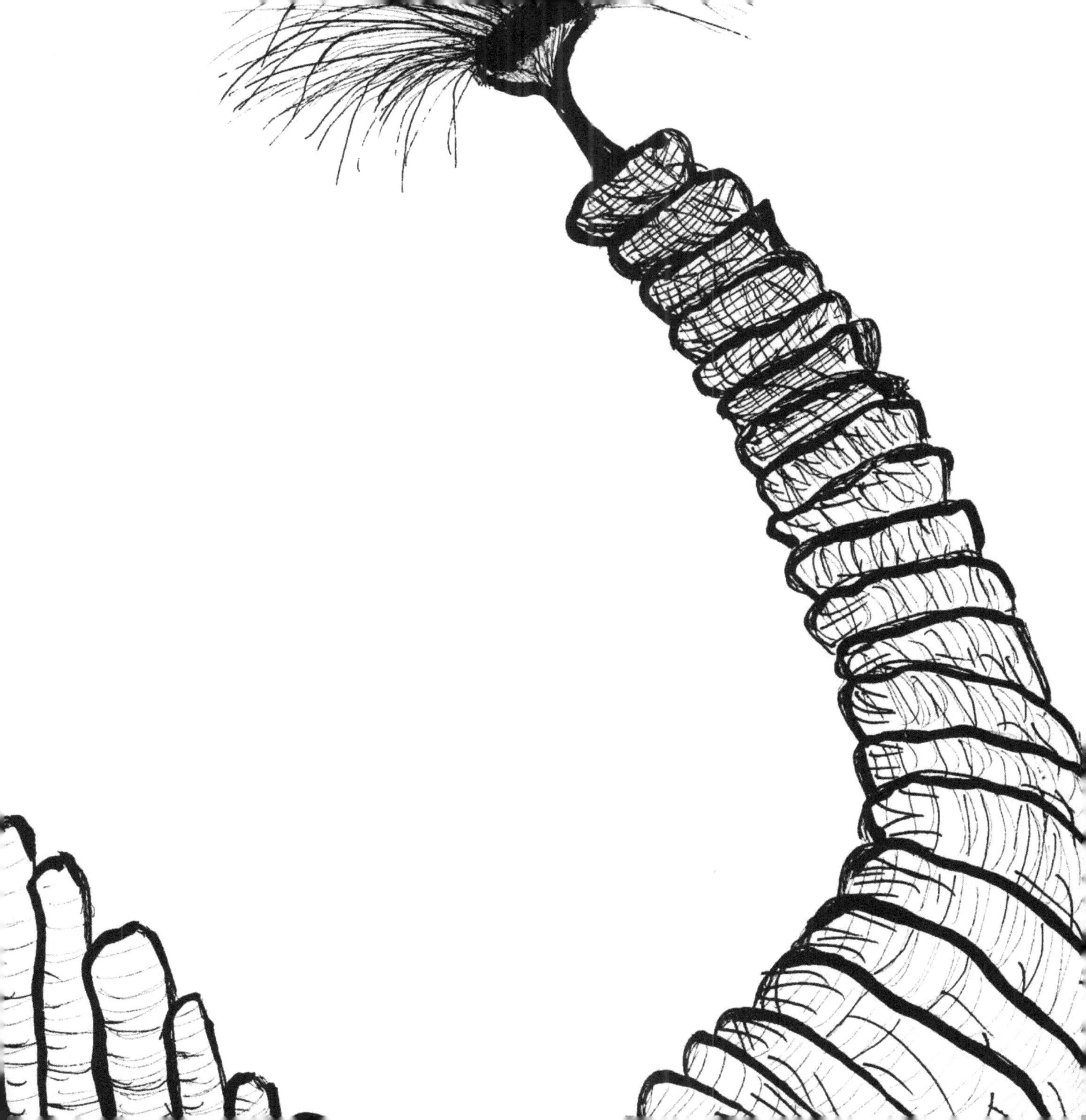

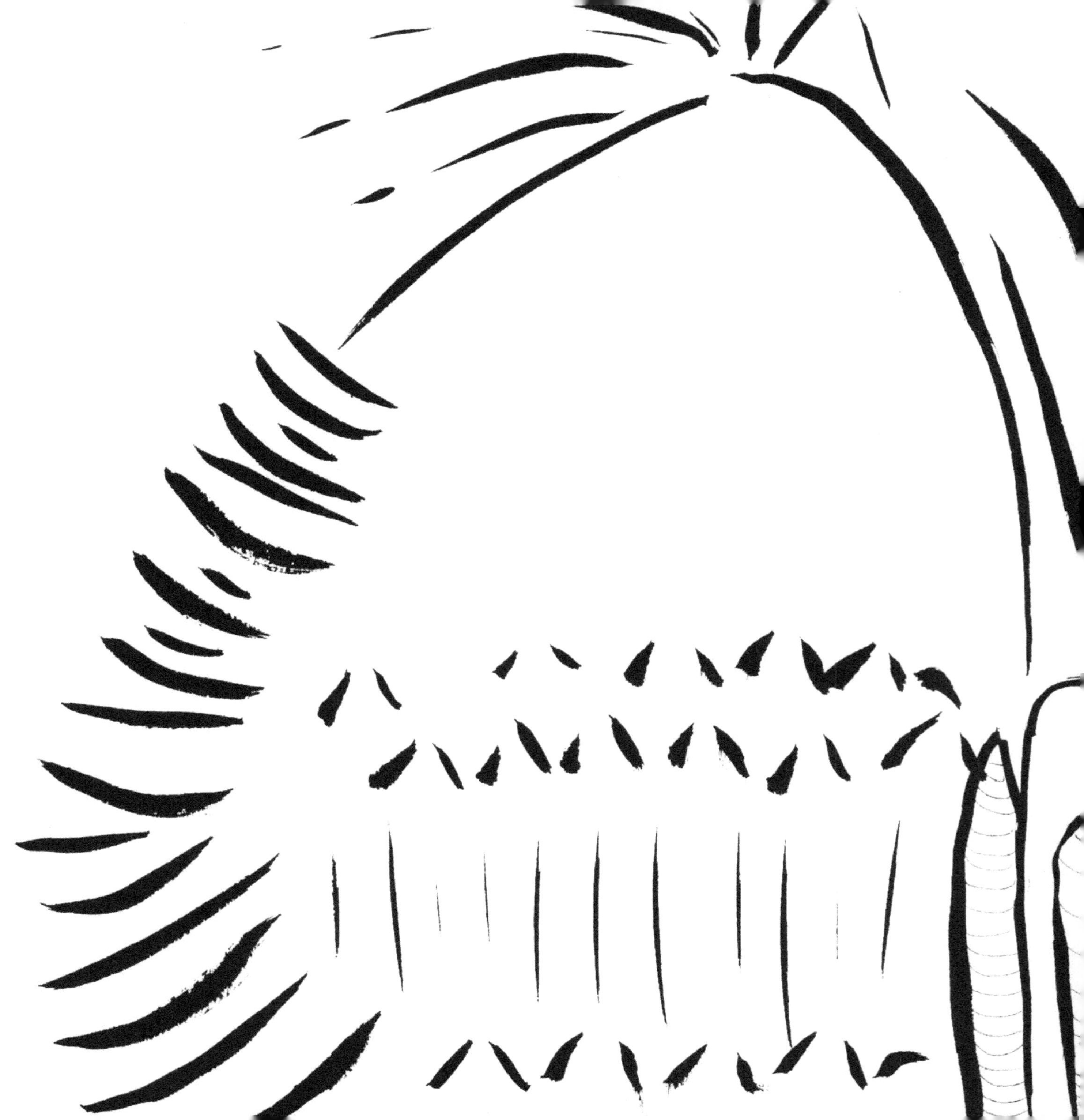

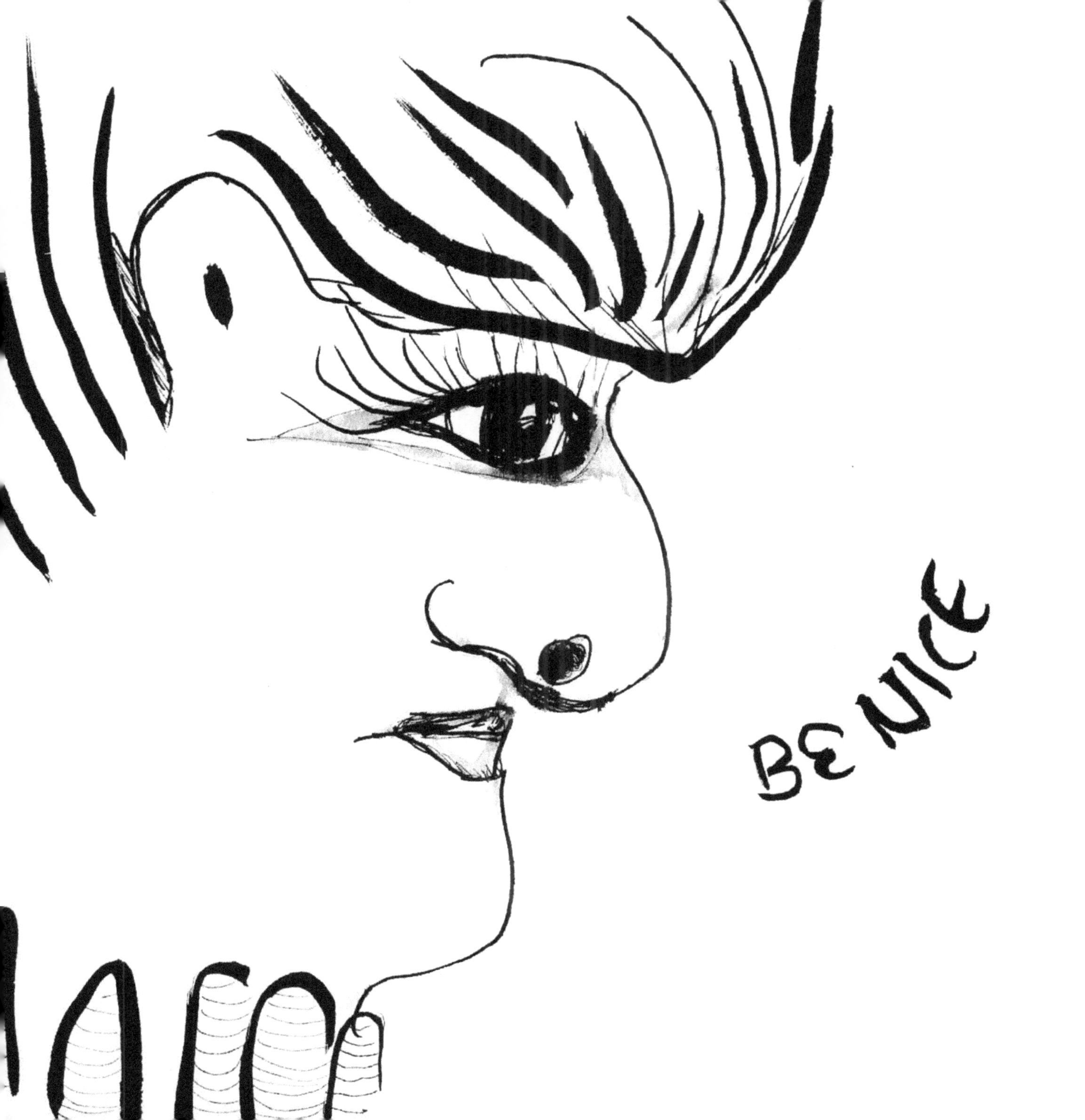
BE NICE

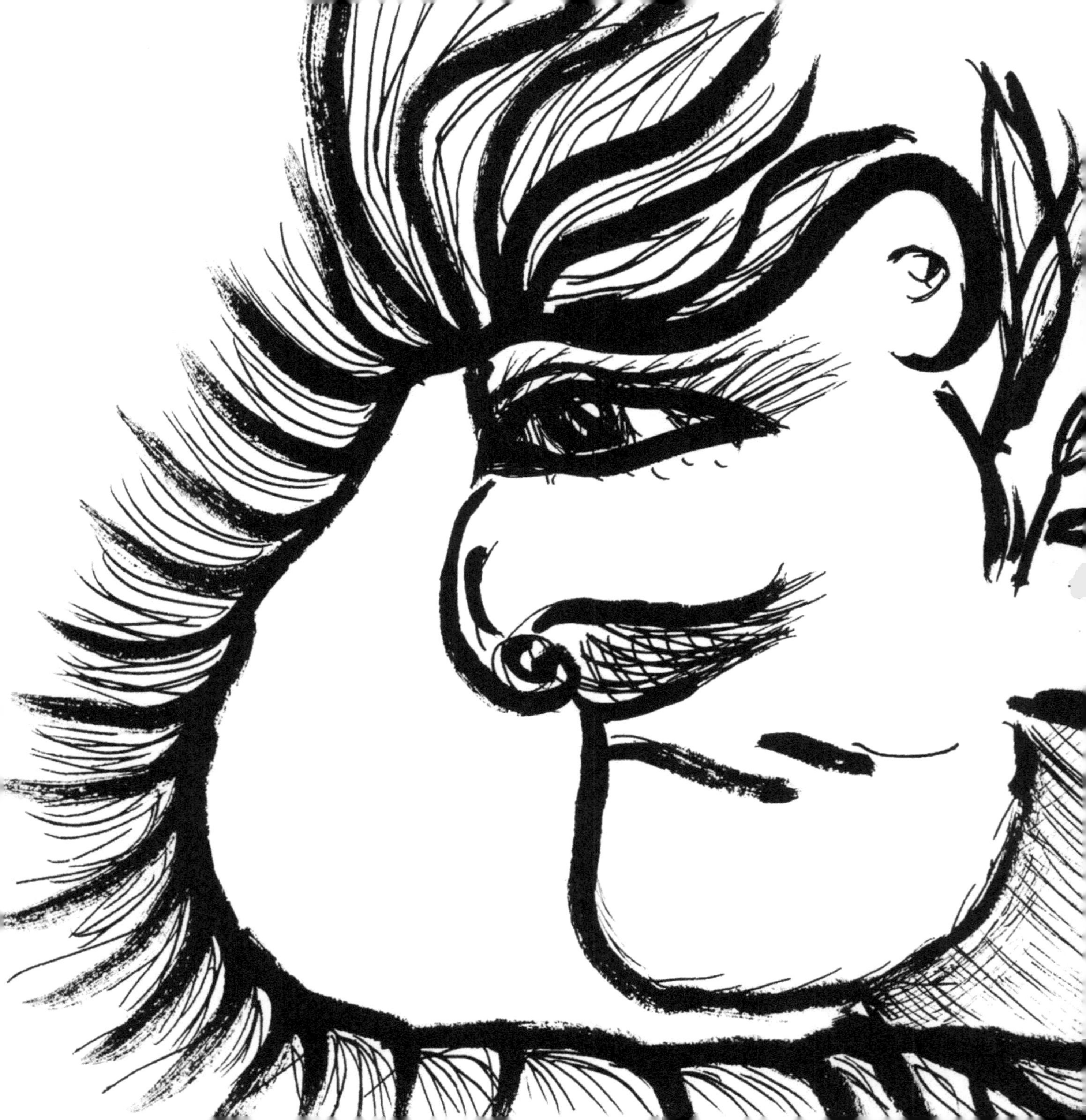

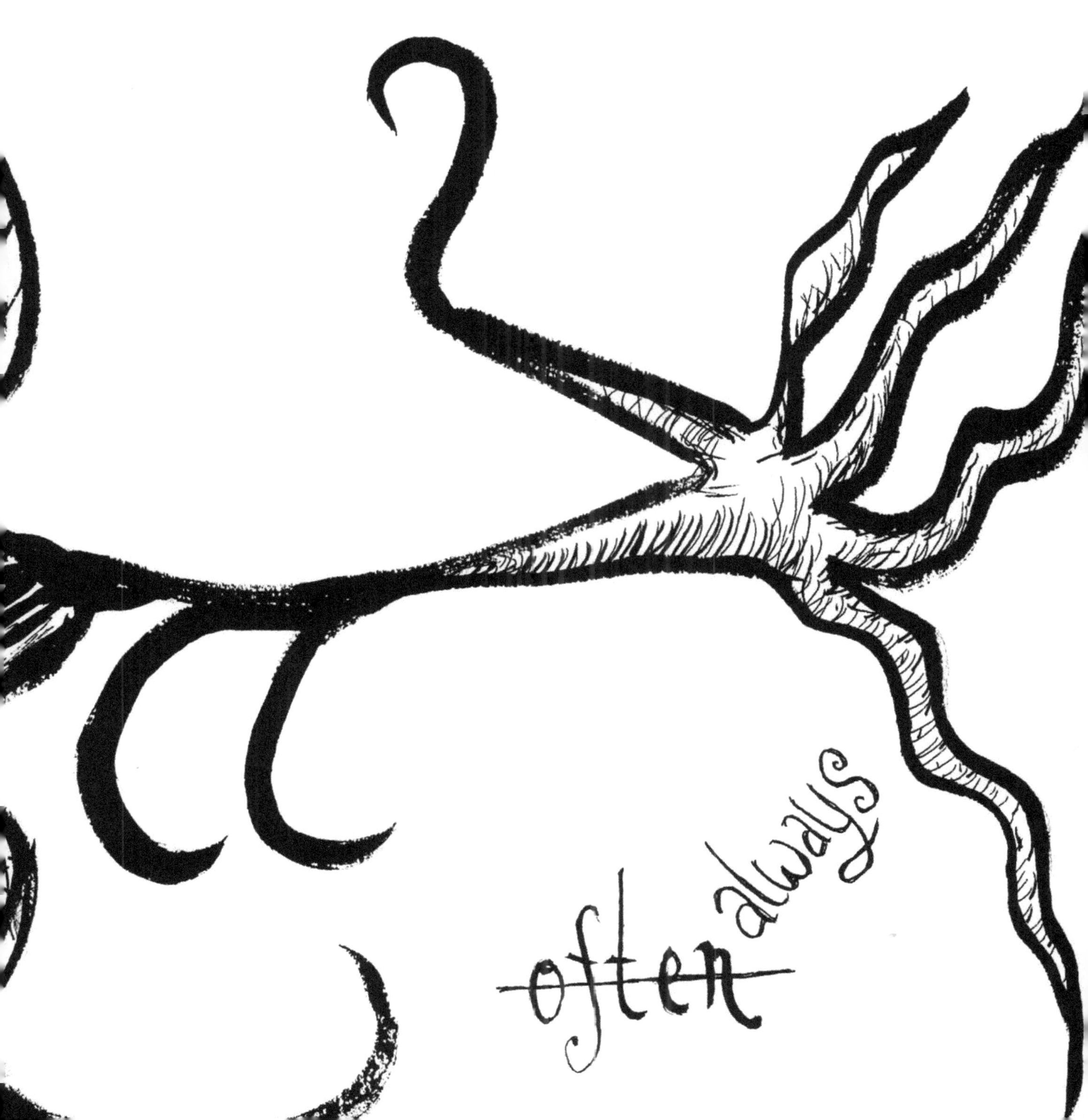

~~often~~ always

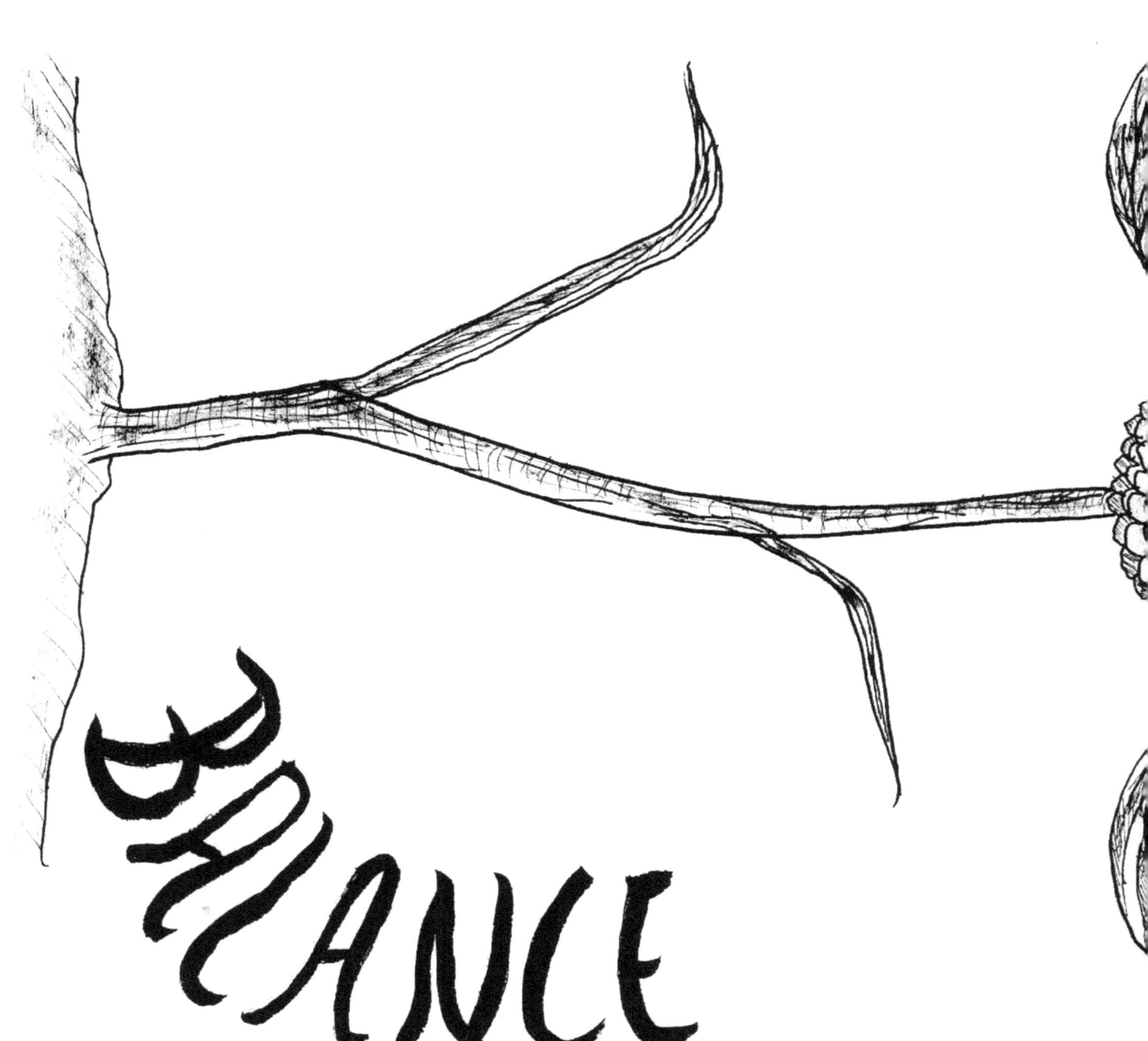

BALANCE

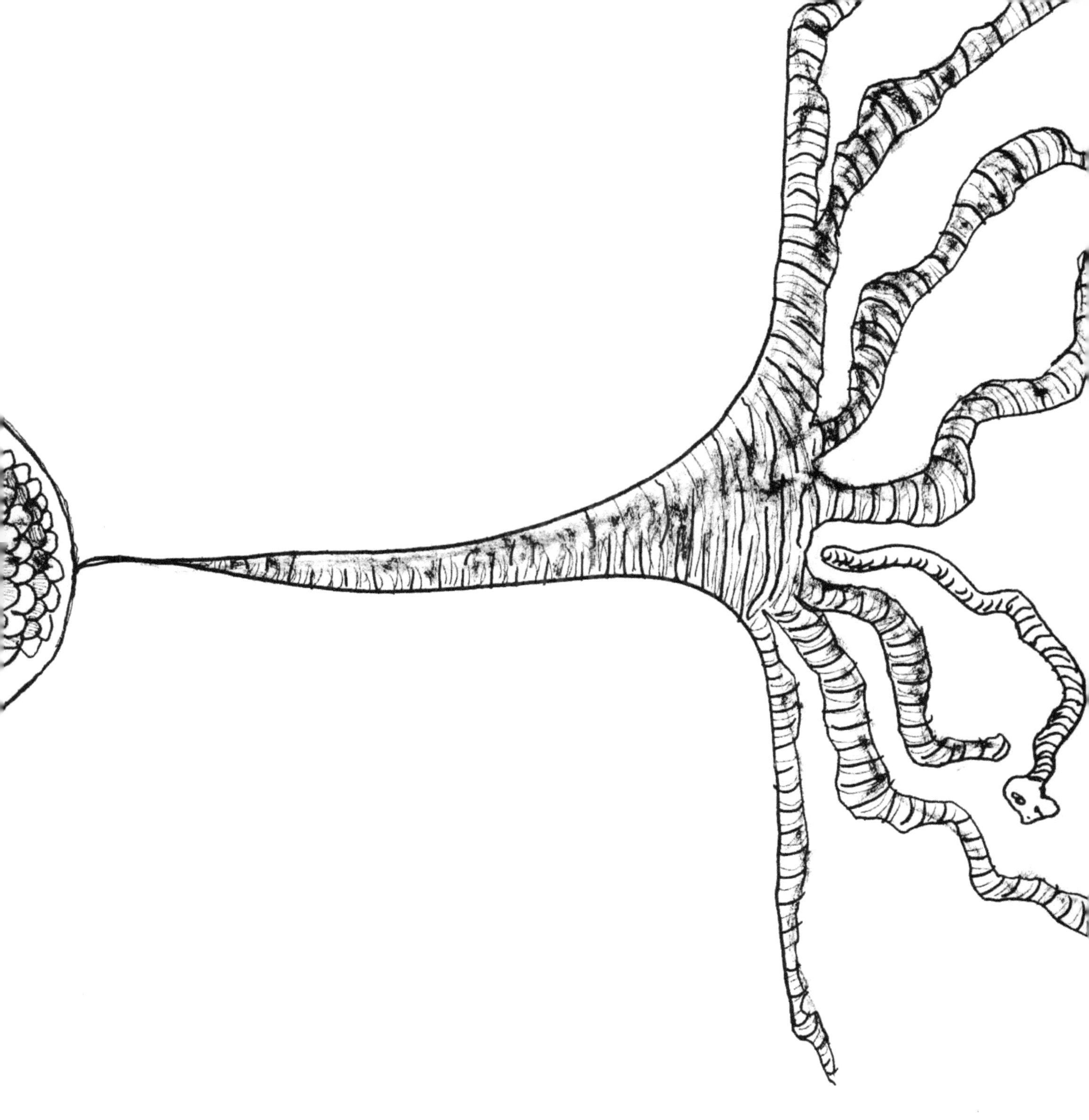

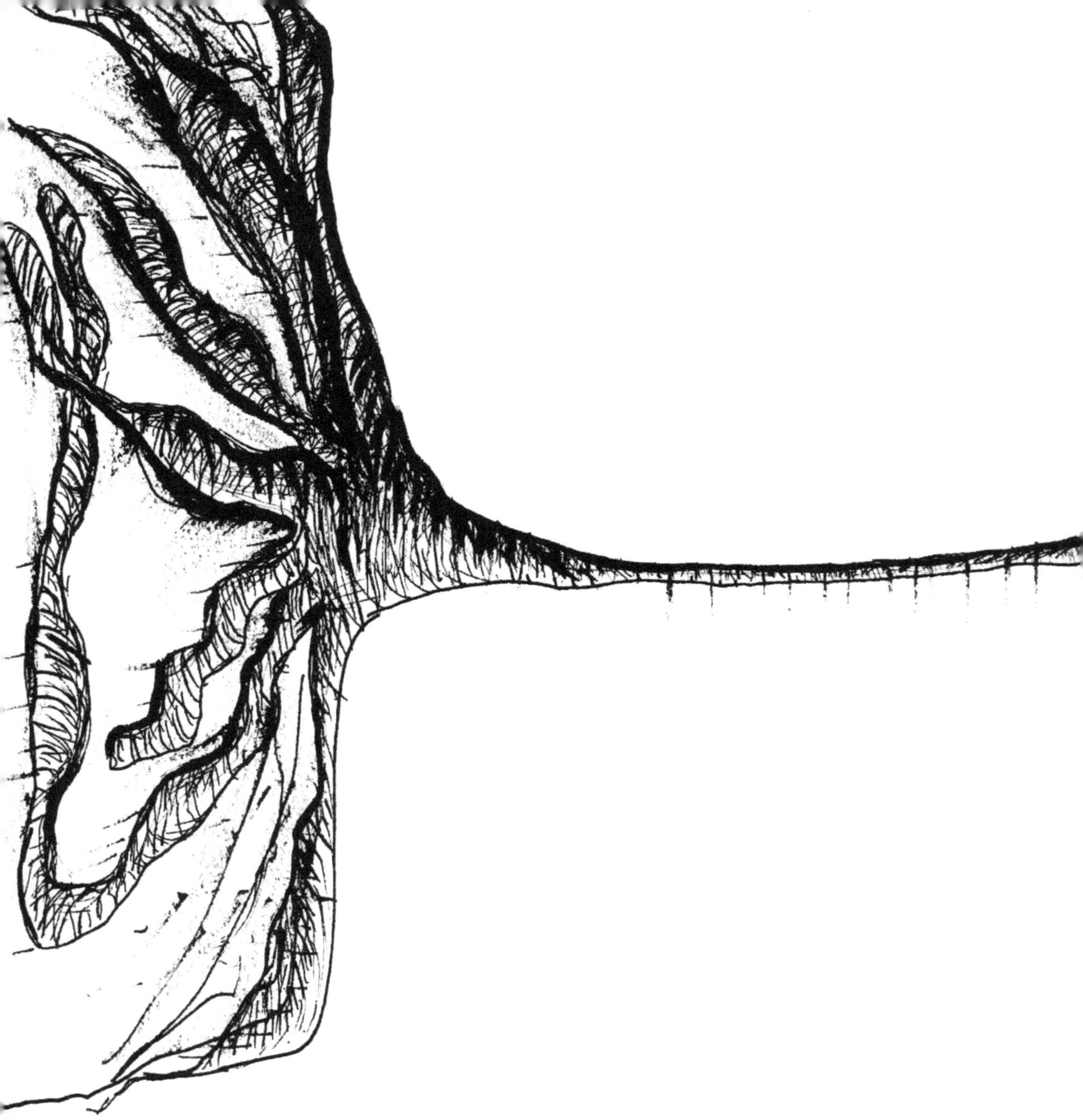

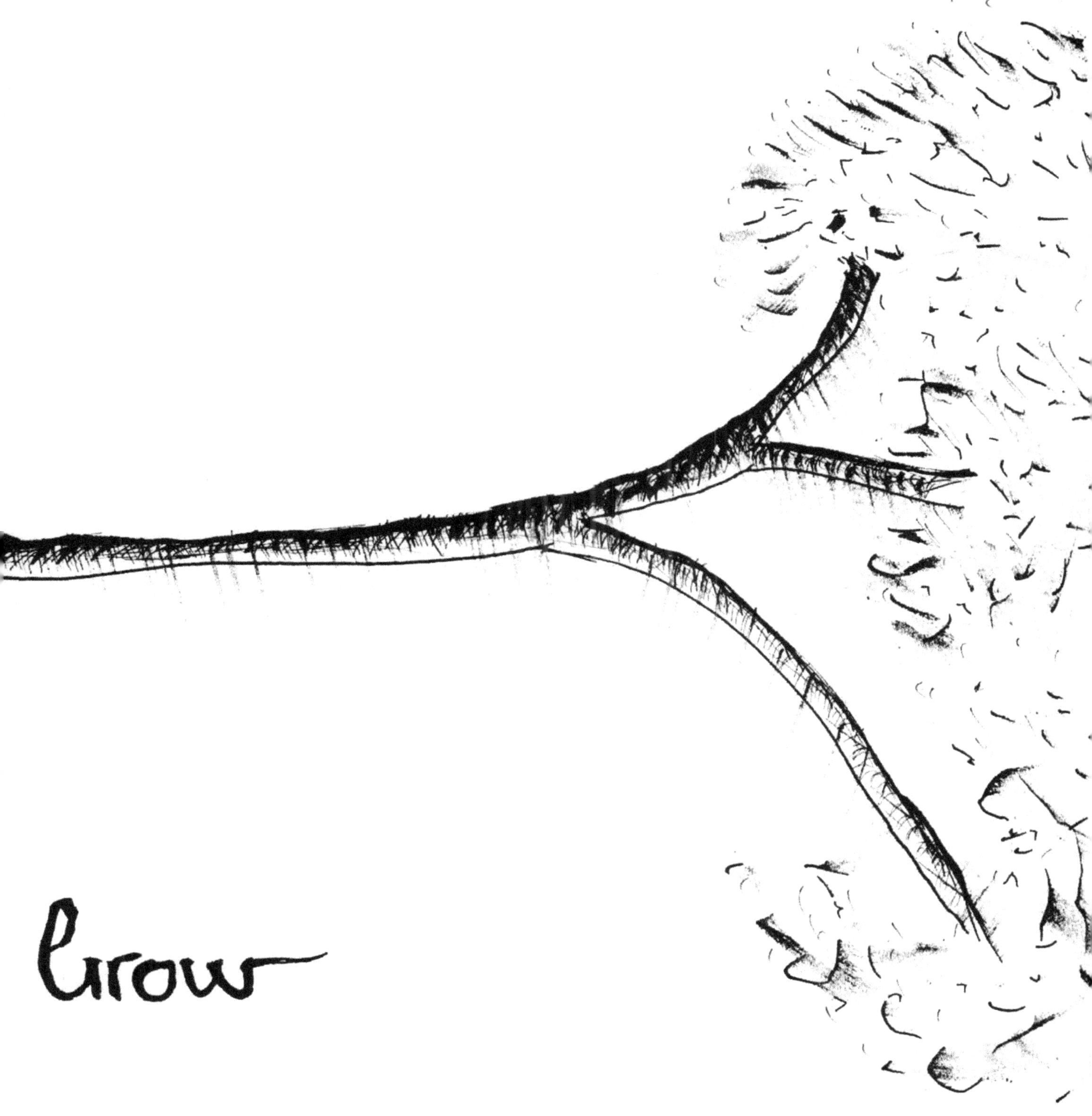
Grow

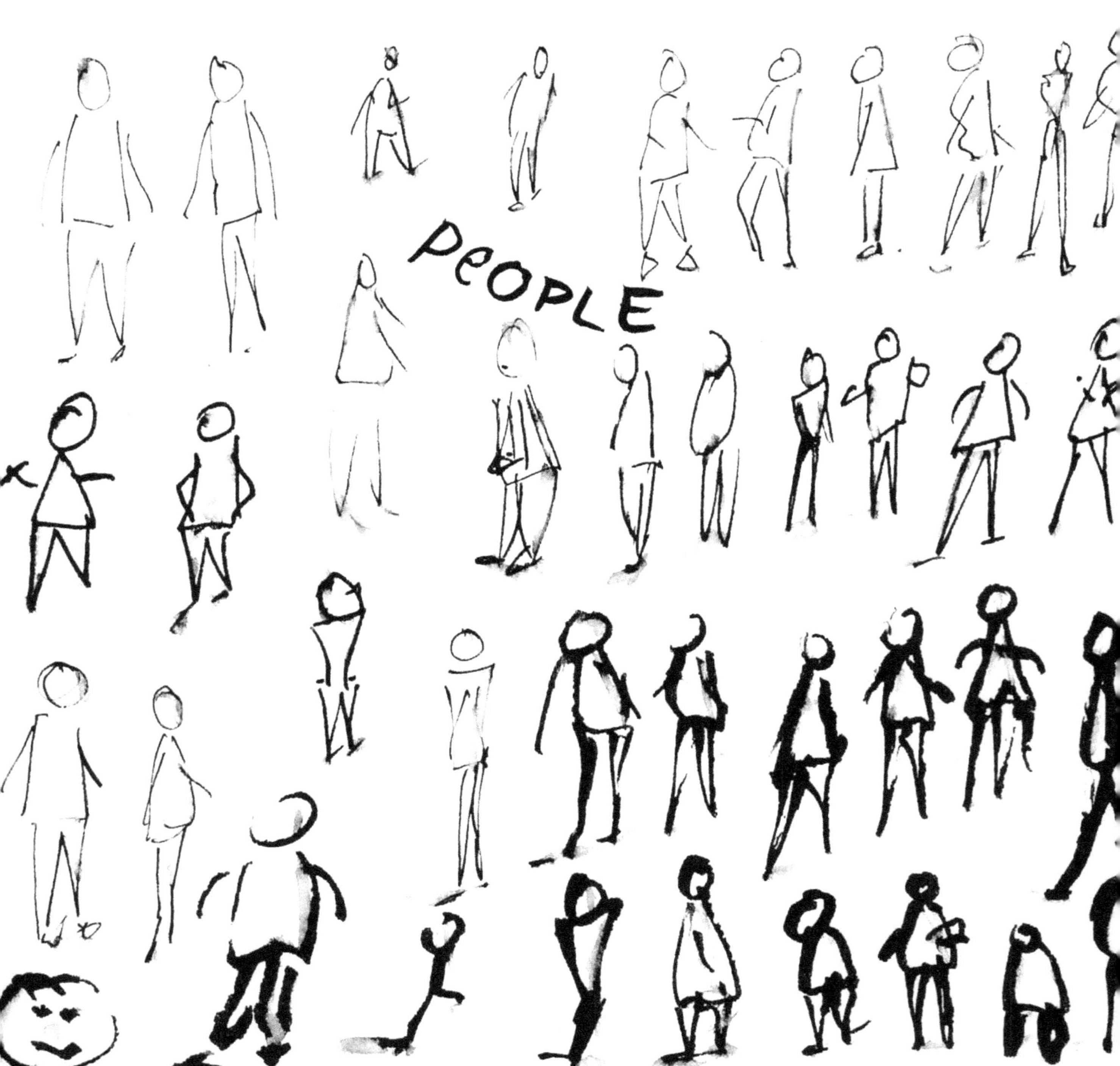
PEOPLE

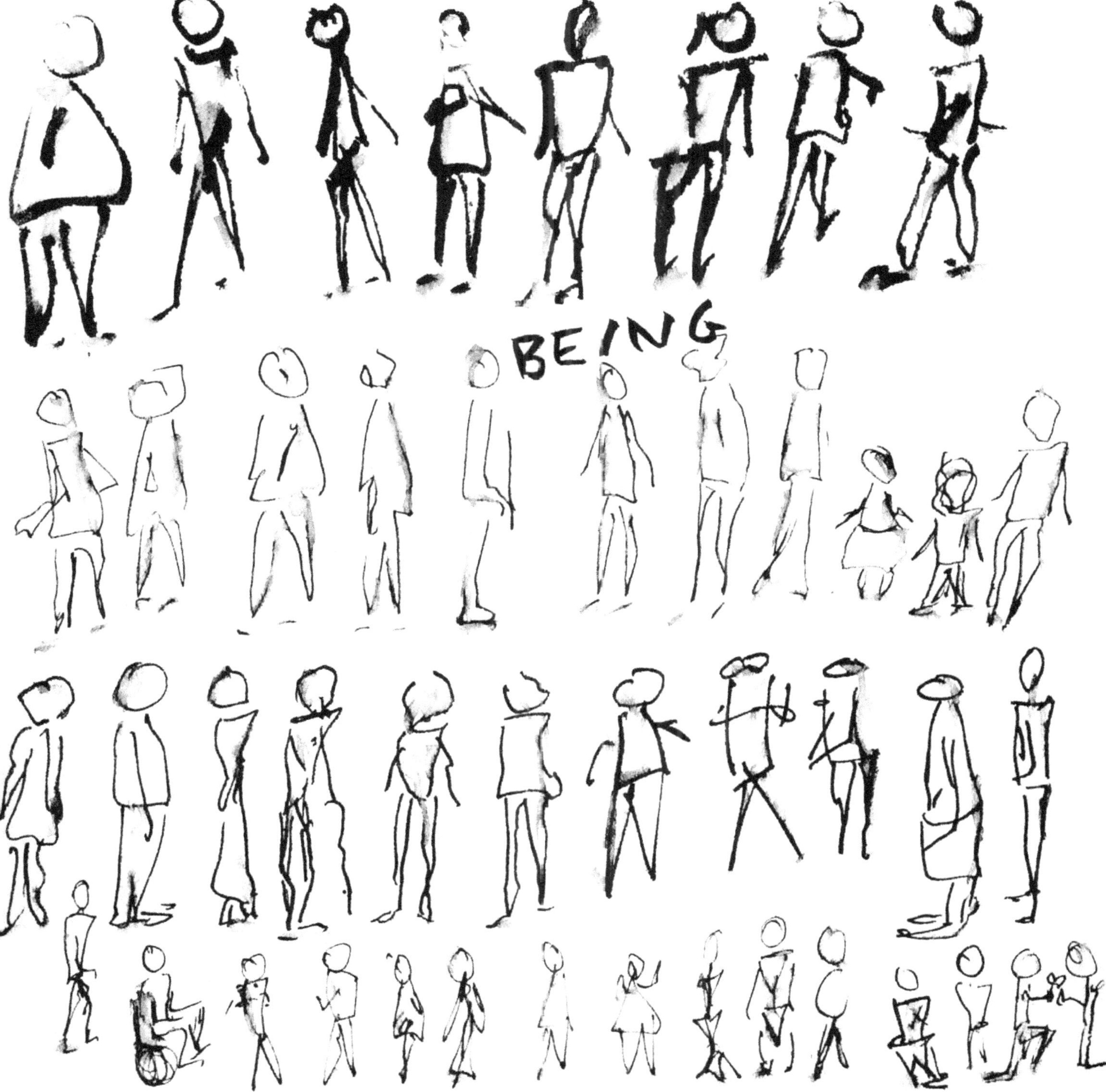
BEING

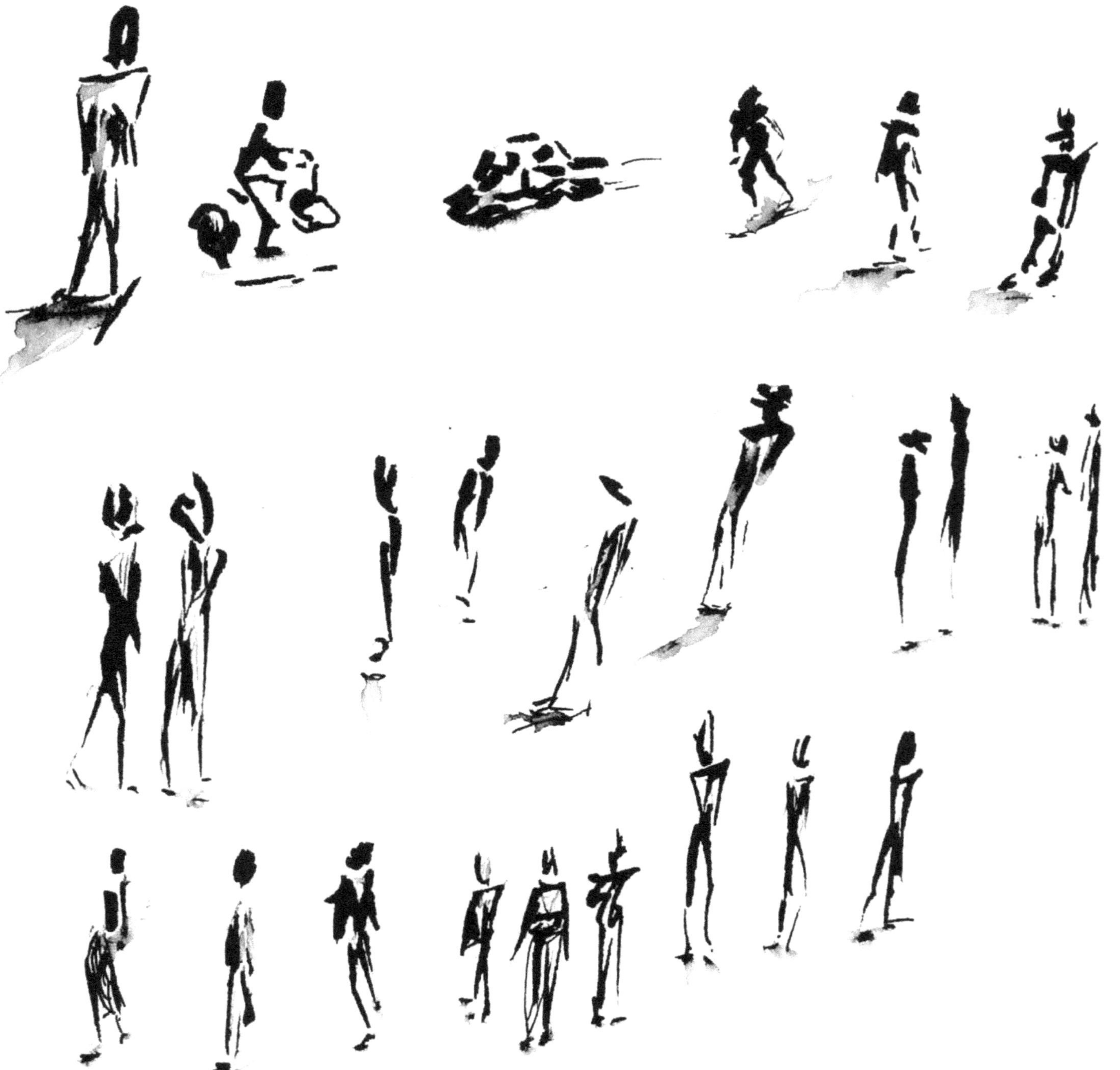

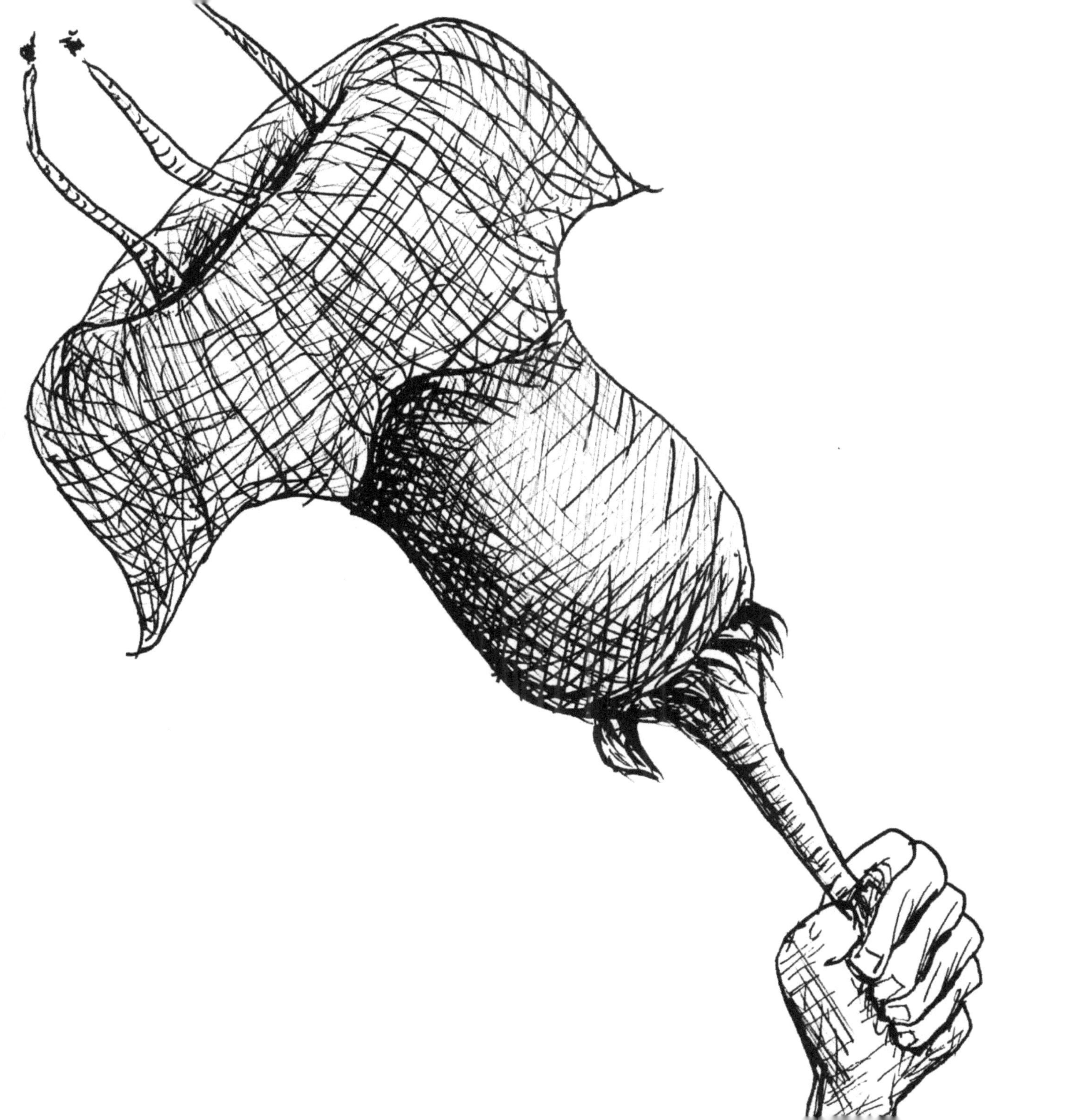

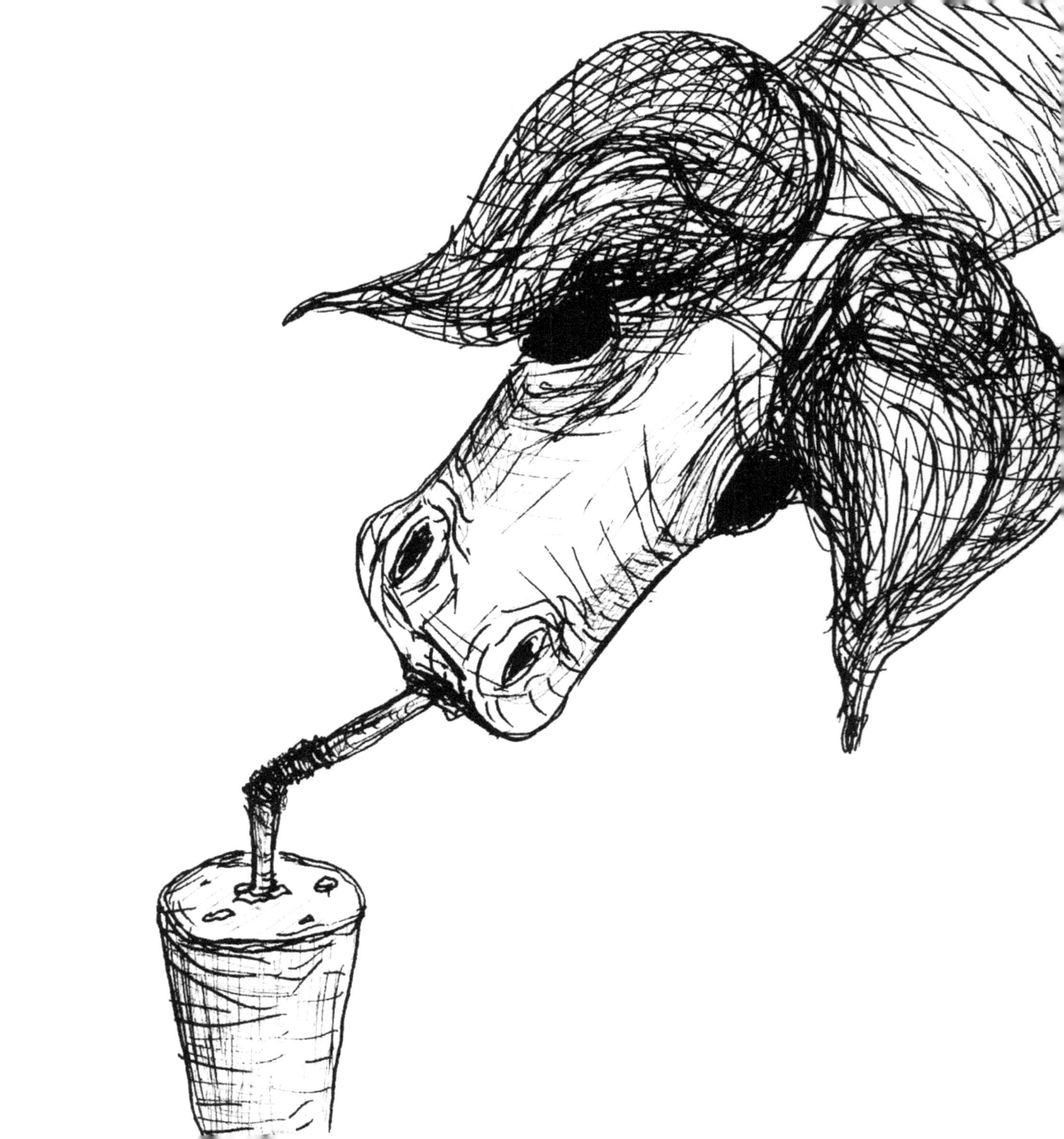

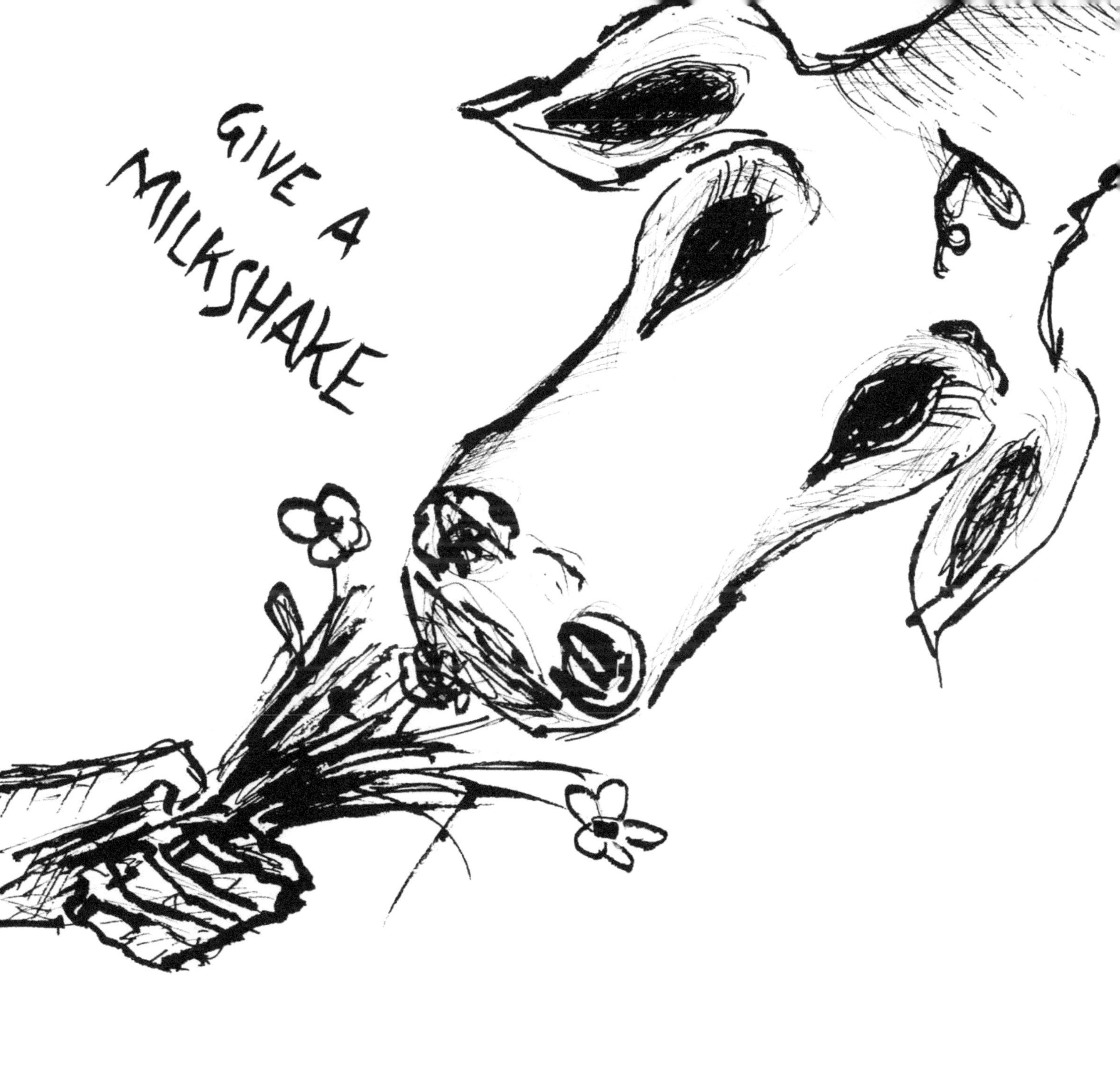
GIVE A
MILKSHAKE

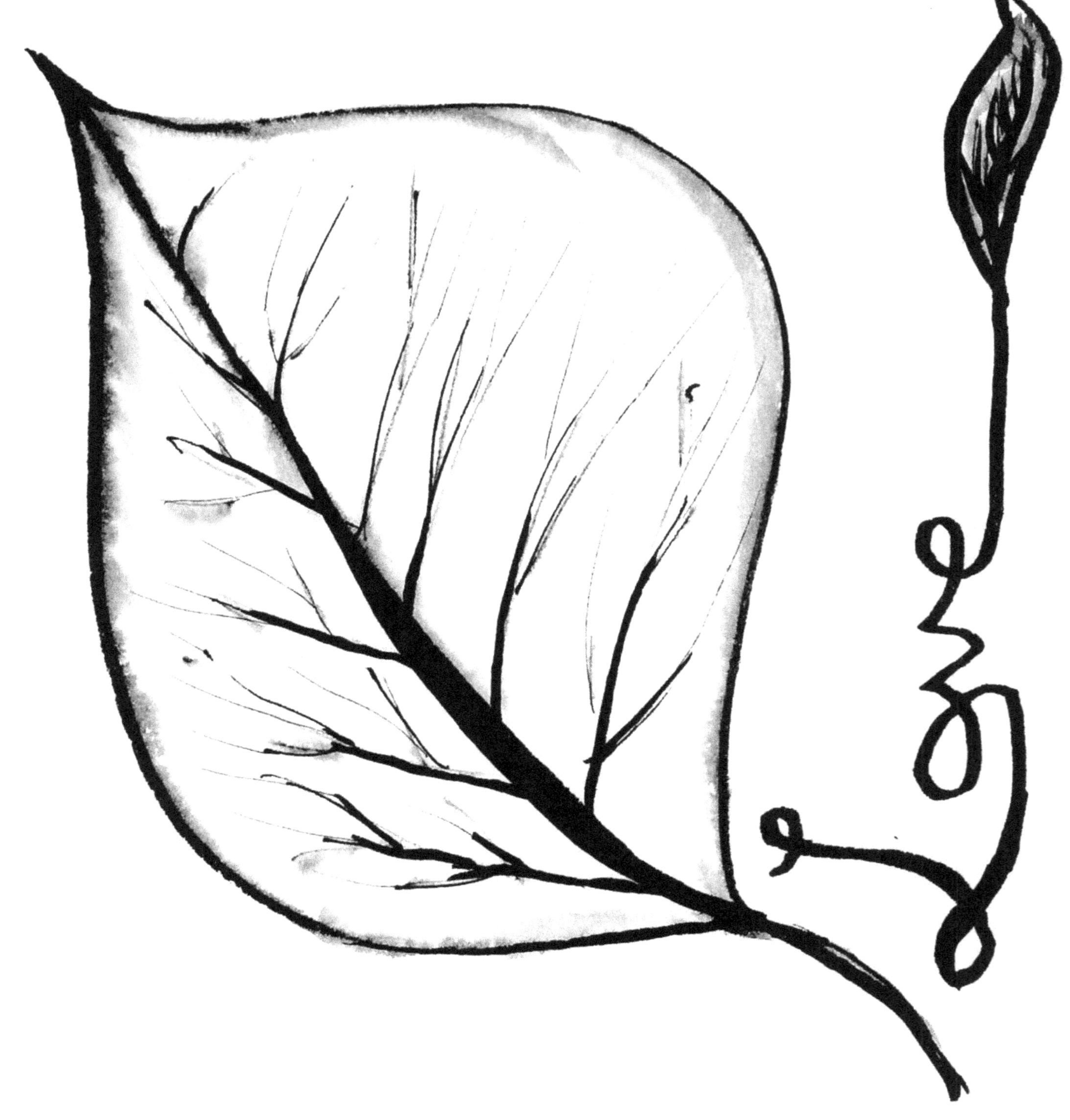

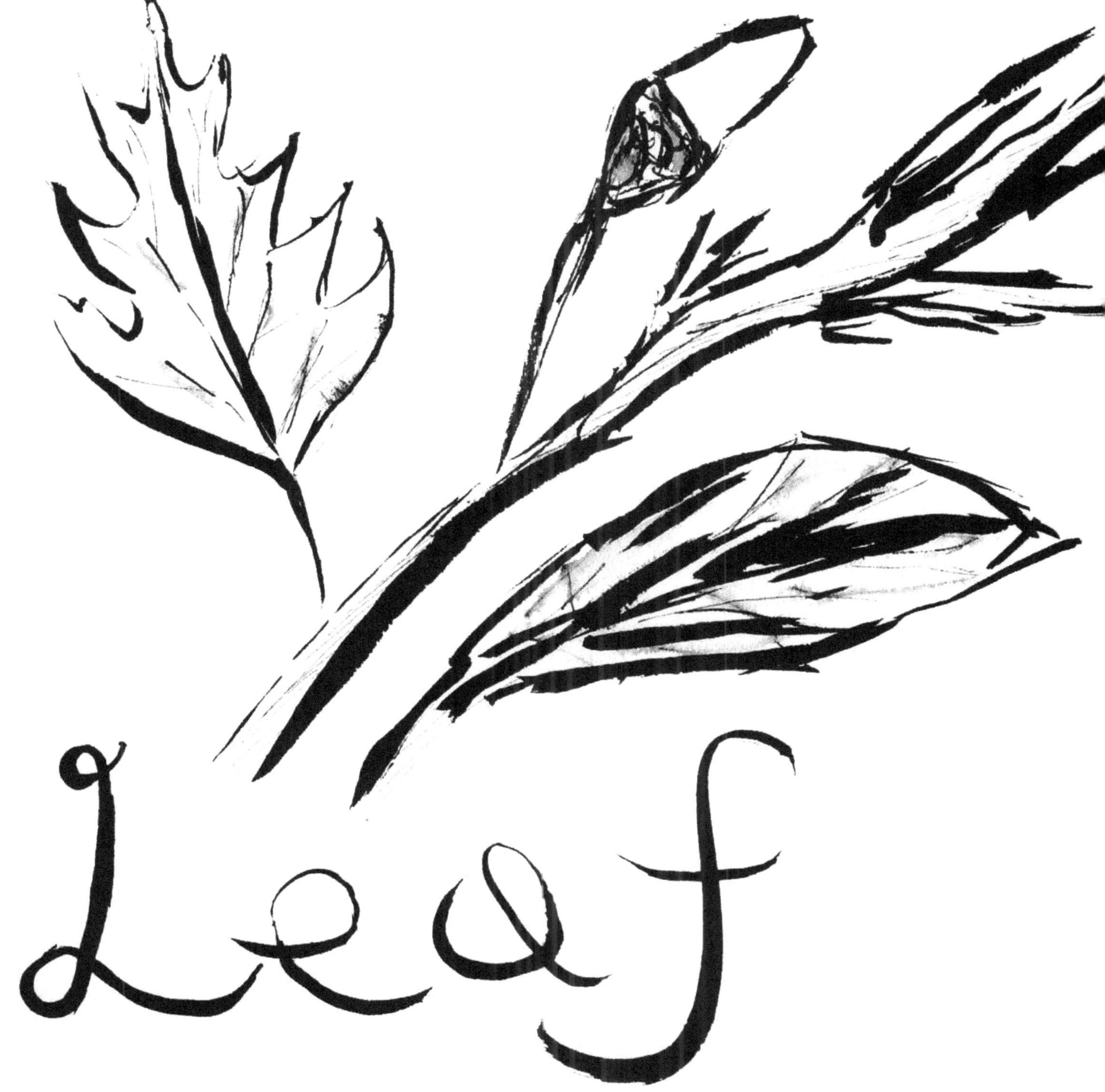
Leaf

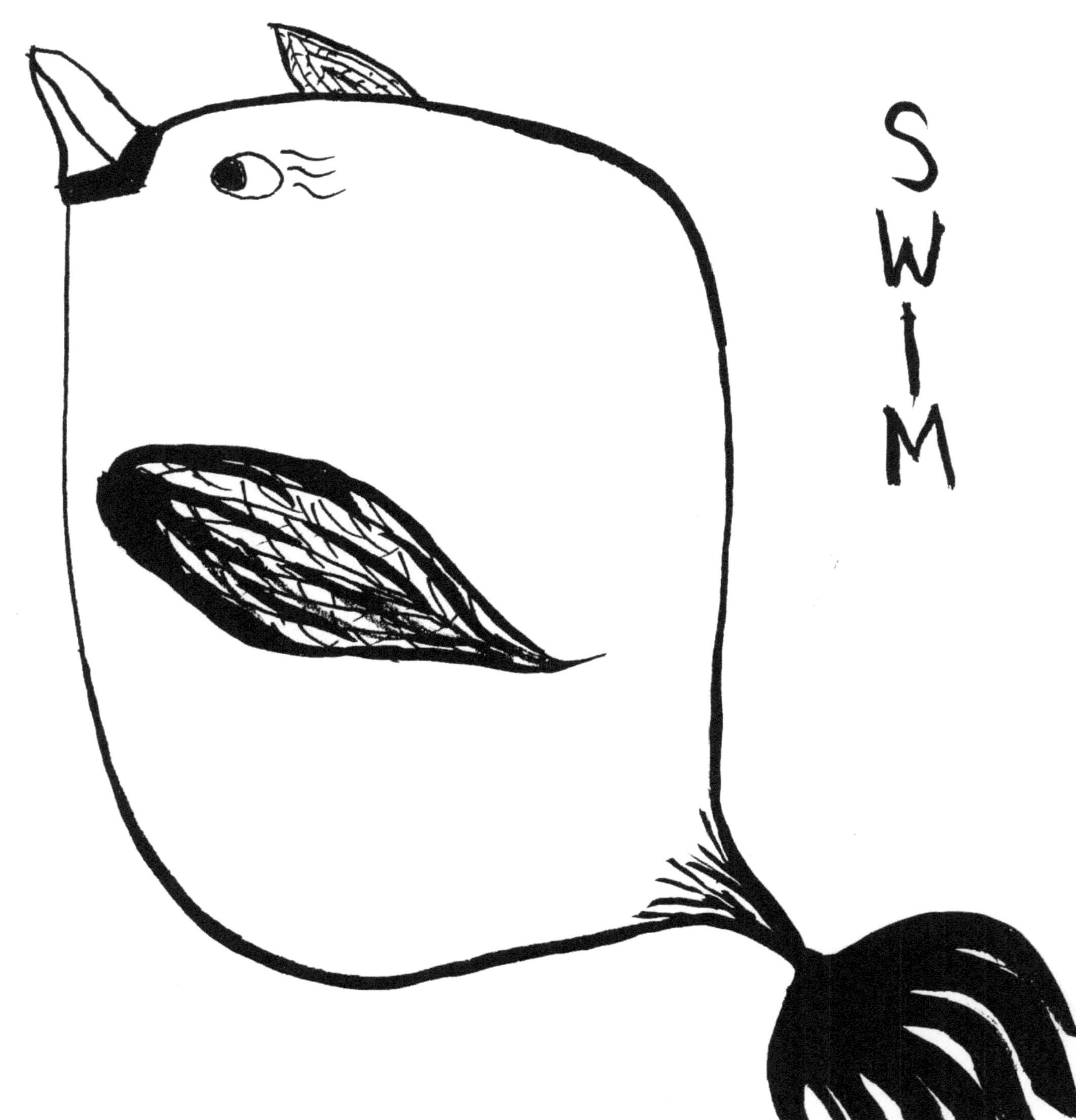
SWIM

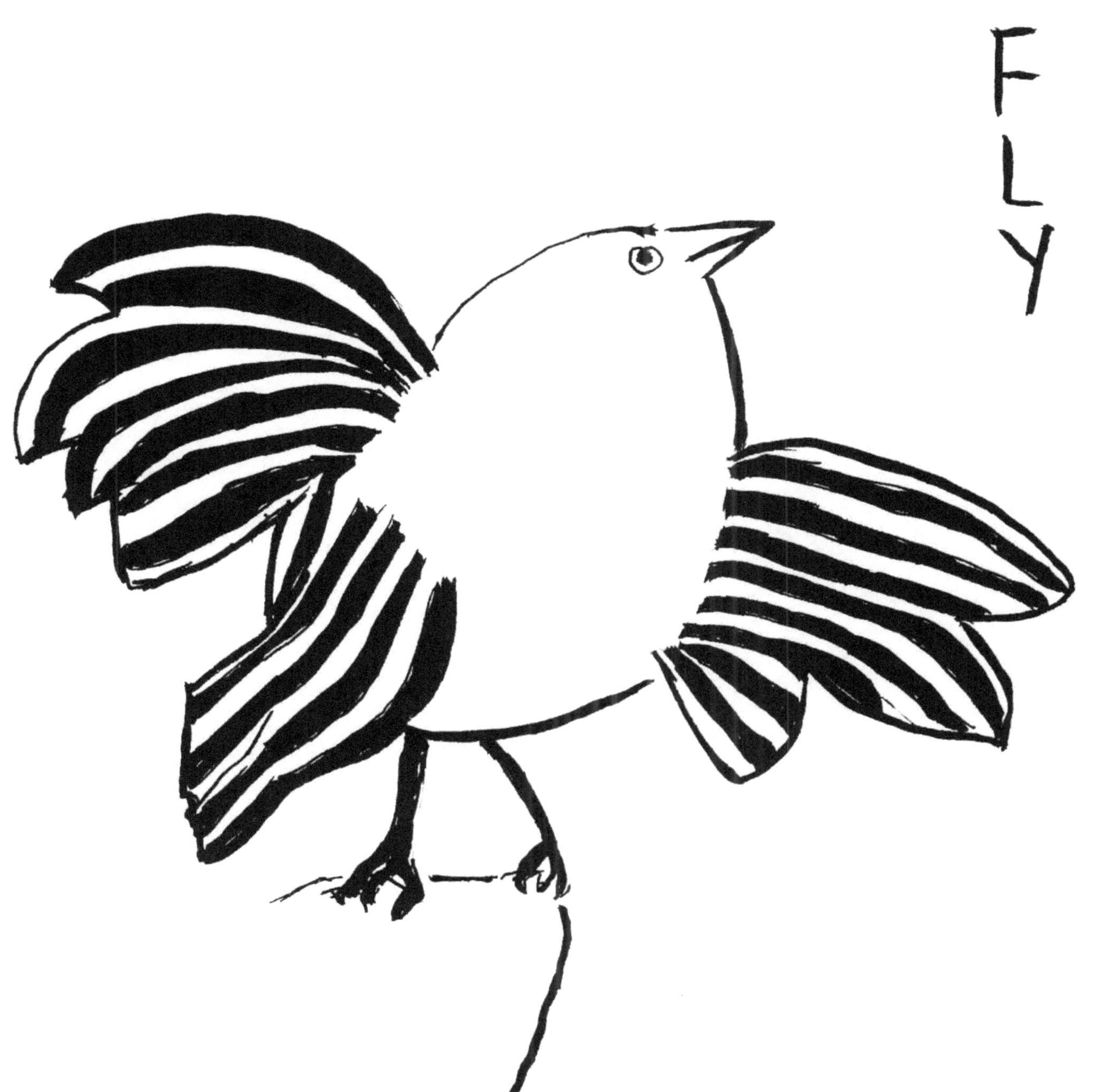
FLY

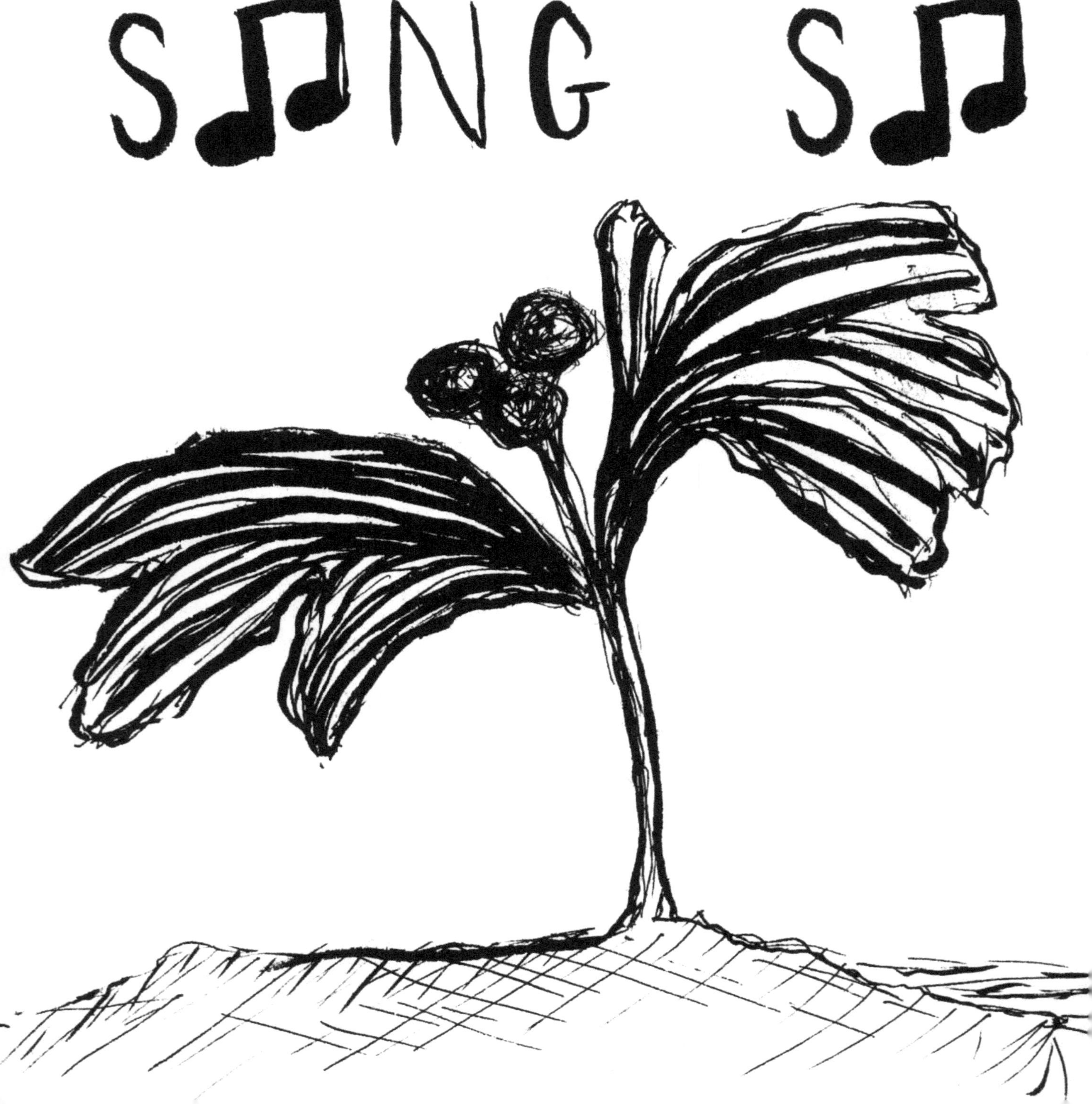

SONGS
SO

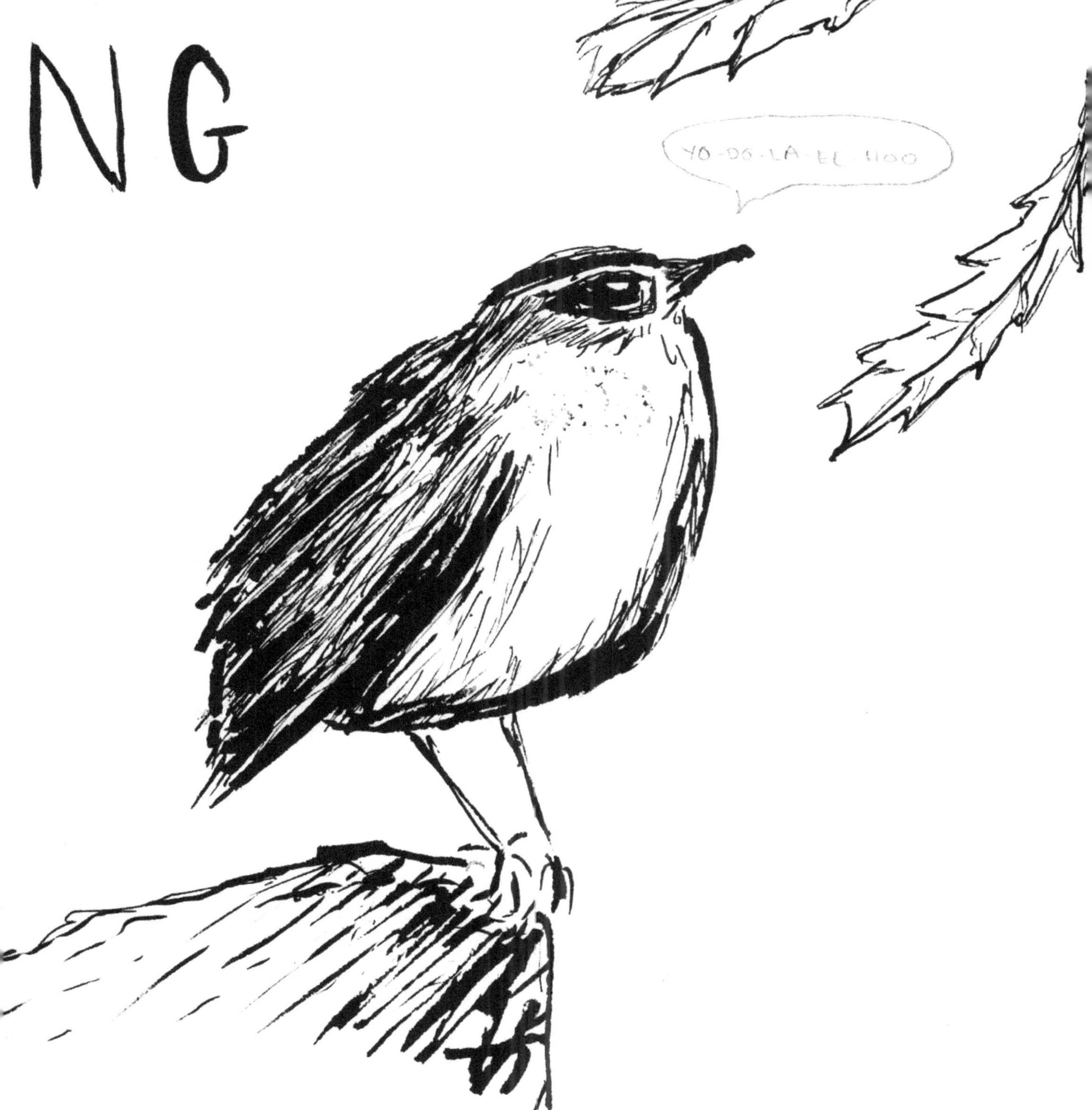

NG
YO-OO-LA-EE-HOO

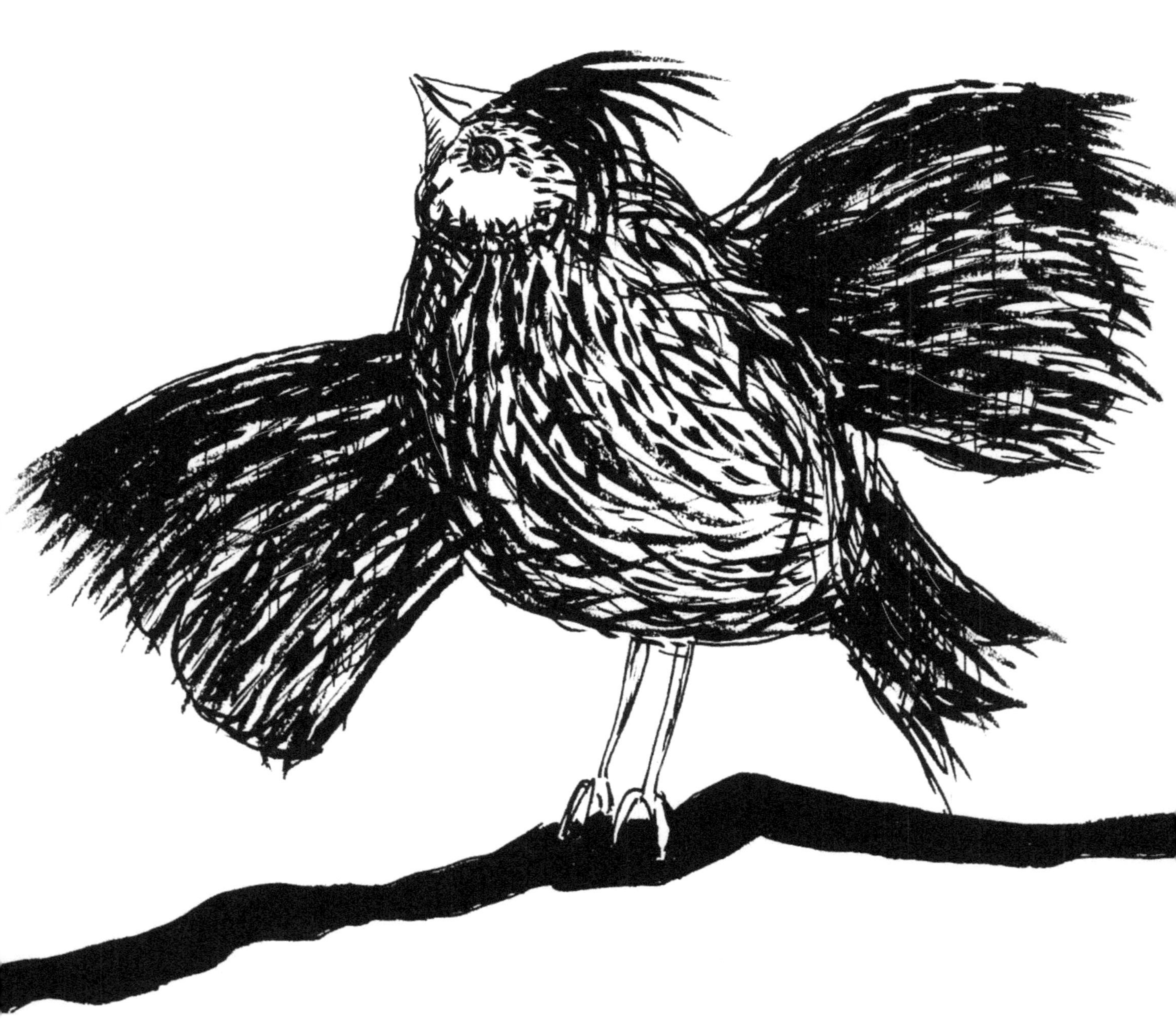

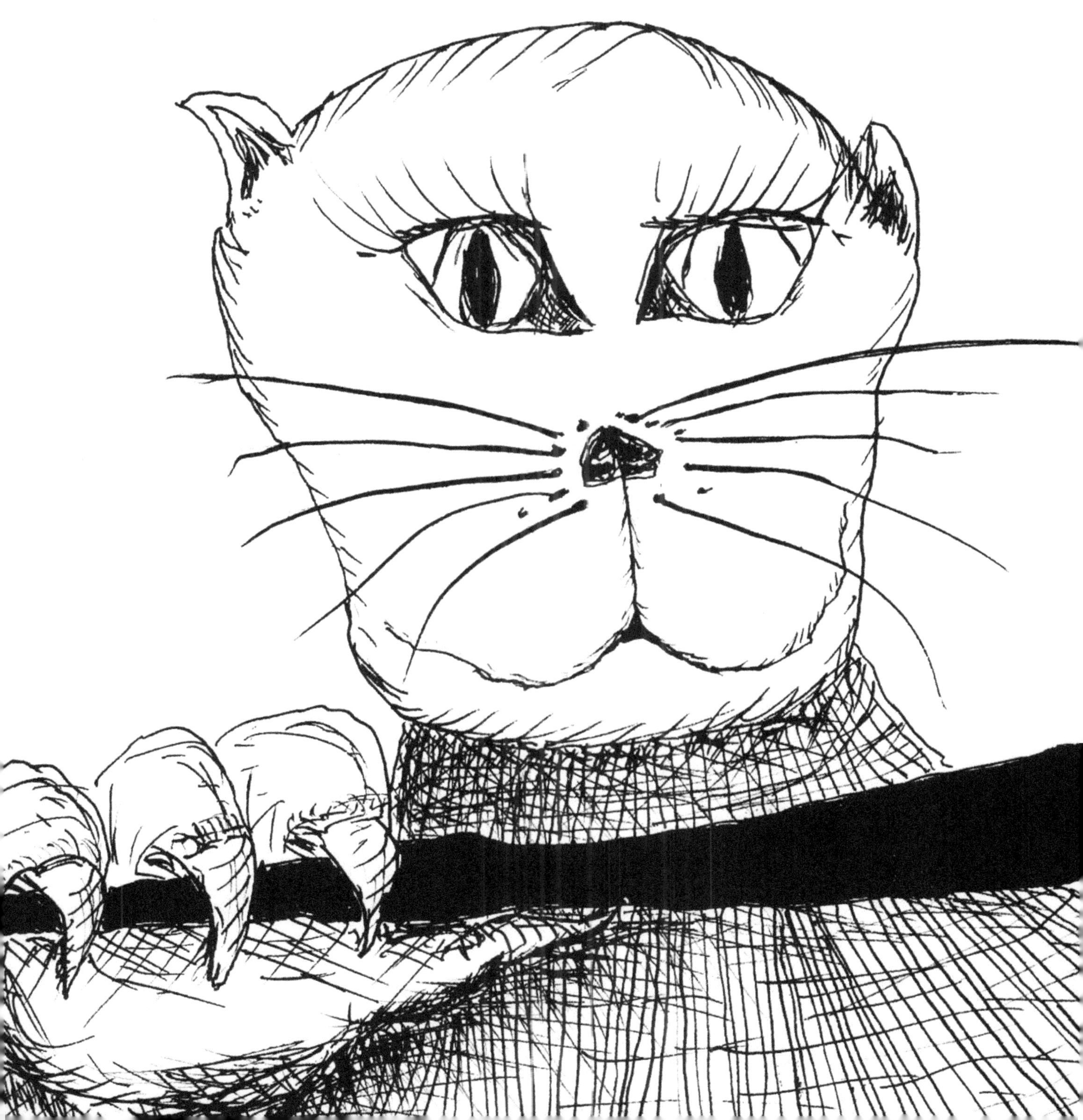

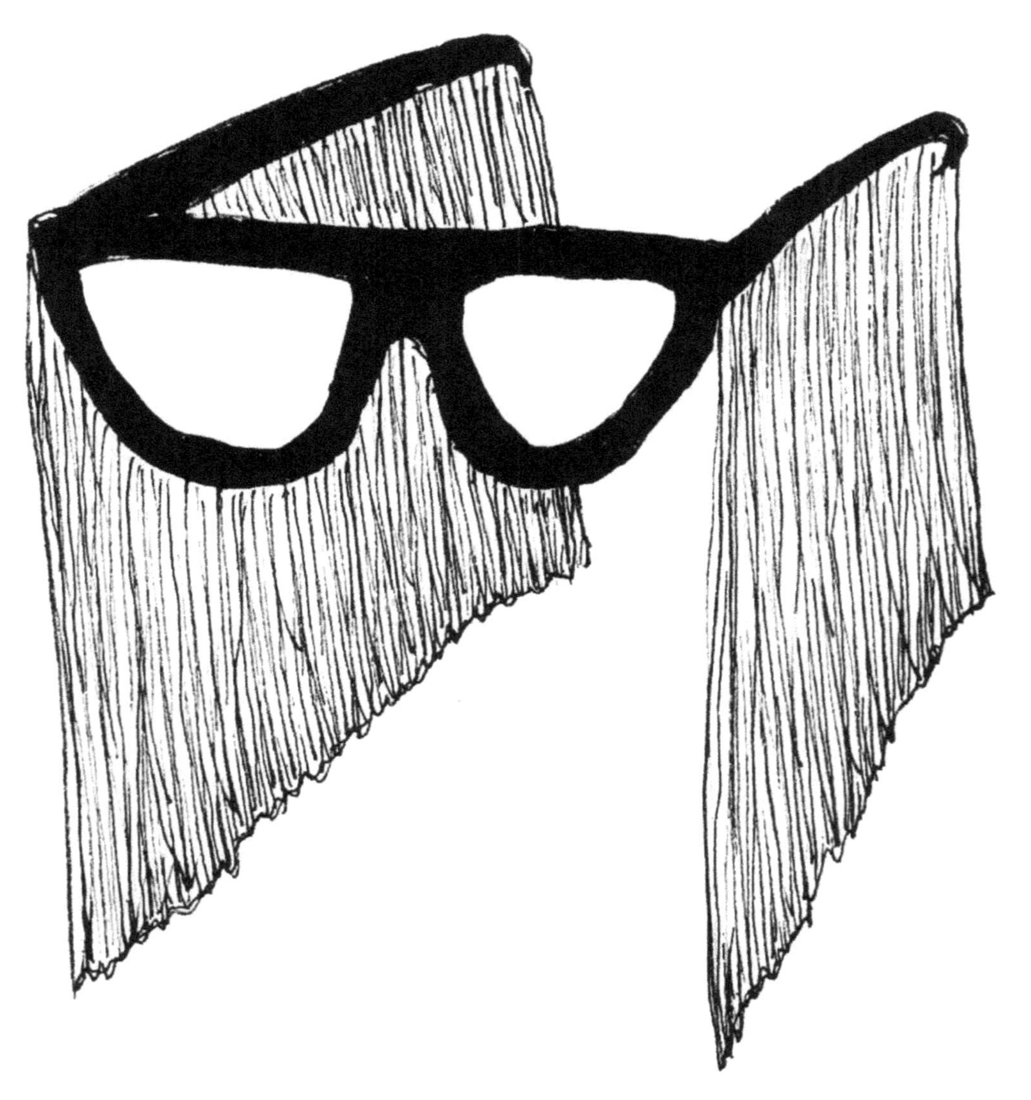

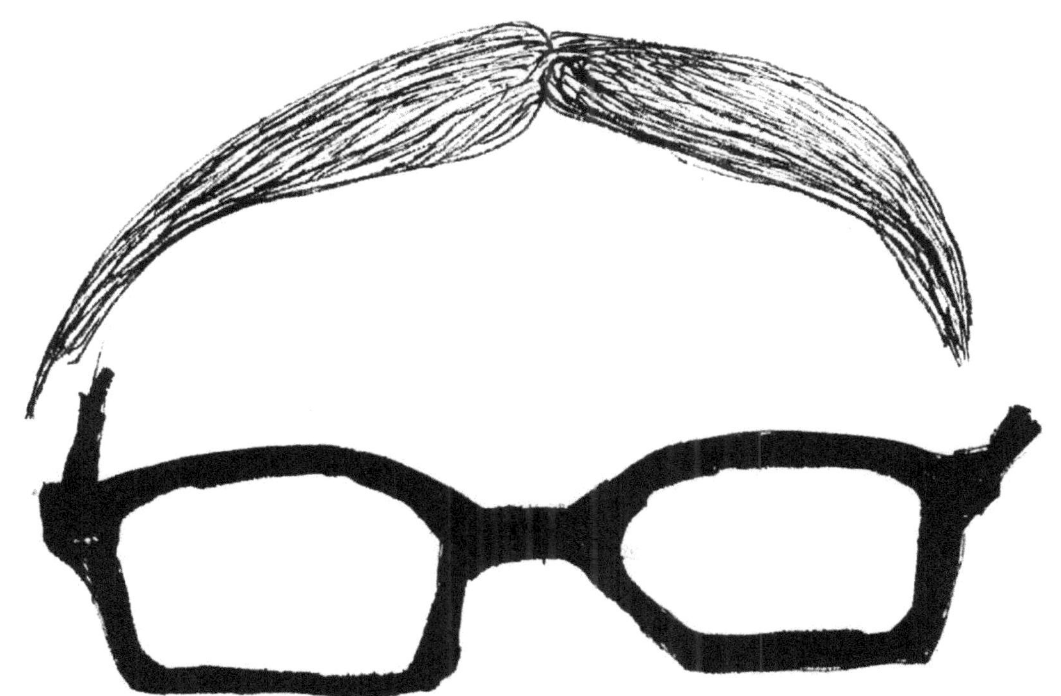
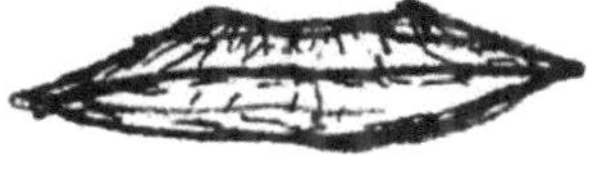

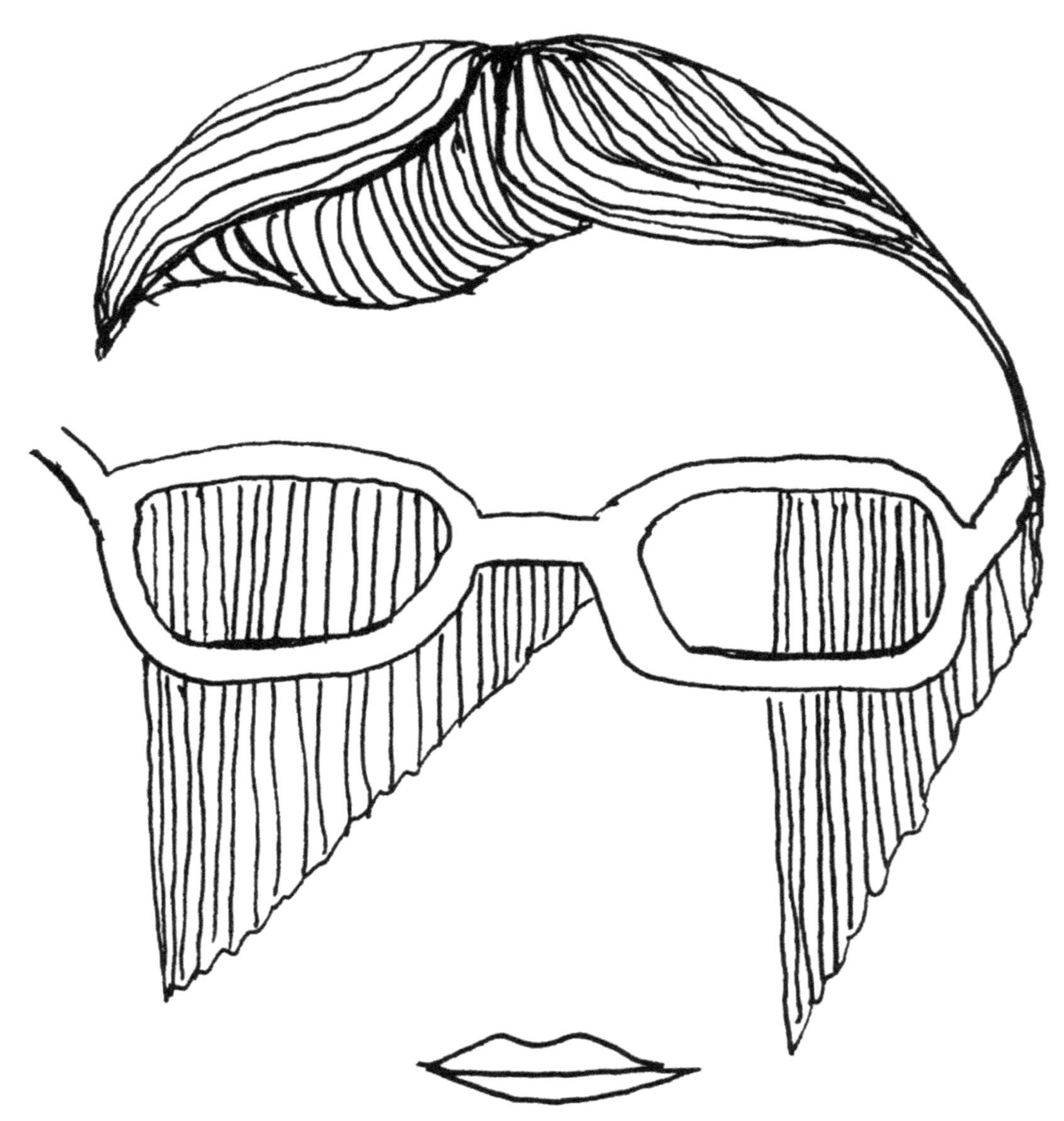

BE
YOUR
OWN
Character

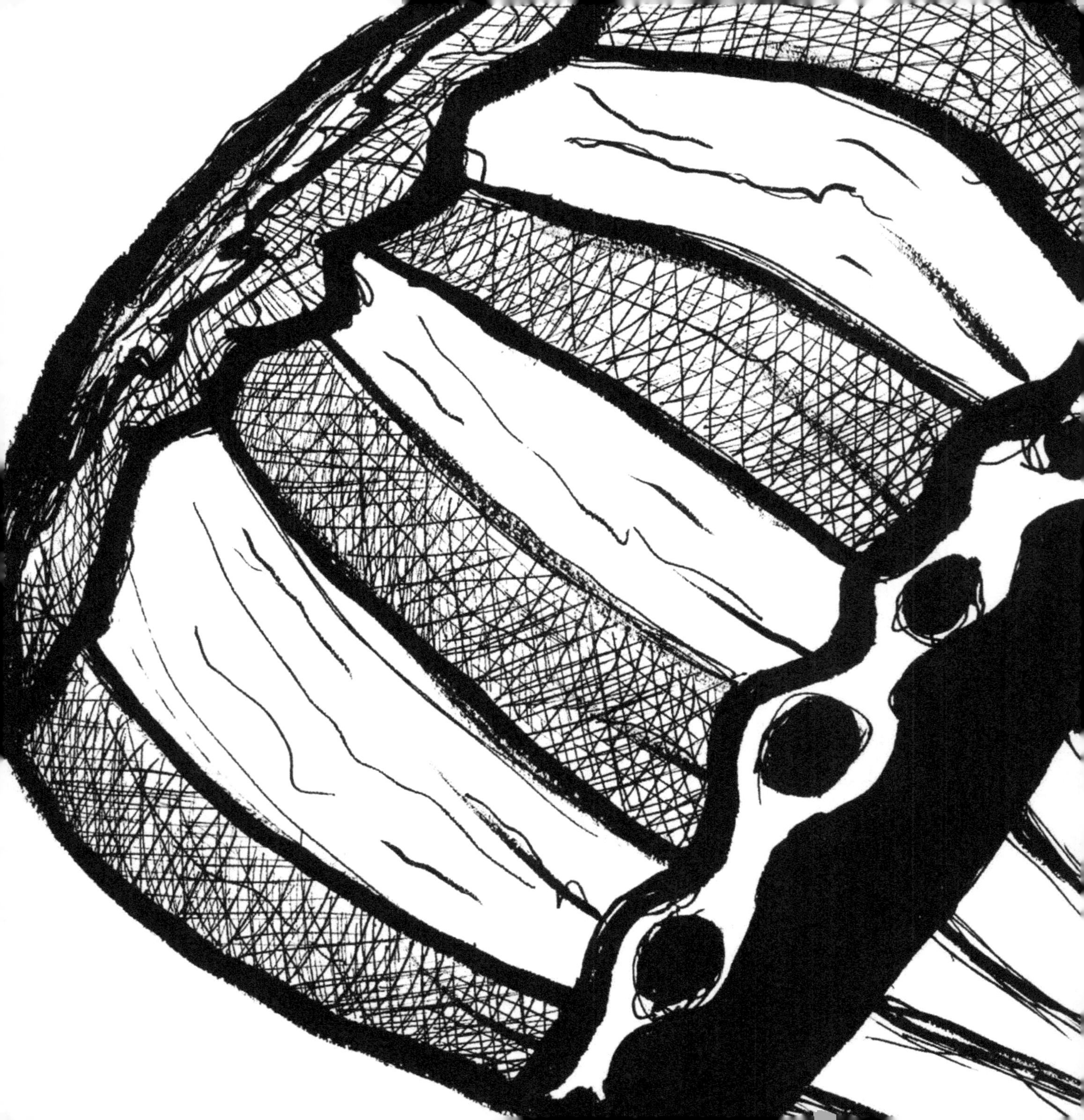

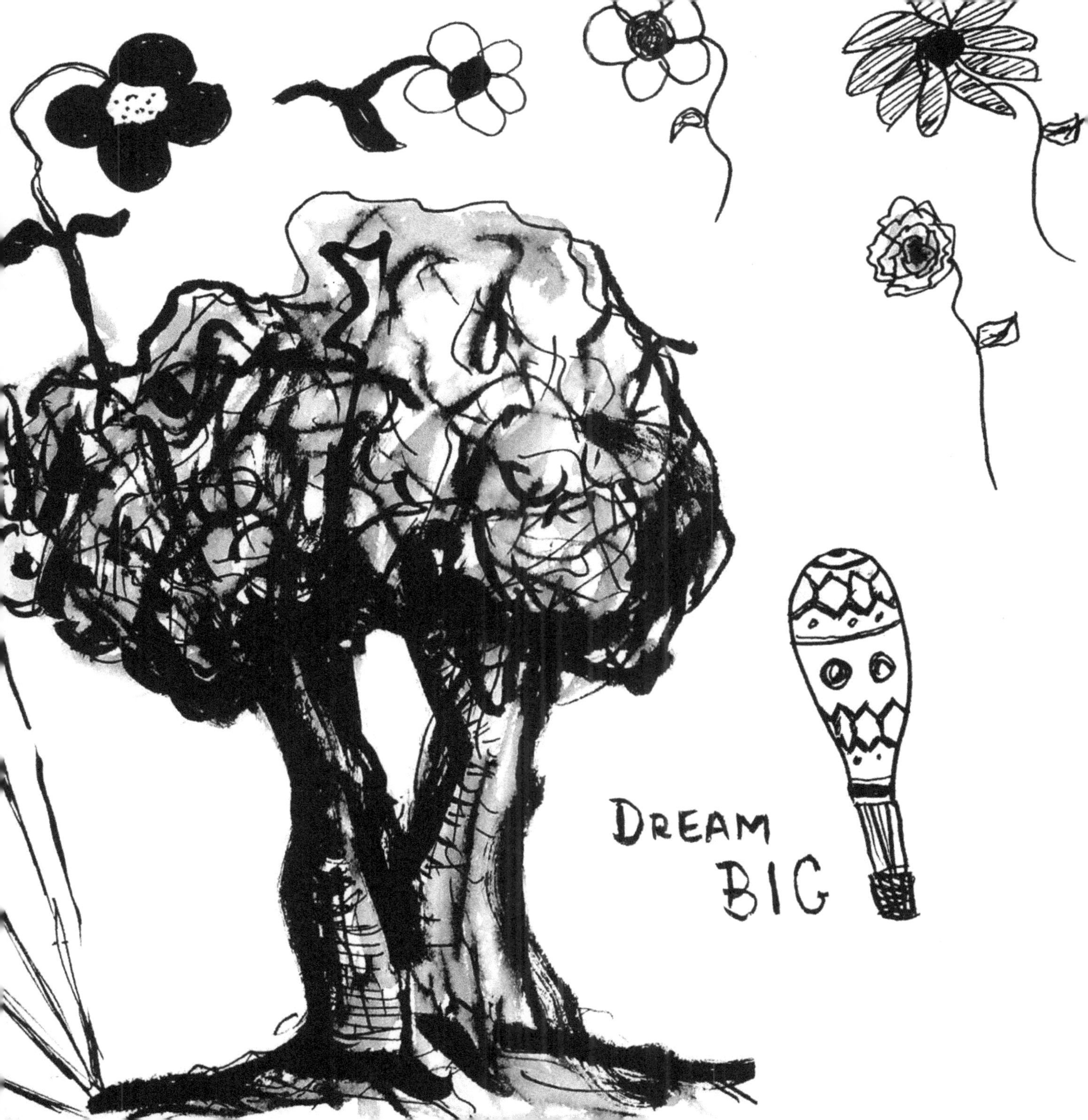

DREAM
BIG

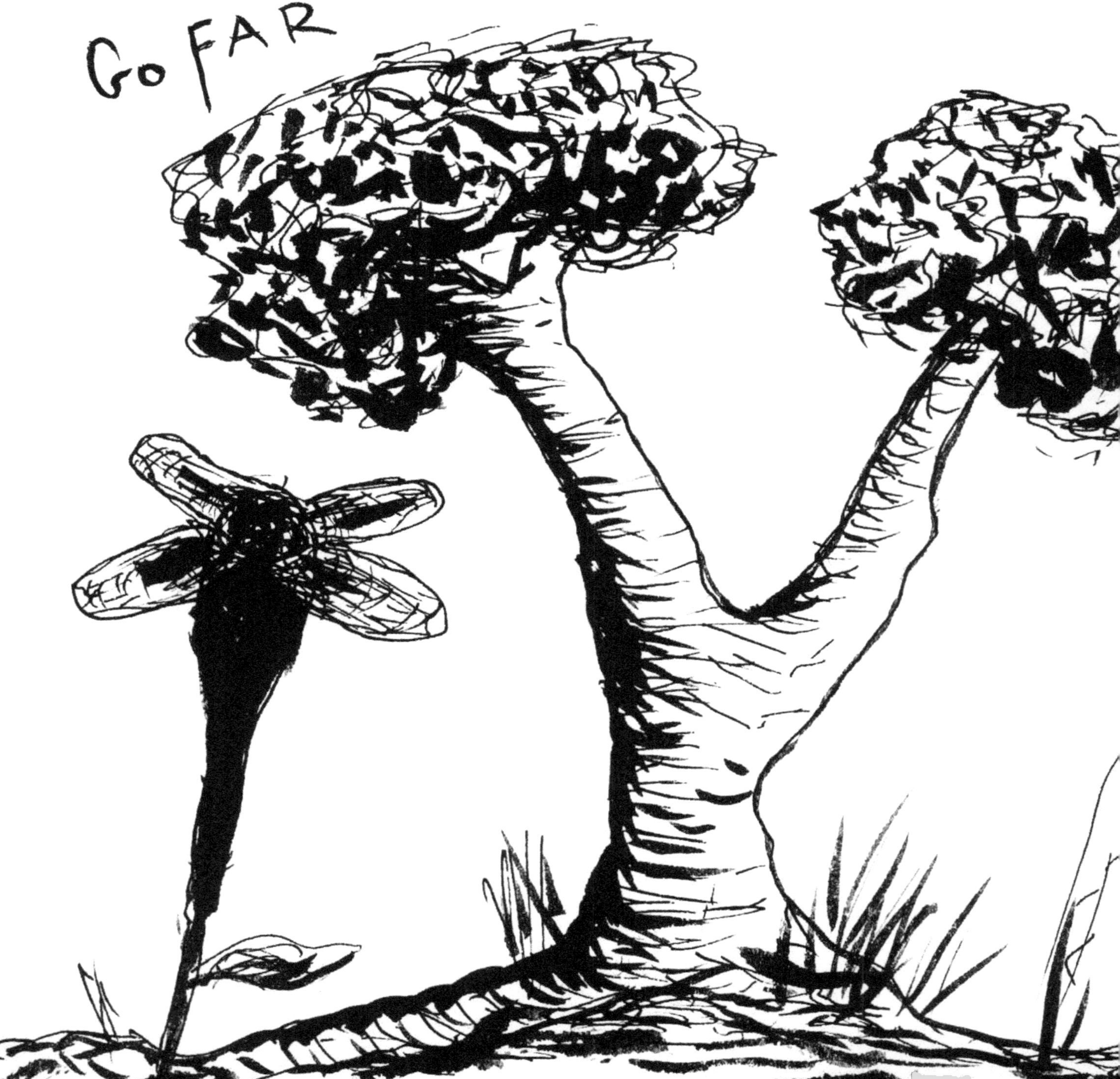
GO FAR

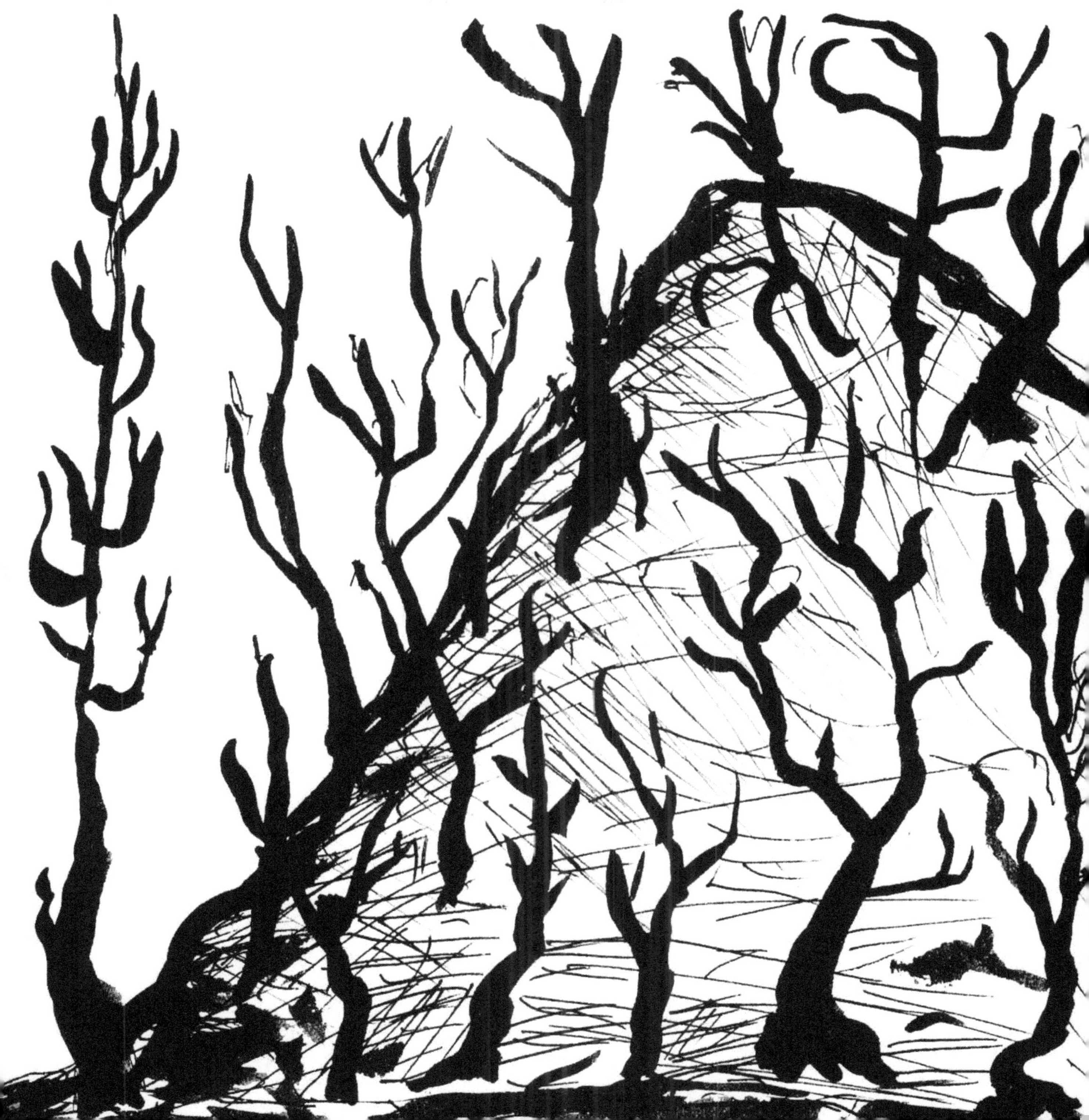

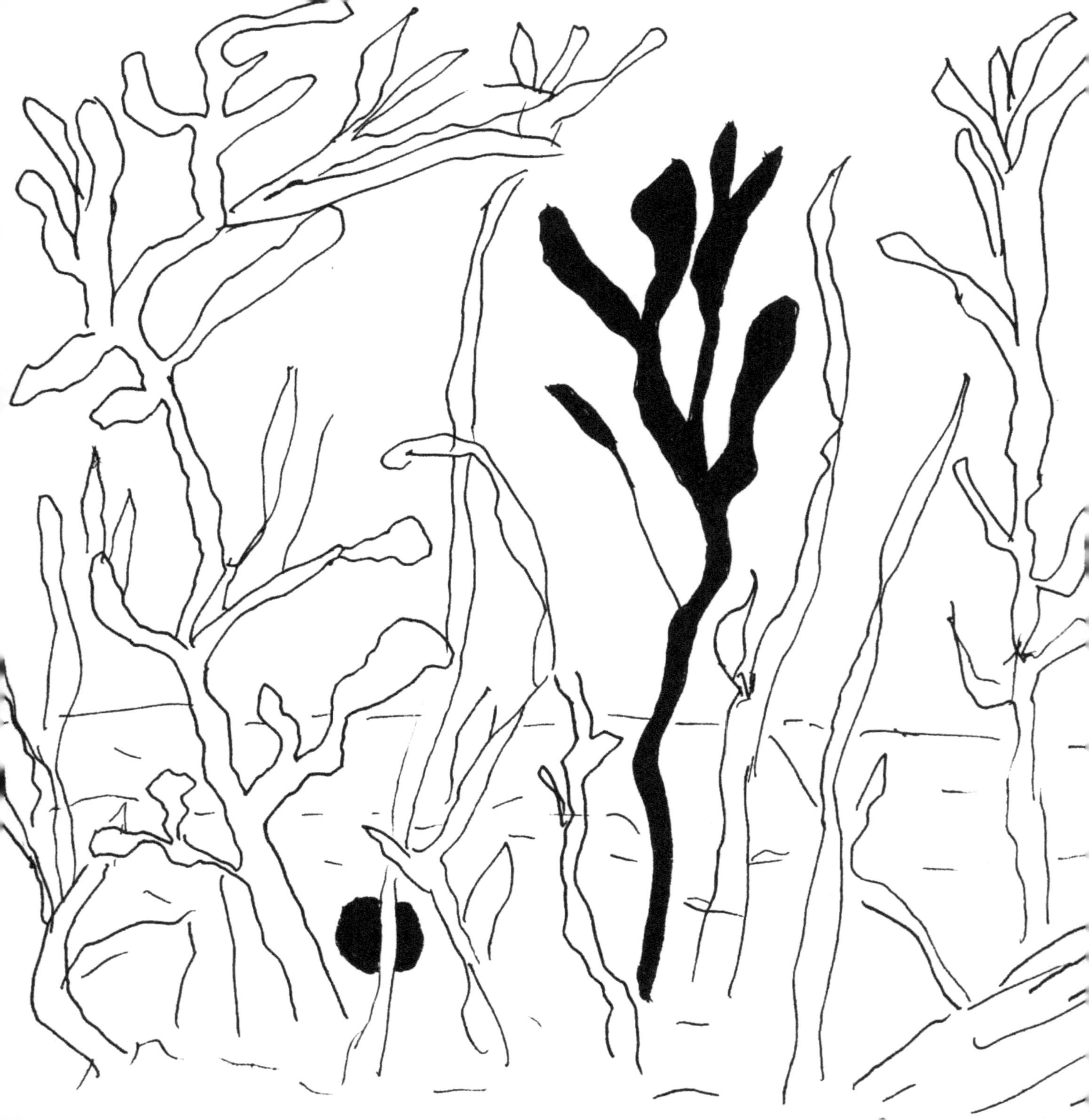

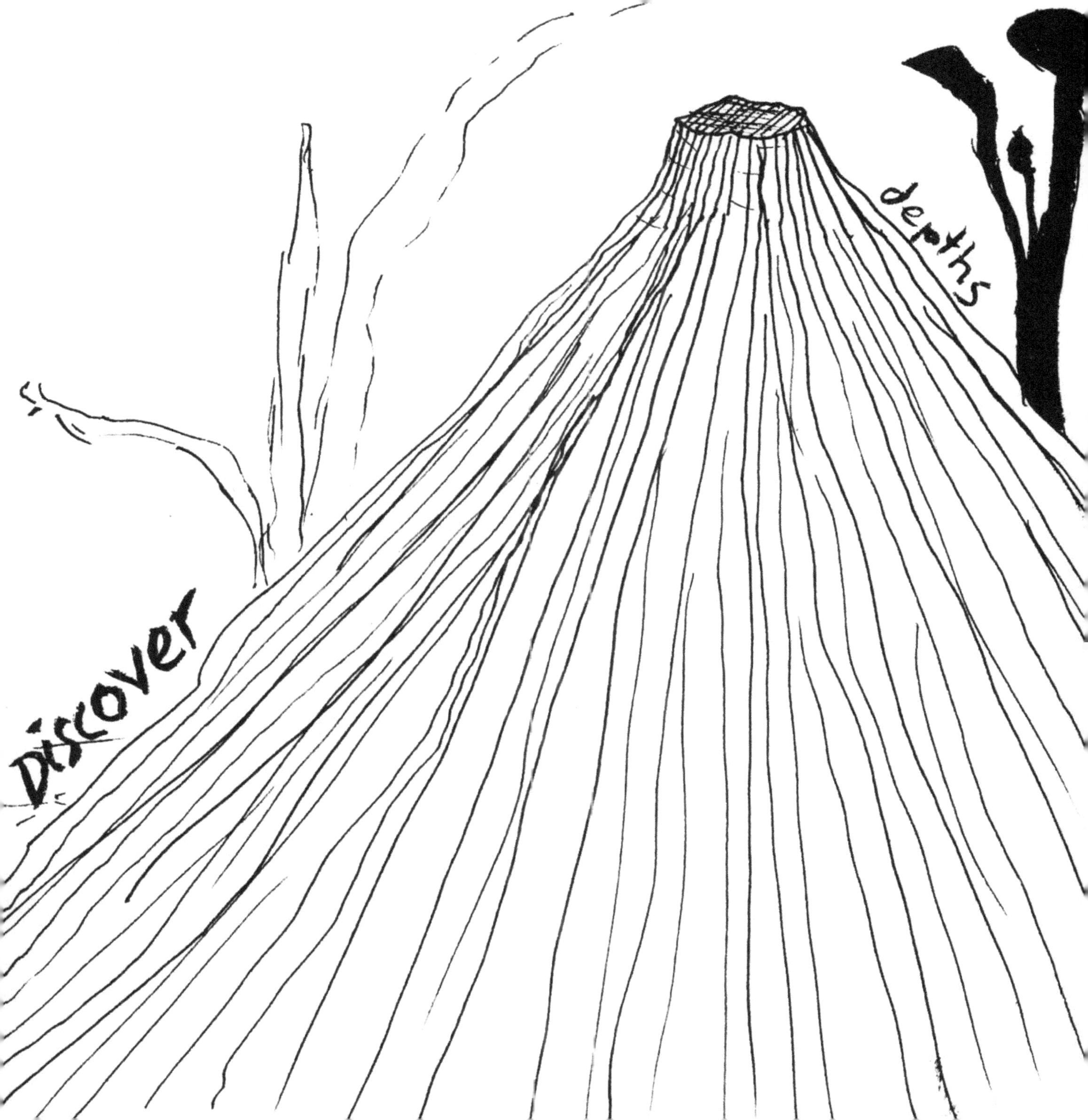

Discover
depths

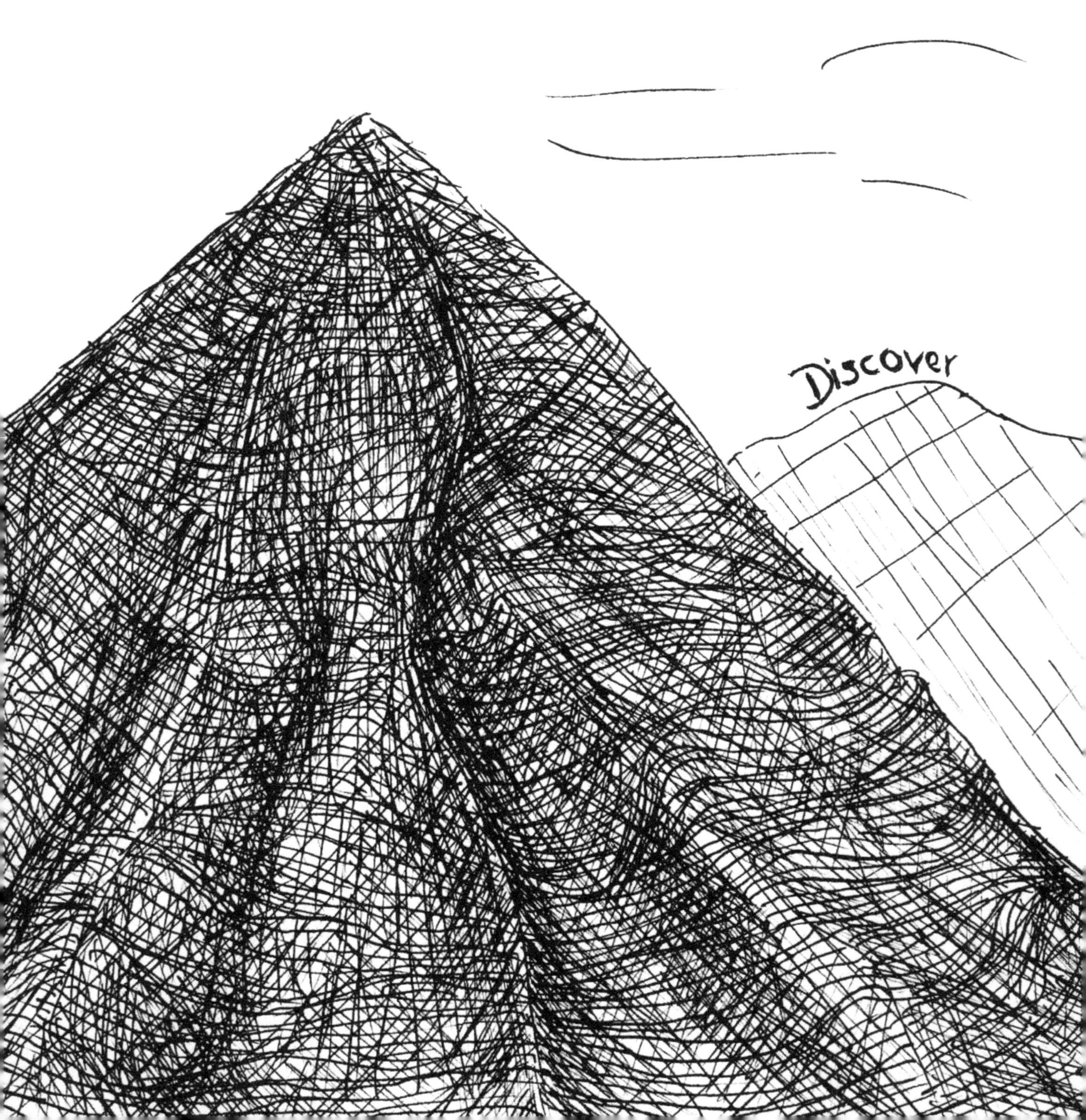

Discover

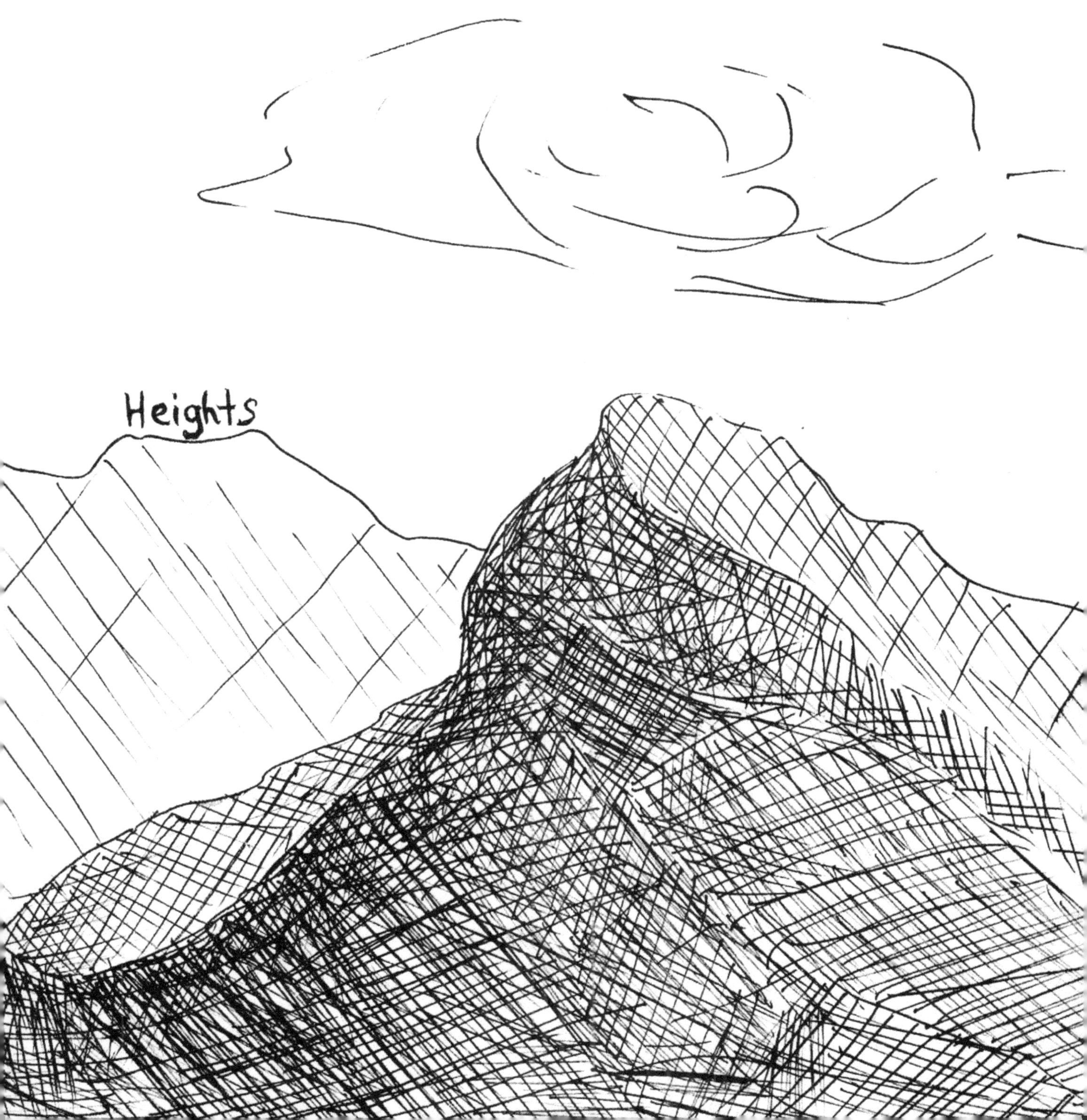
Heights

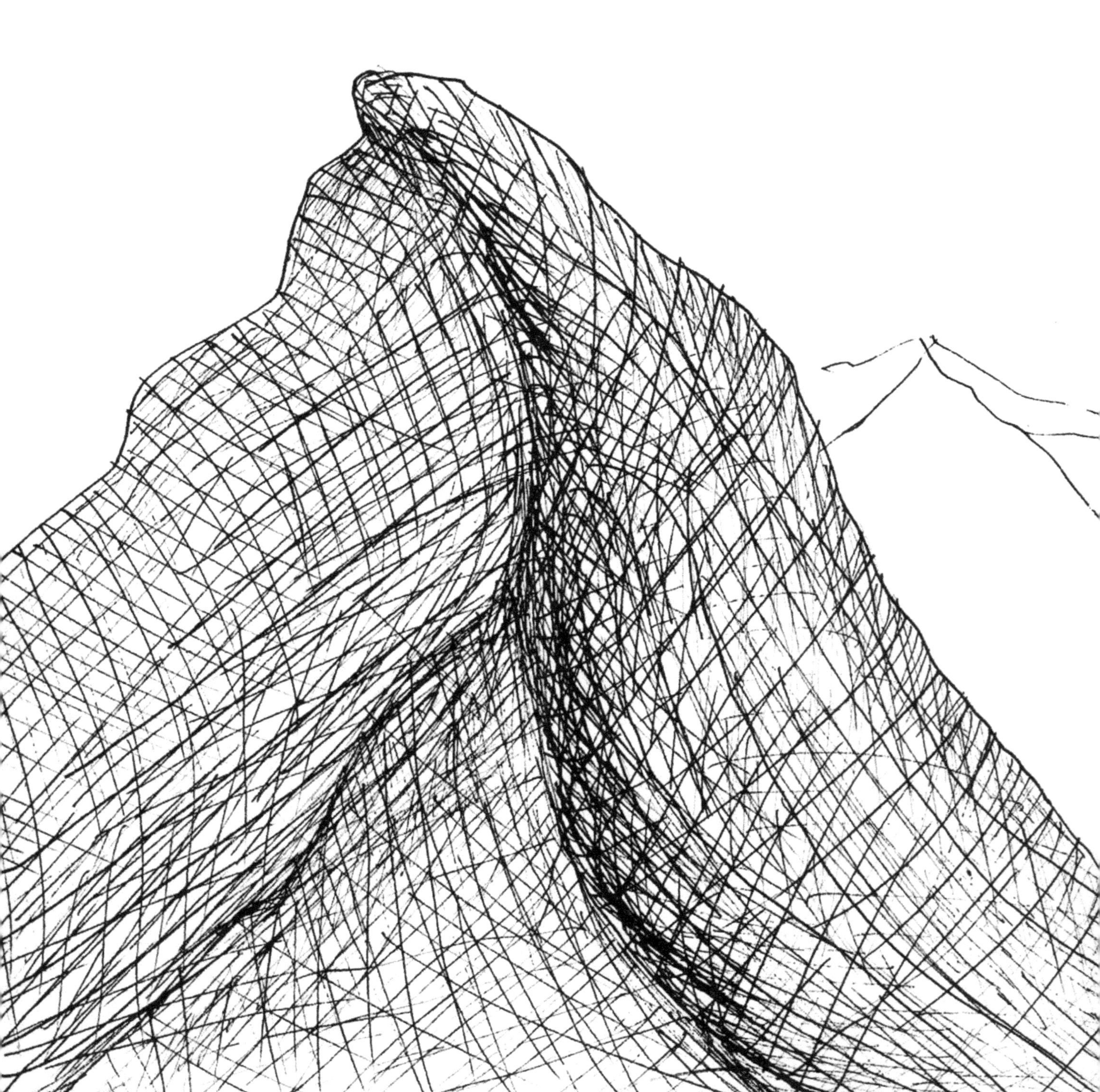

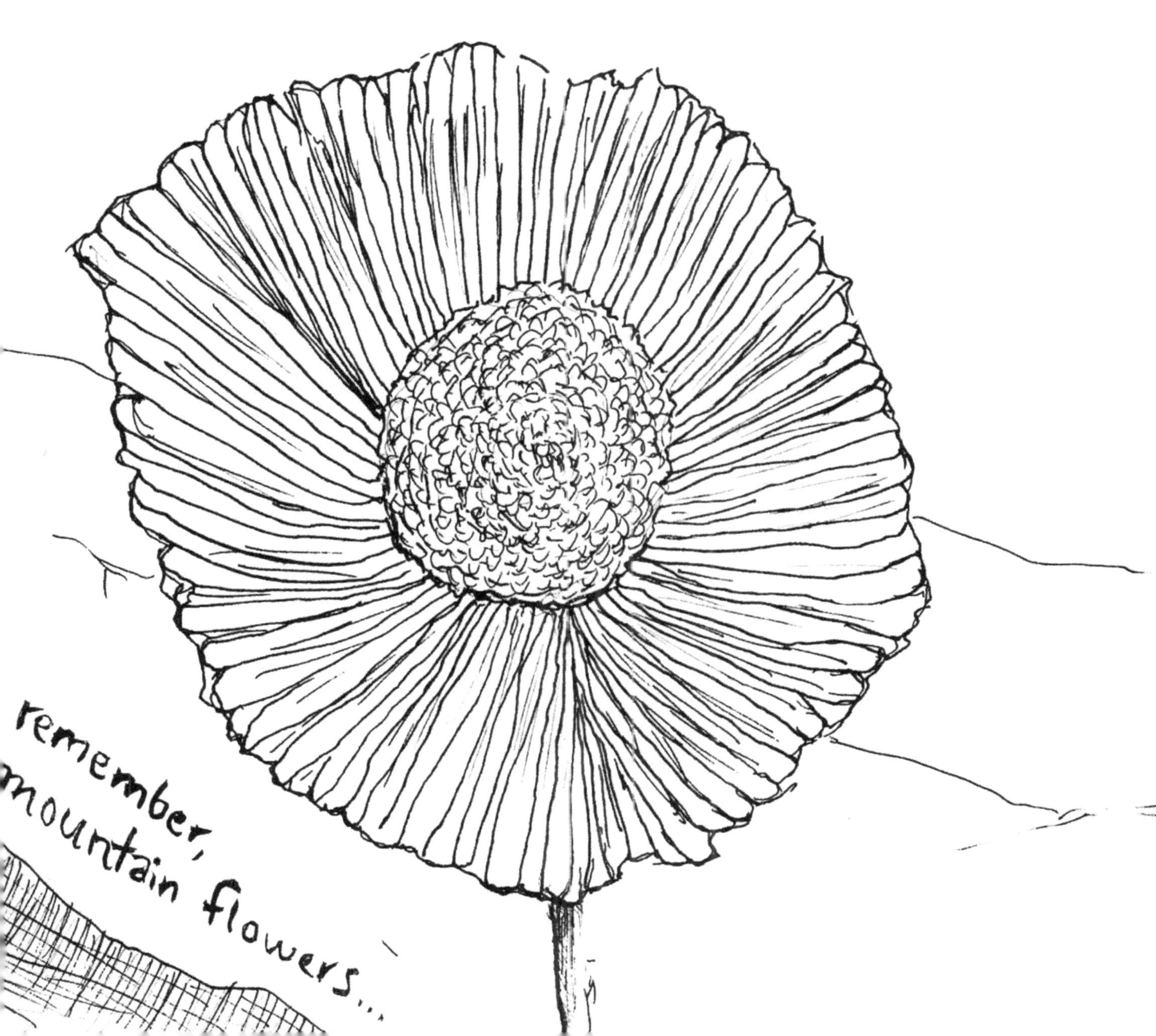
remember,
mountain flowers...

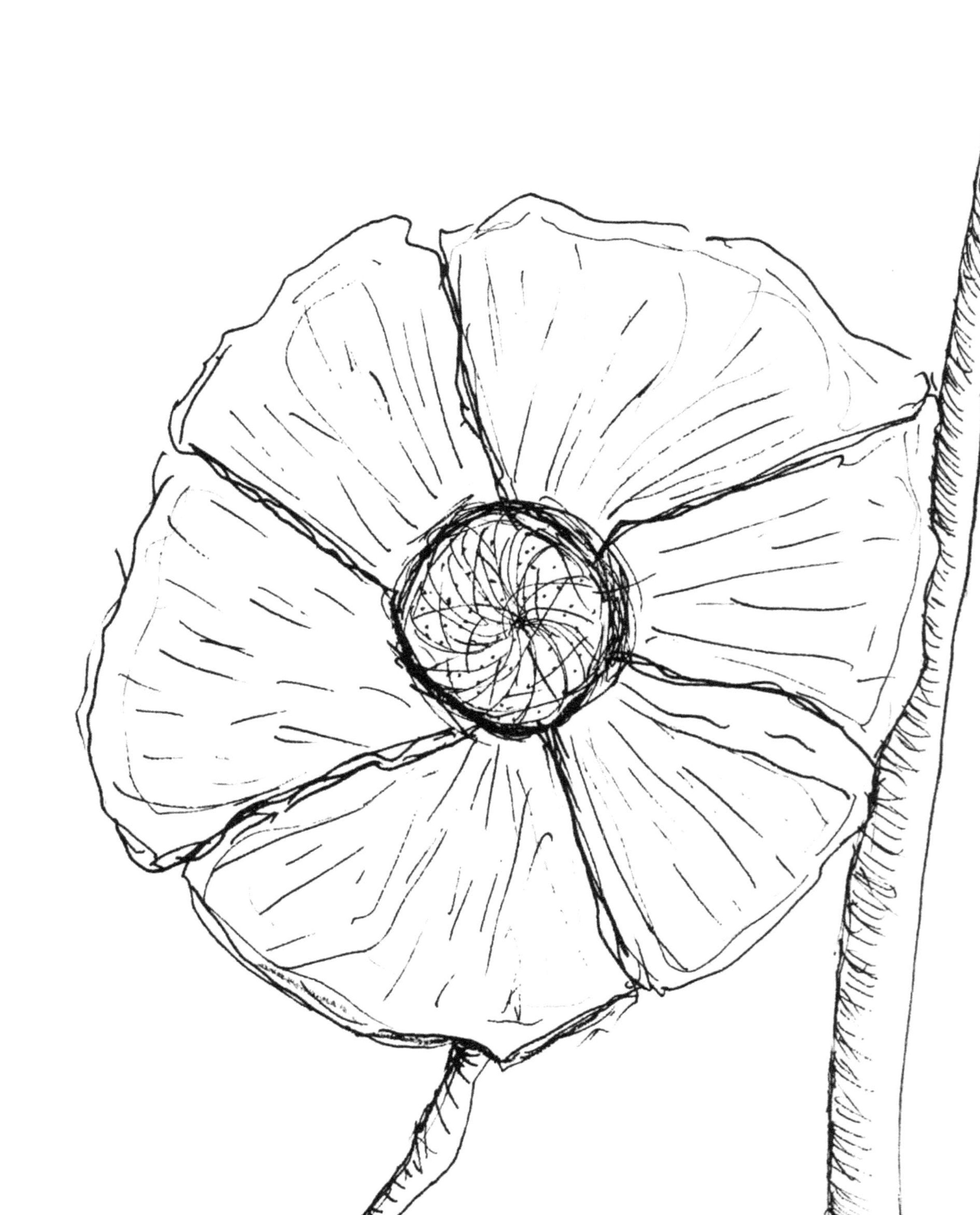

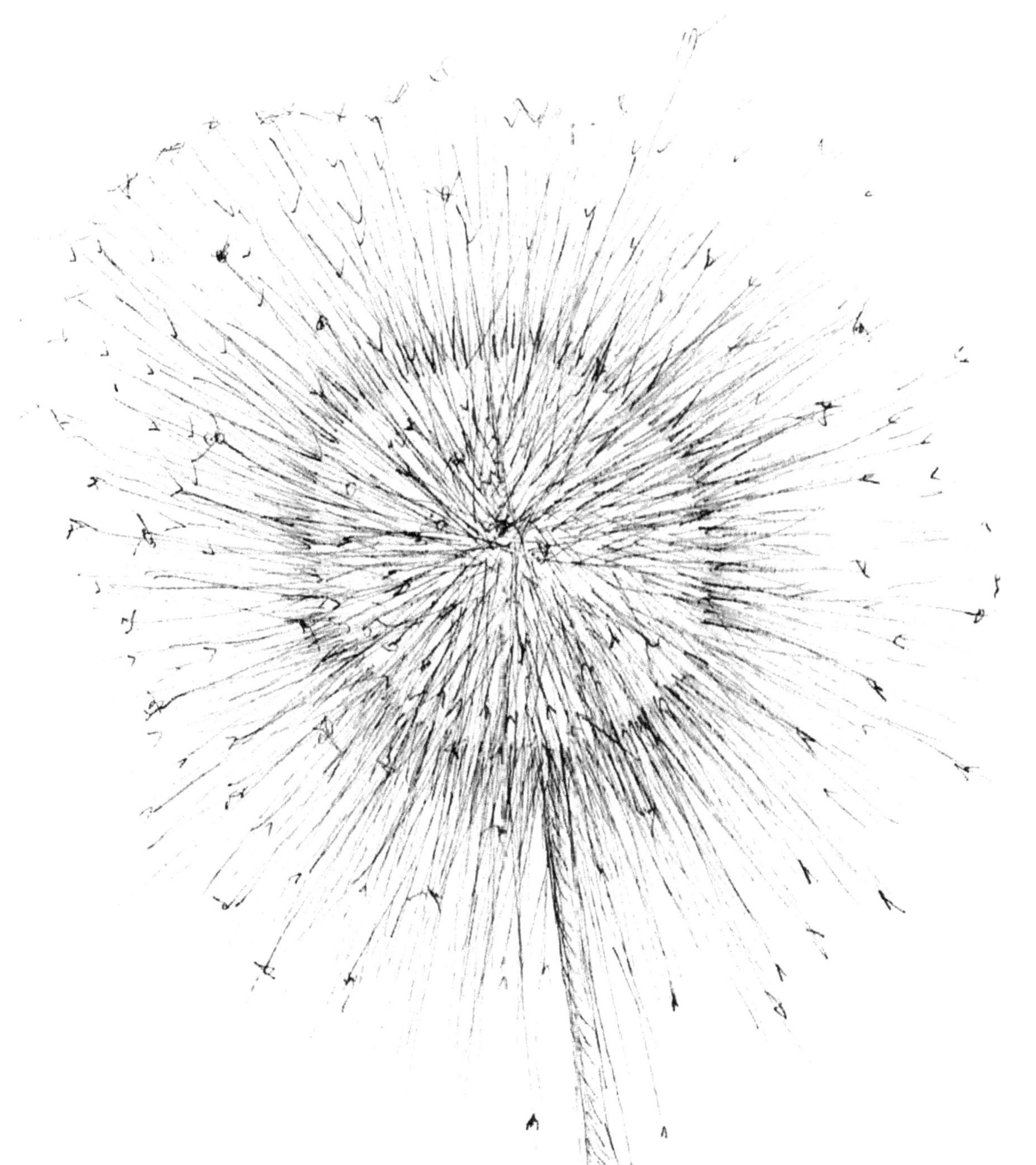

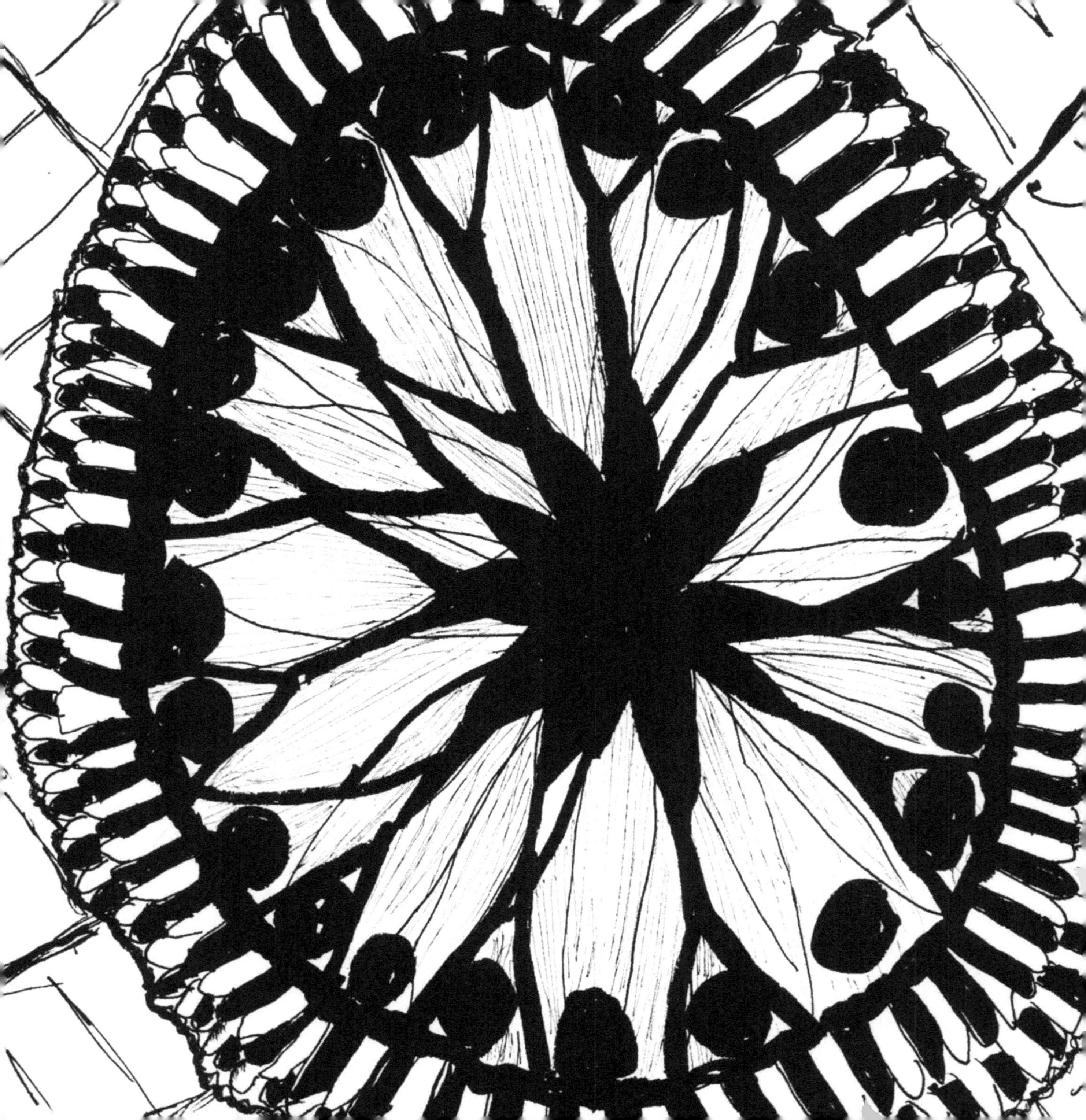

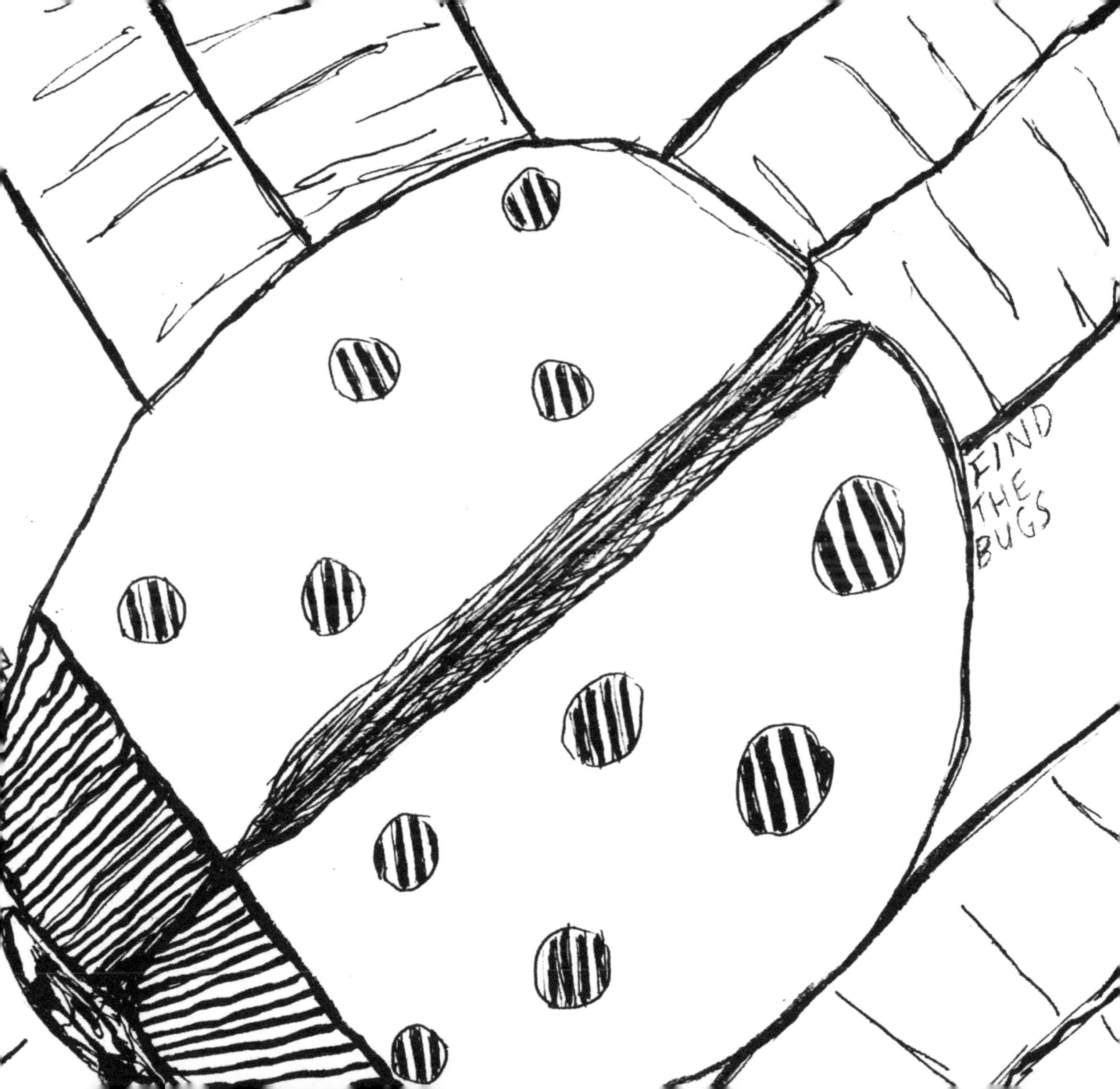

FIND
THE
BUGS

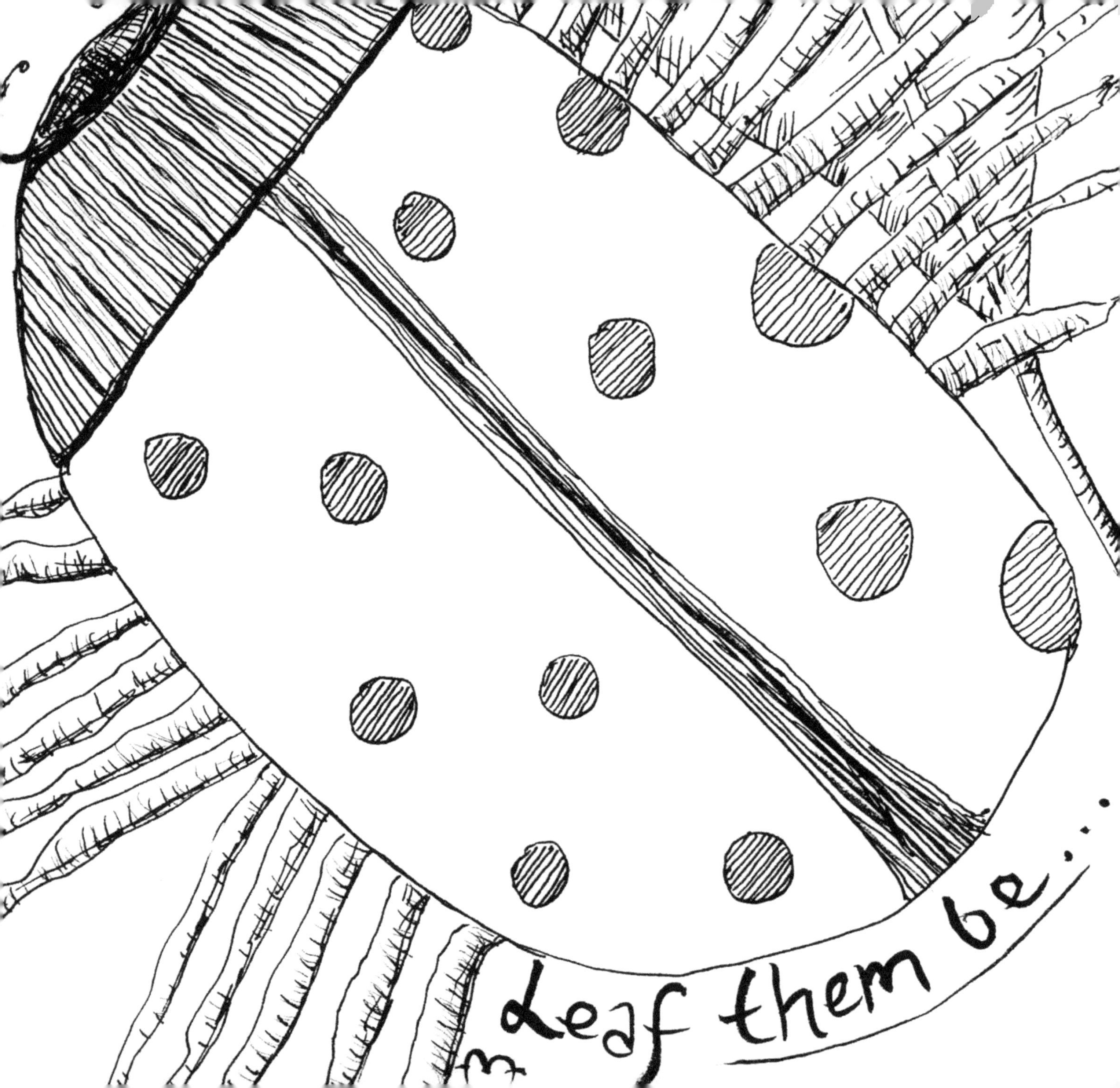
Leaf them be...

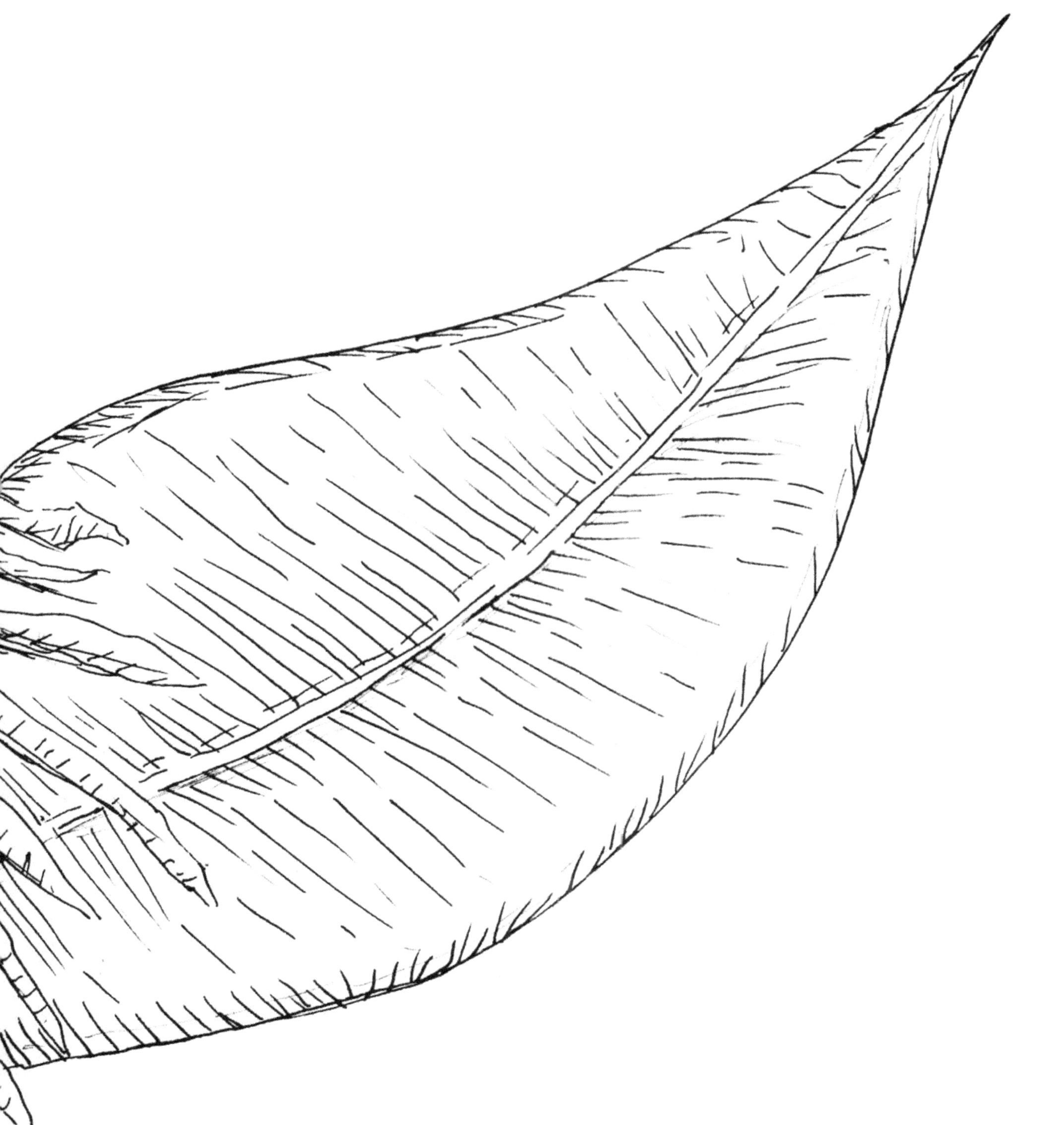

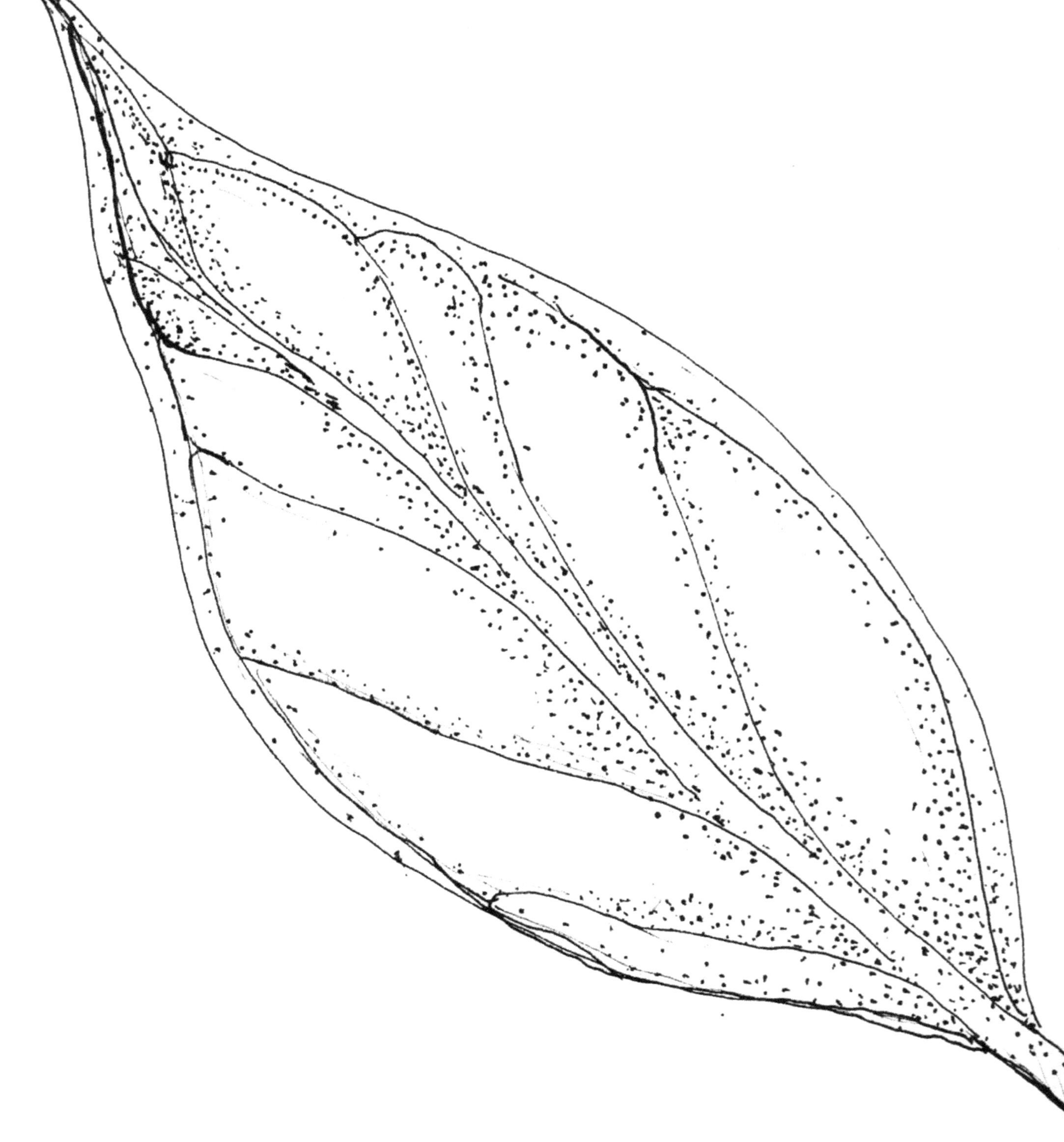

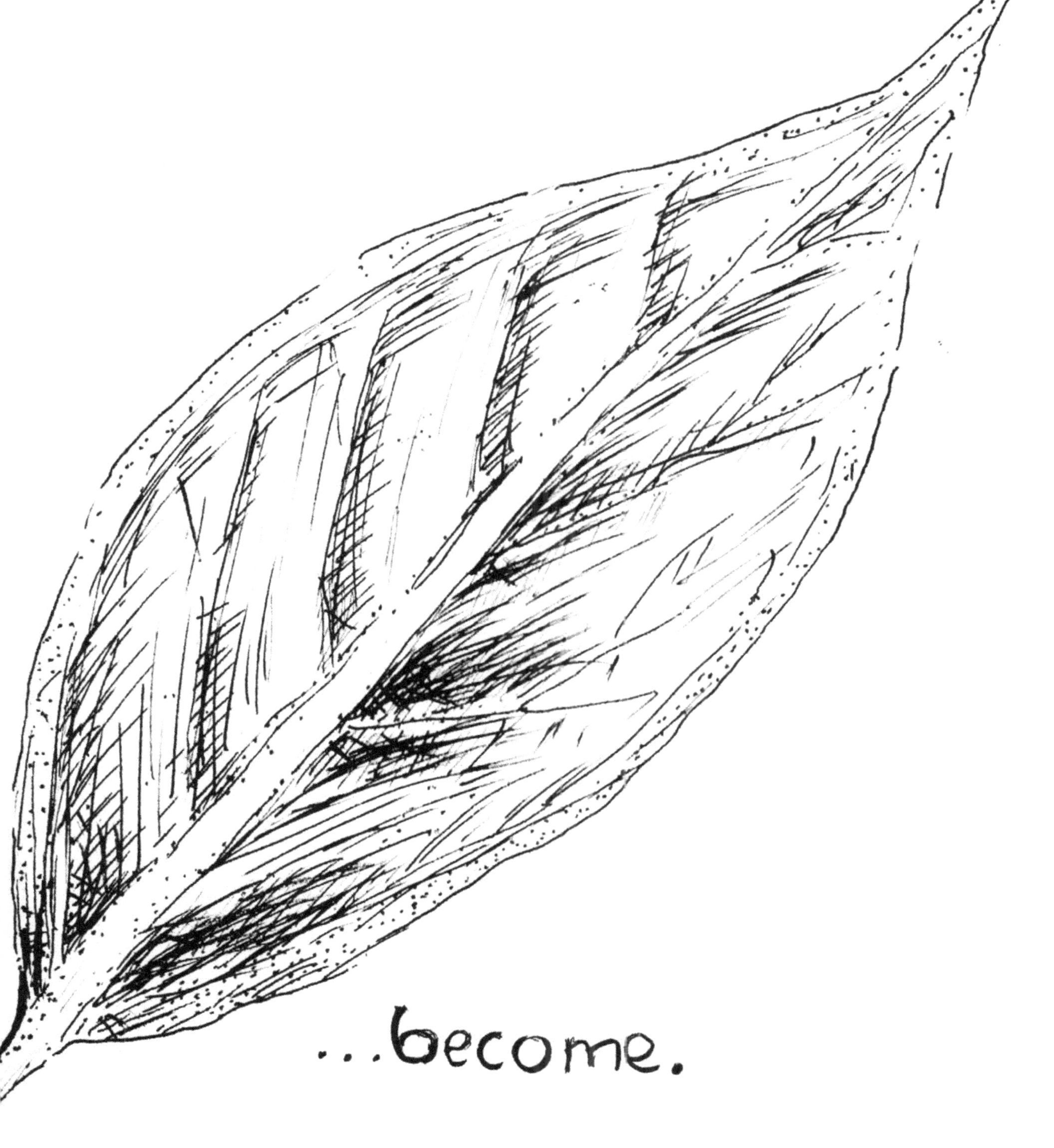
...become.

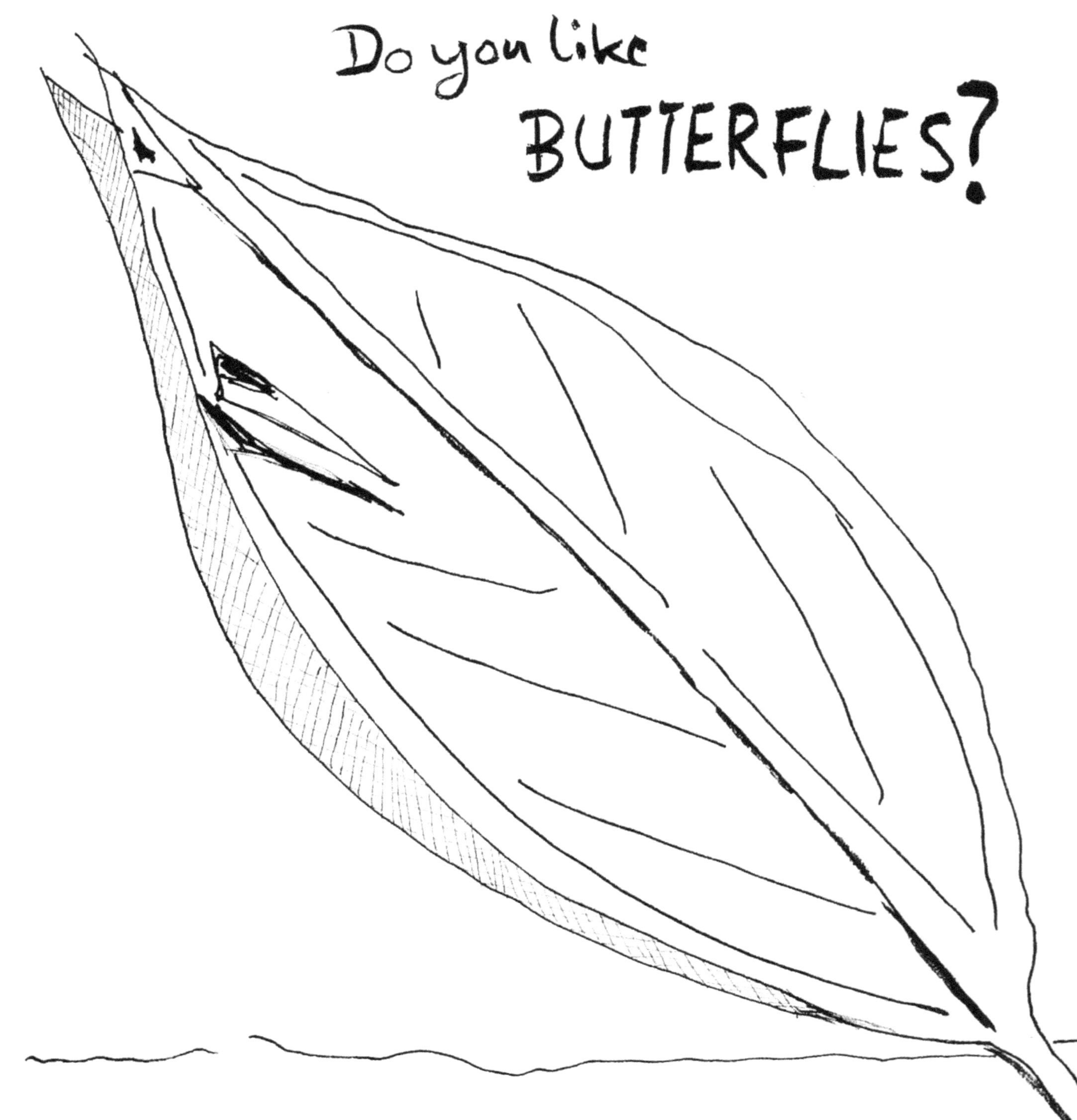
Do you like
BUTTERFLIES?

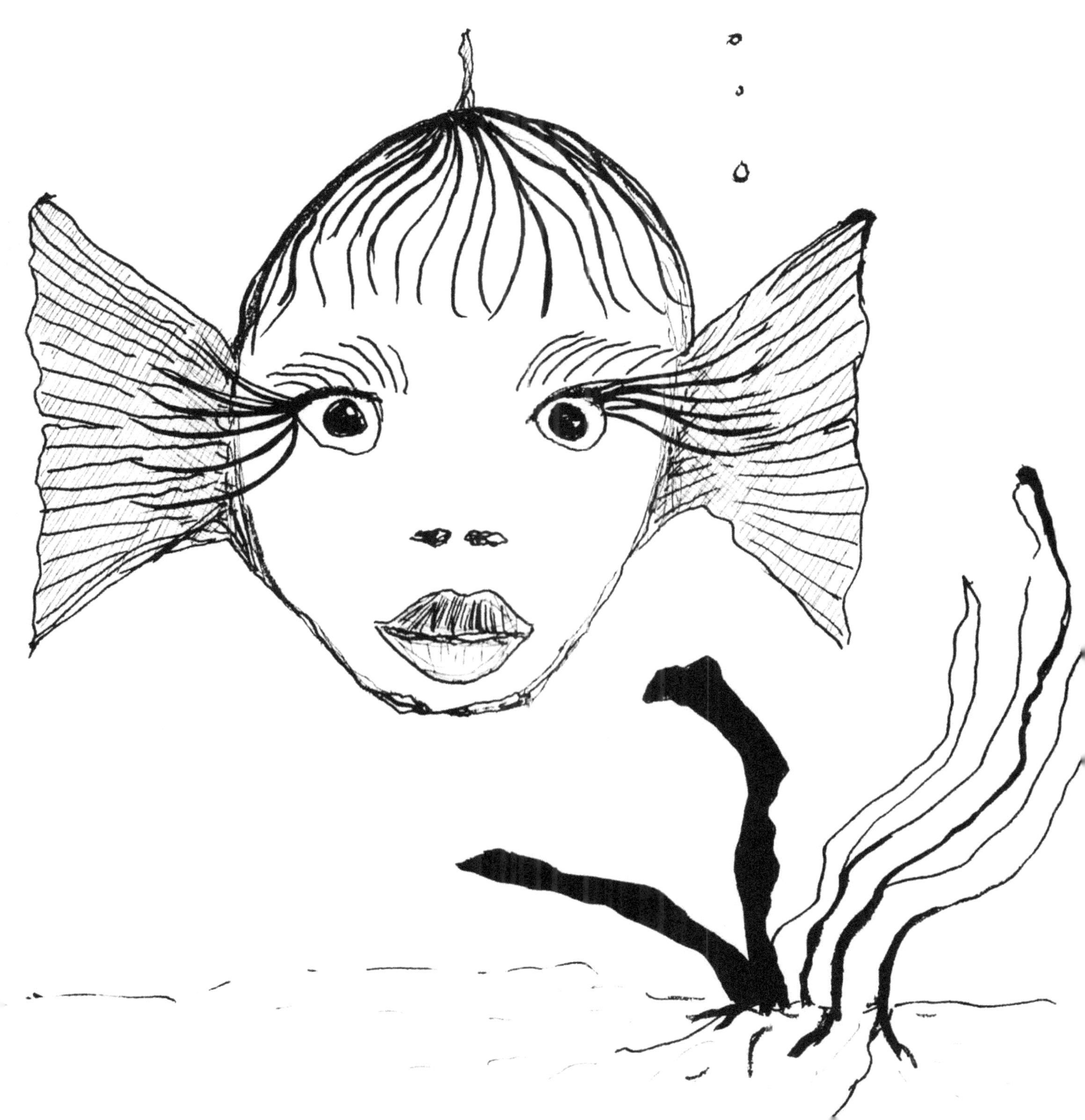

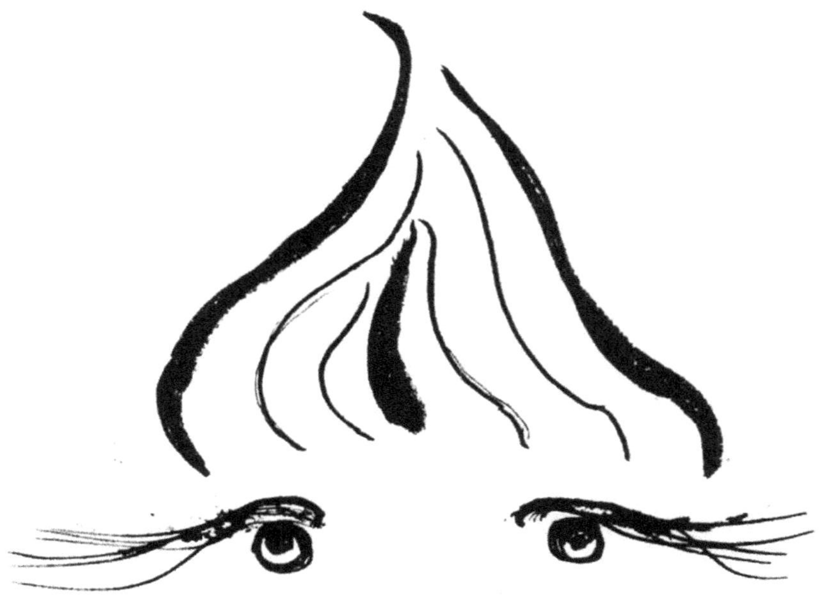
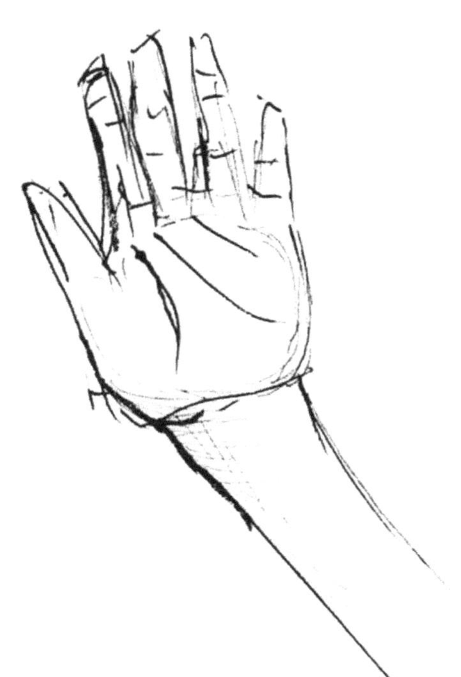

Our World

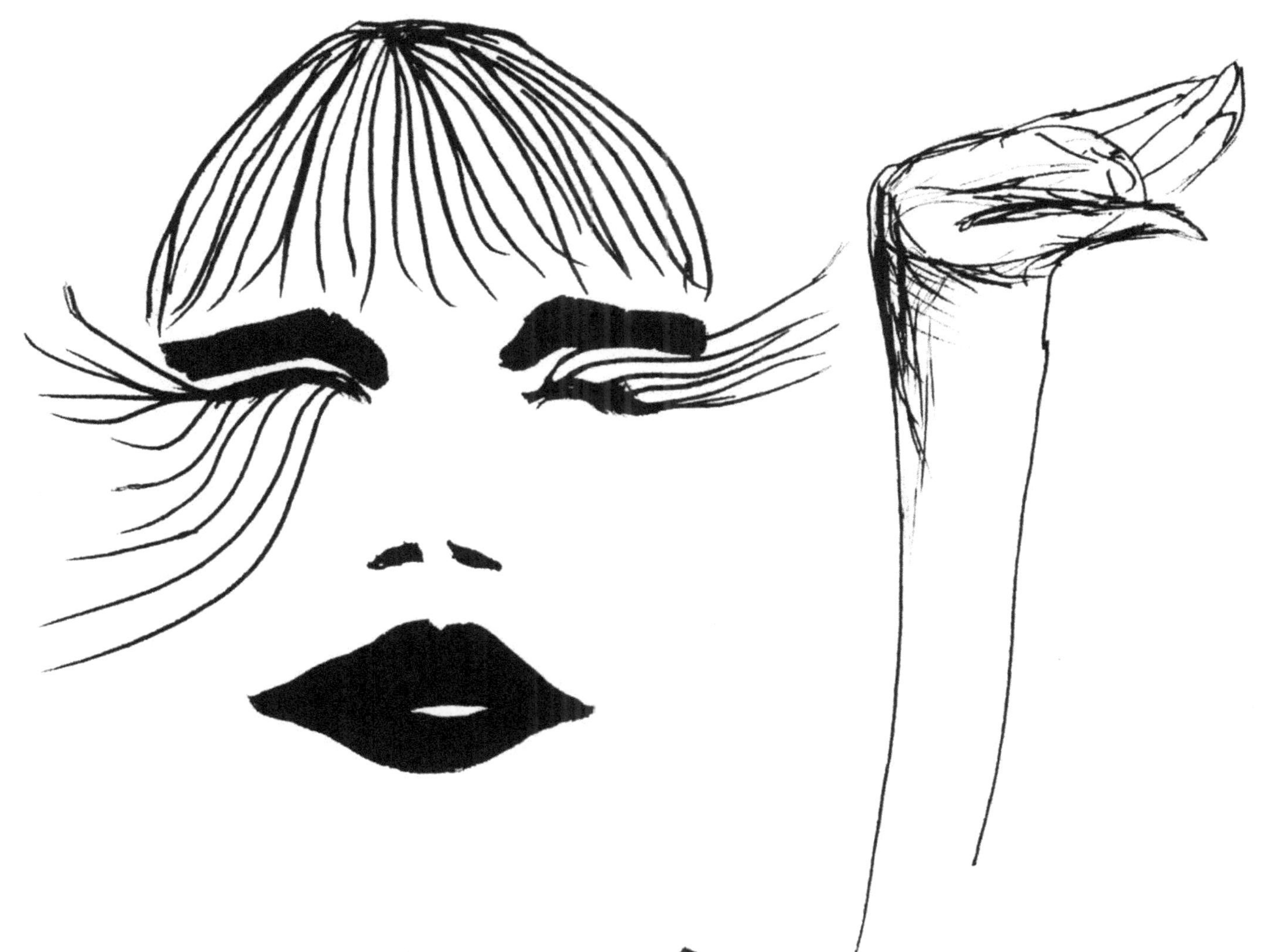

needs Butterflies

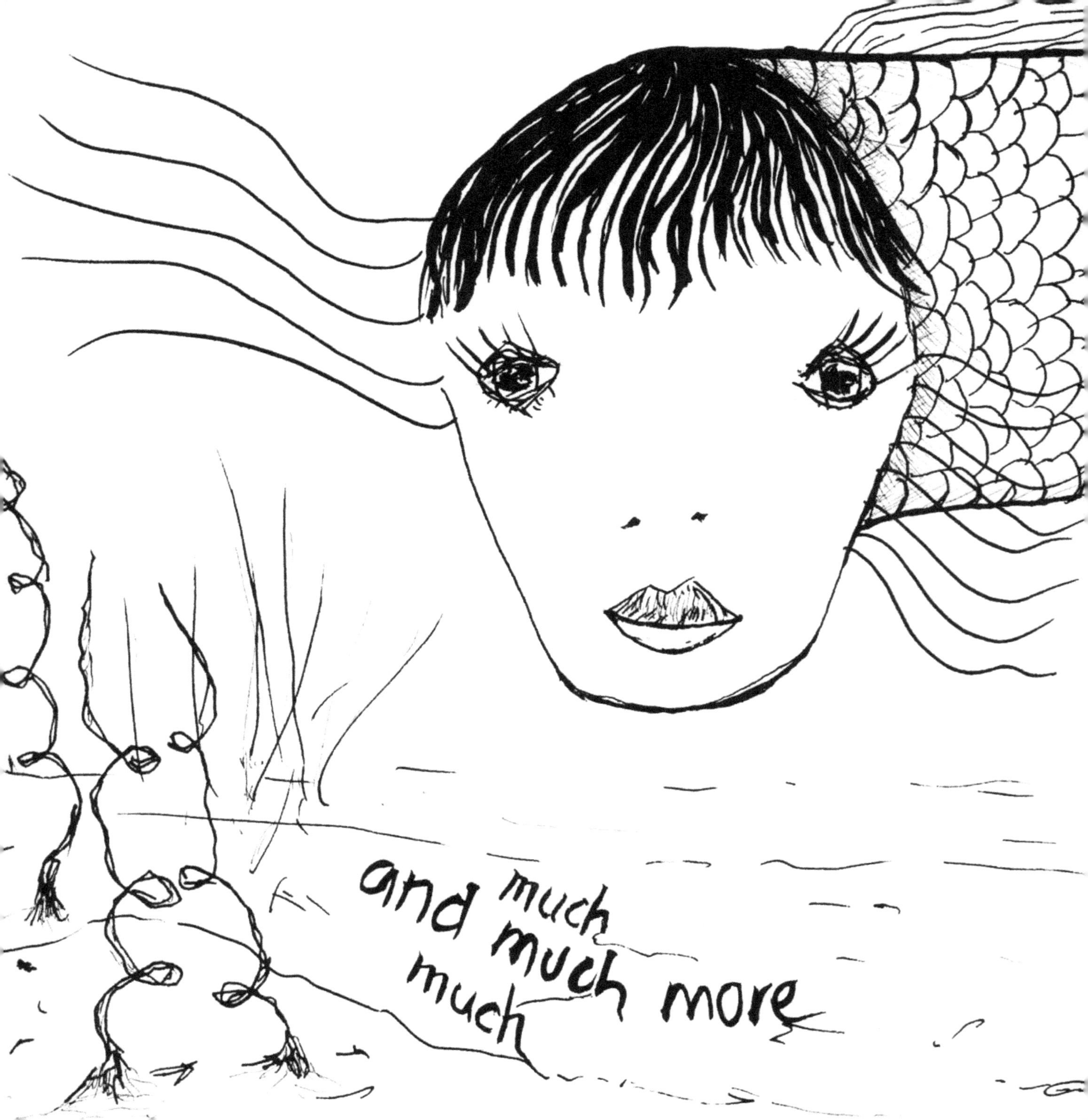
and much
much more
much

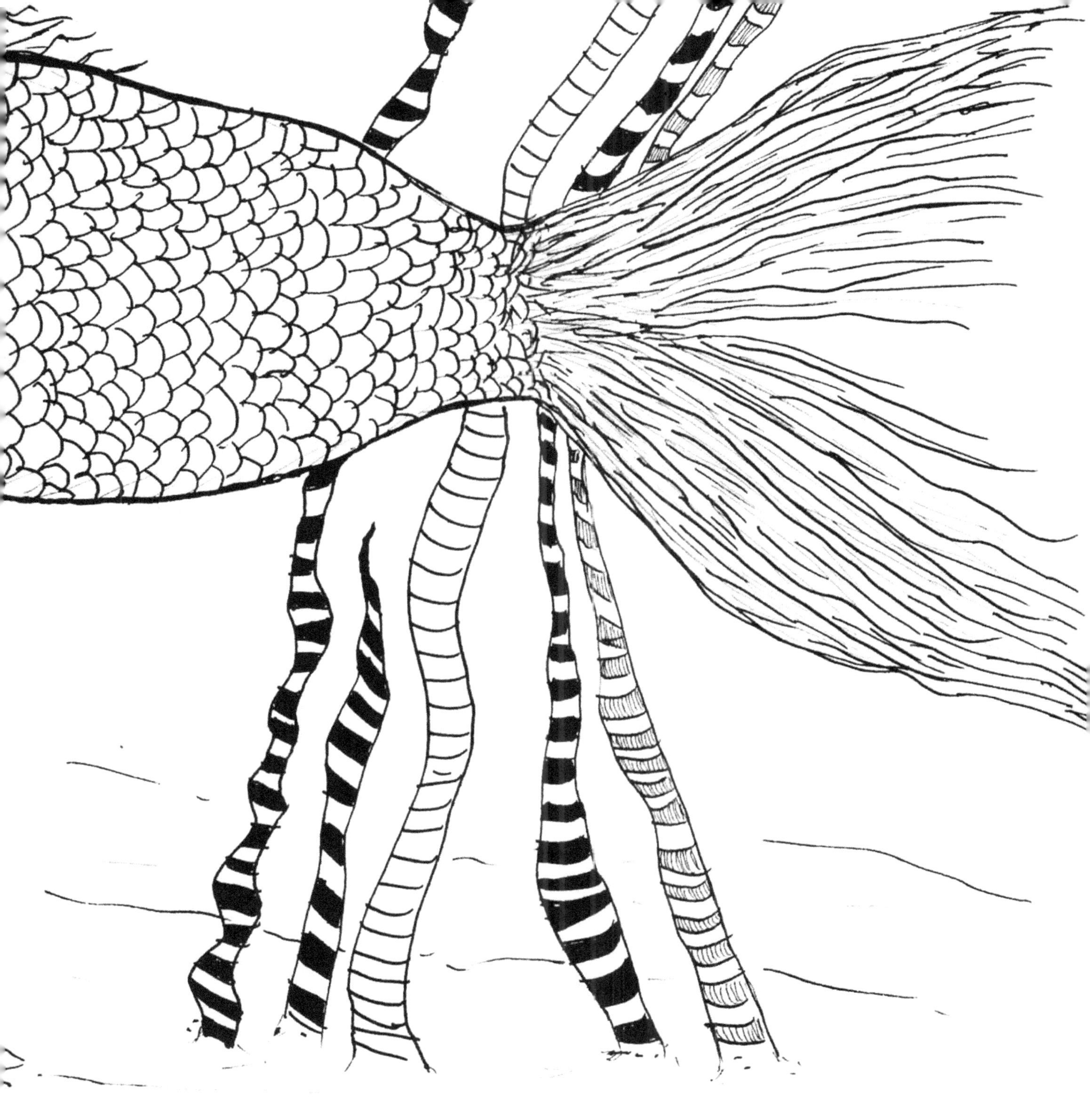

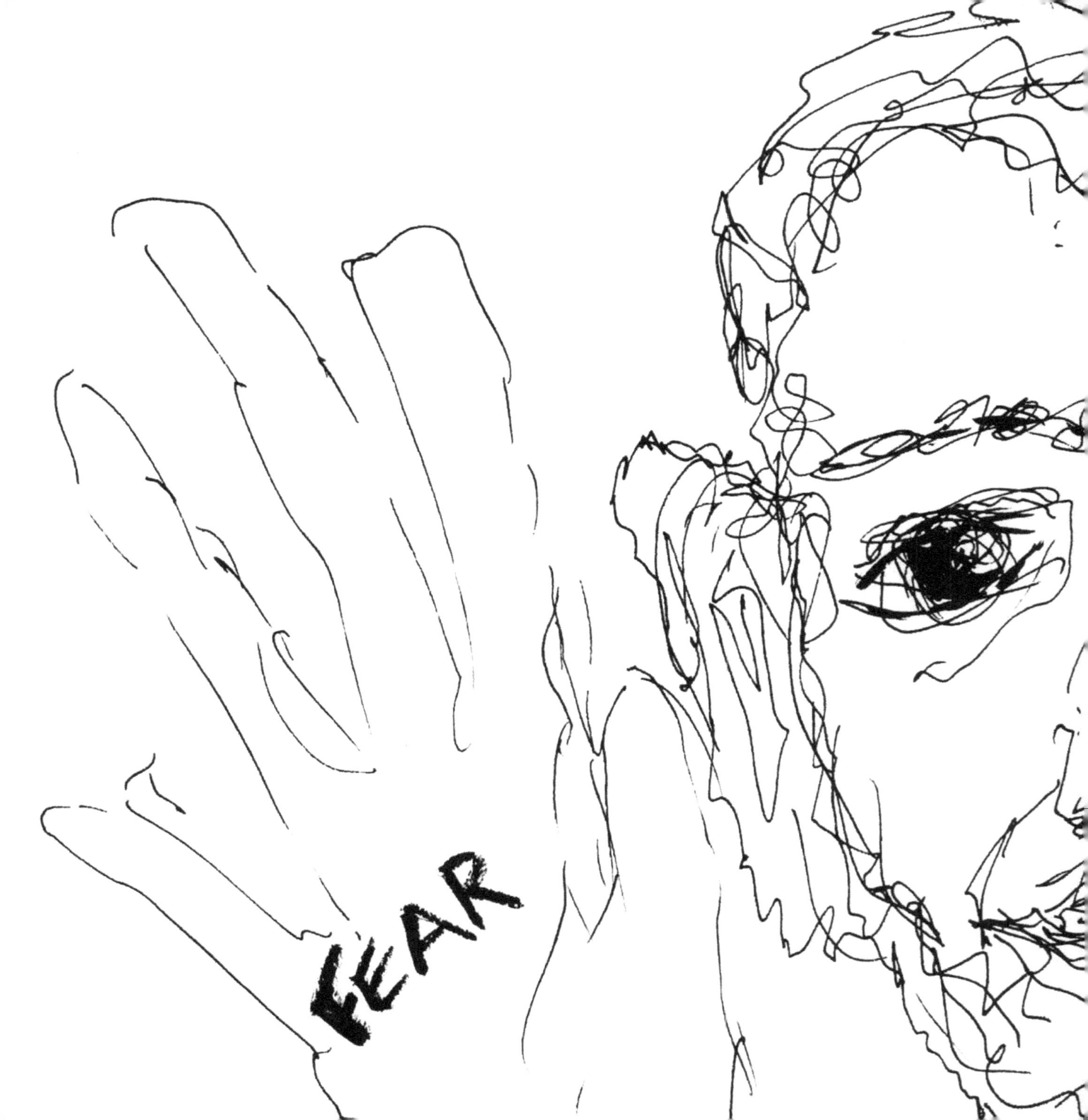

FEAR

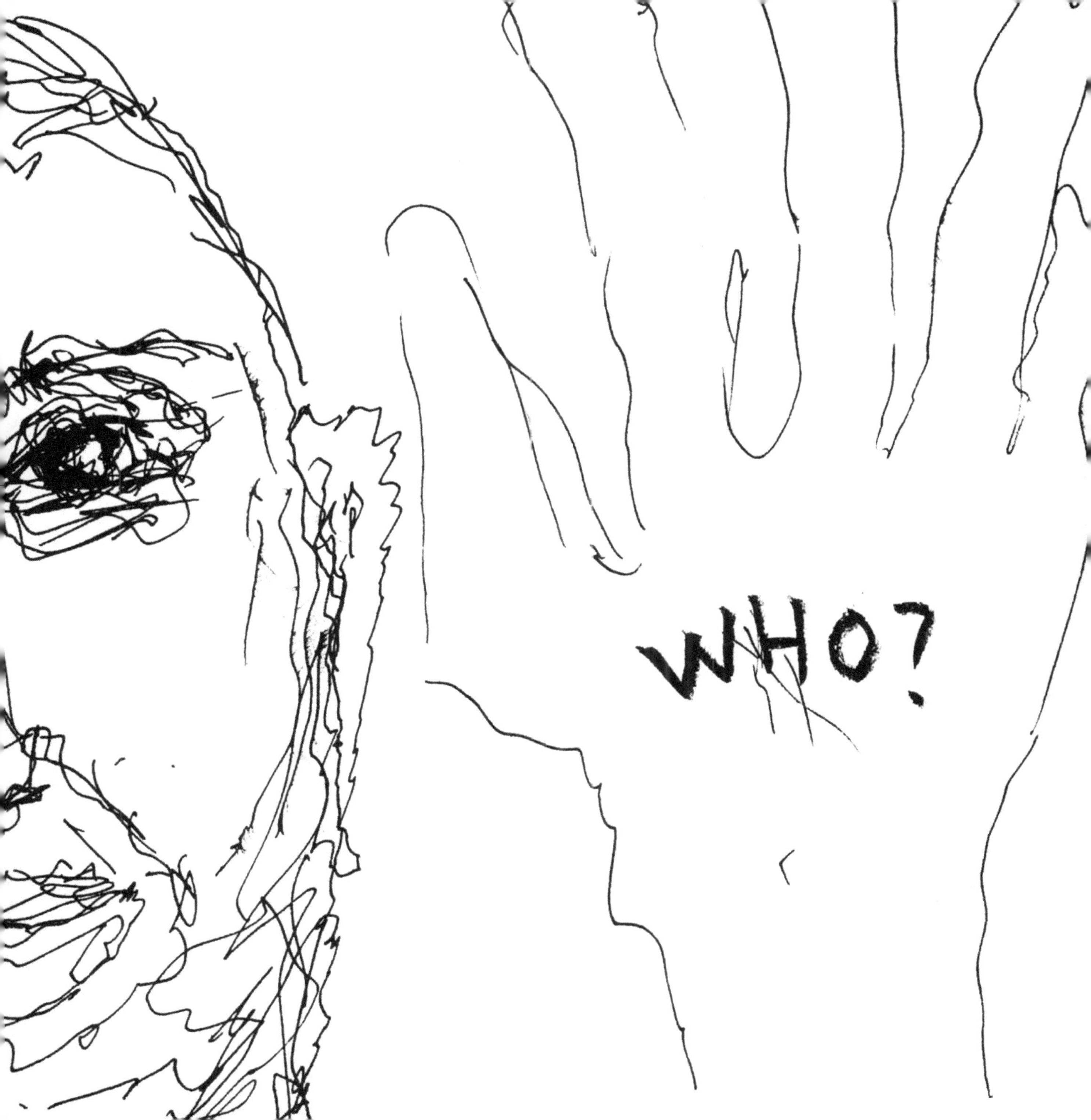

WHO?

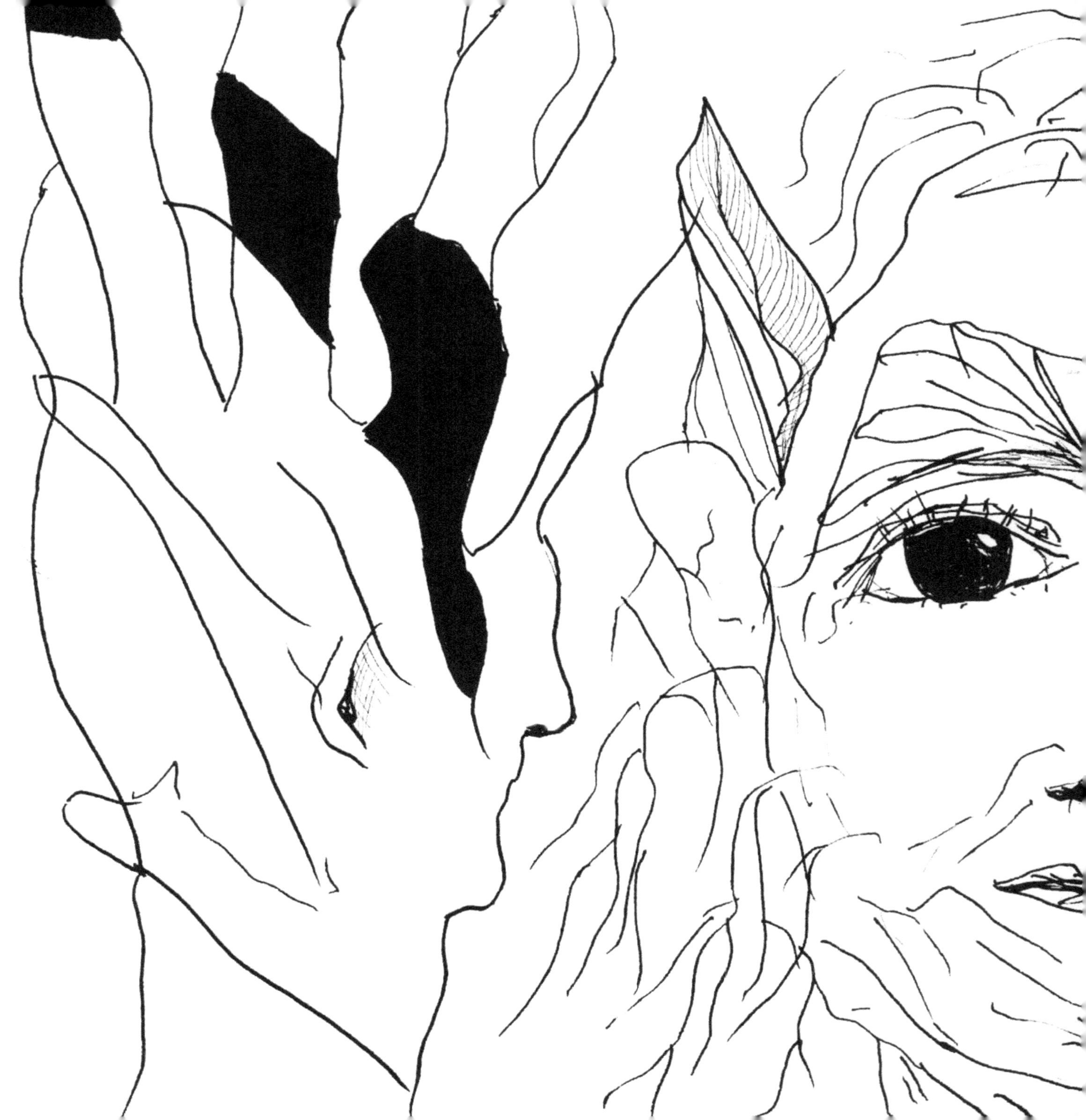

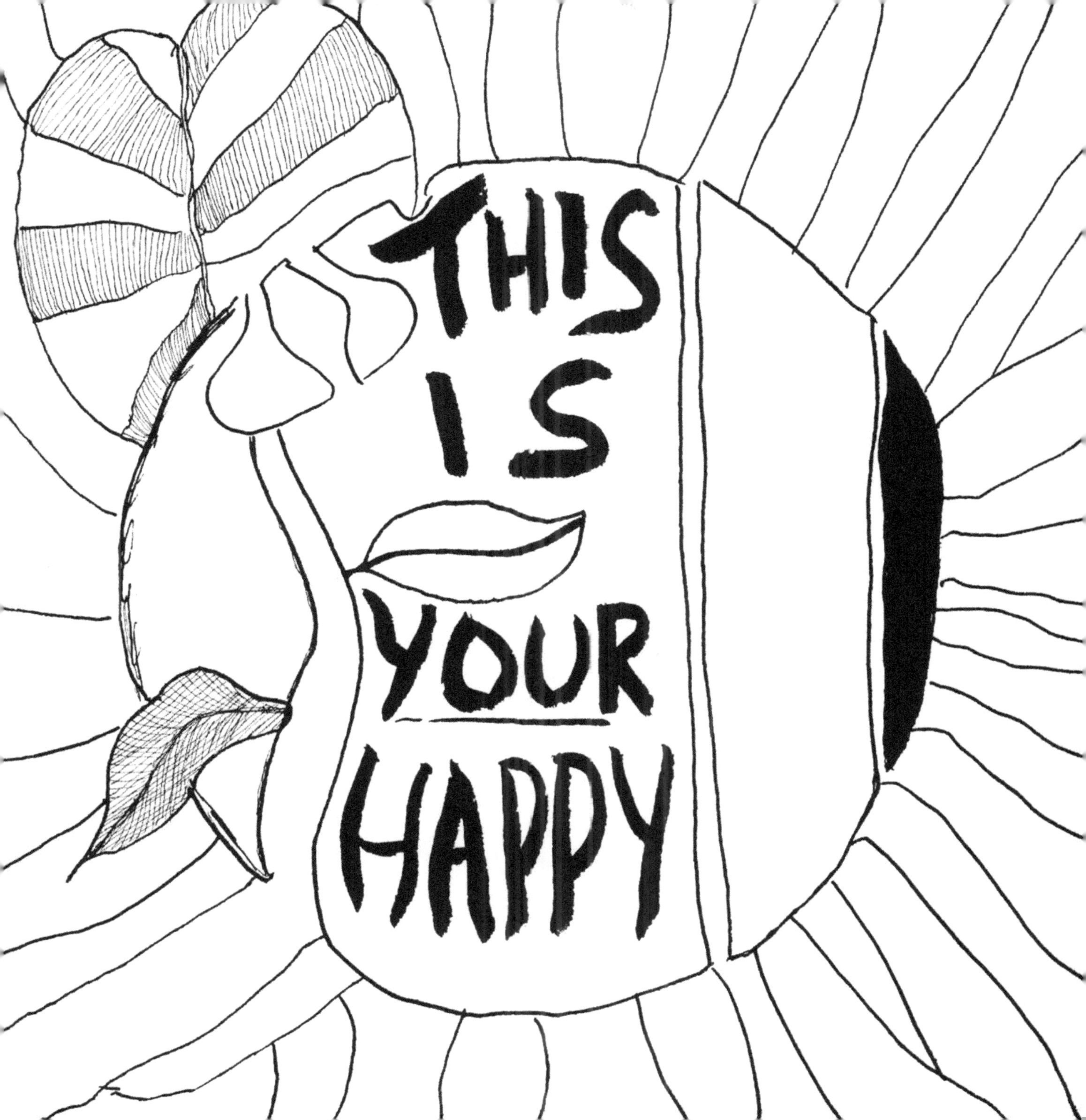

THIS
IS
YOUR
HAPPY

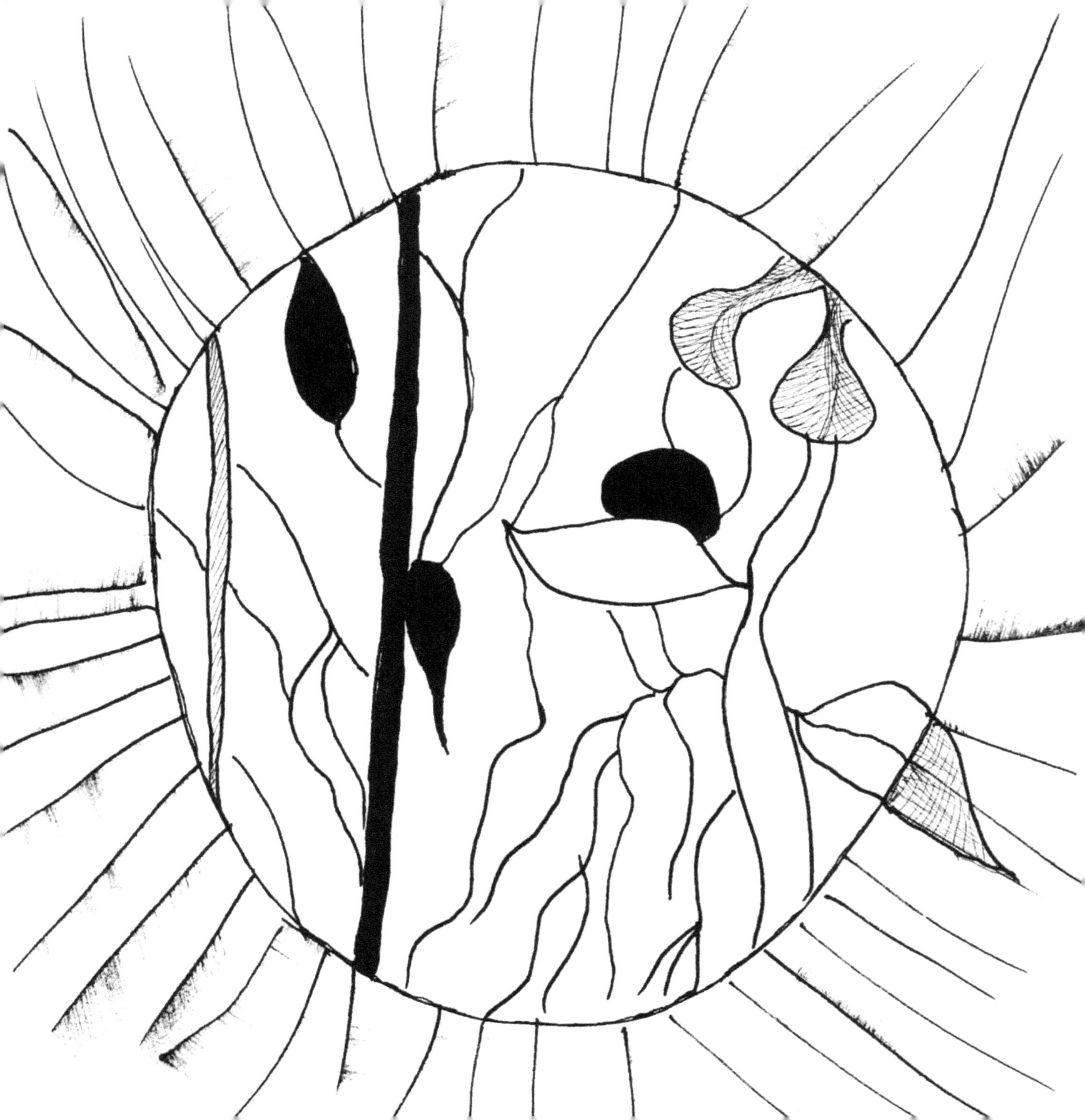

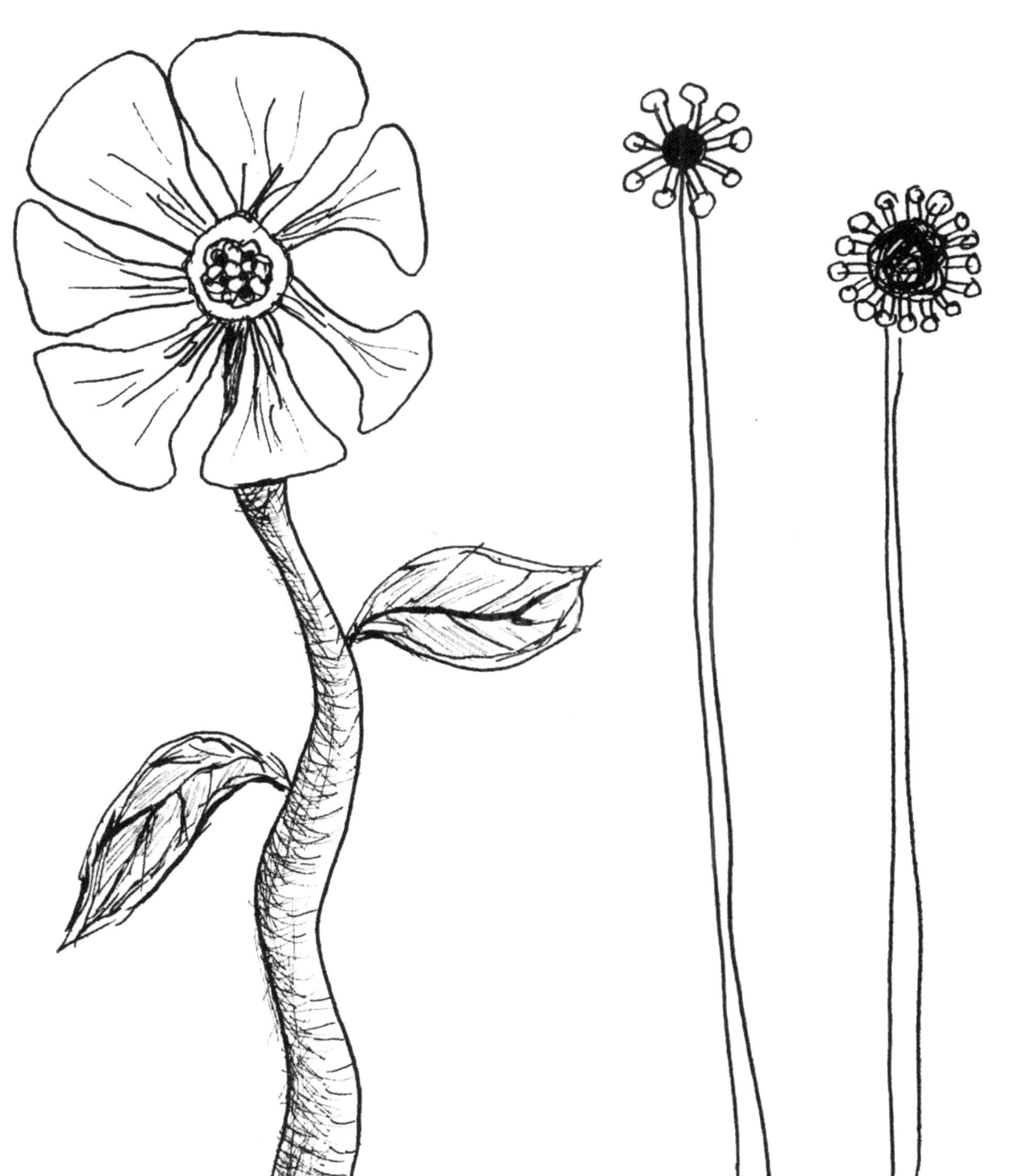

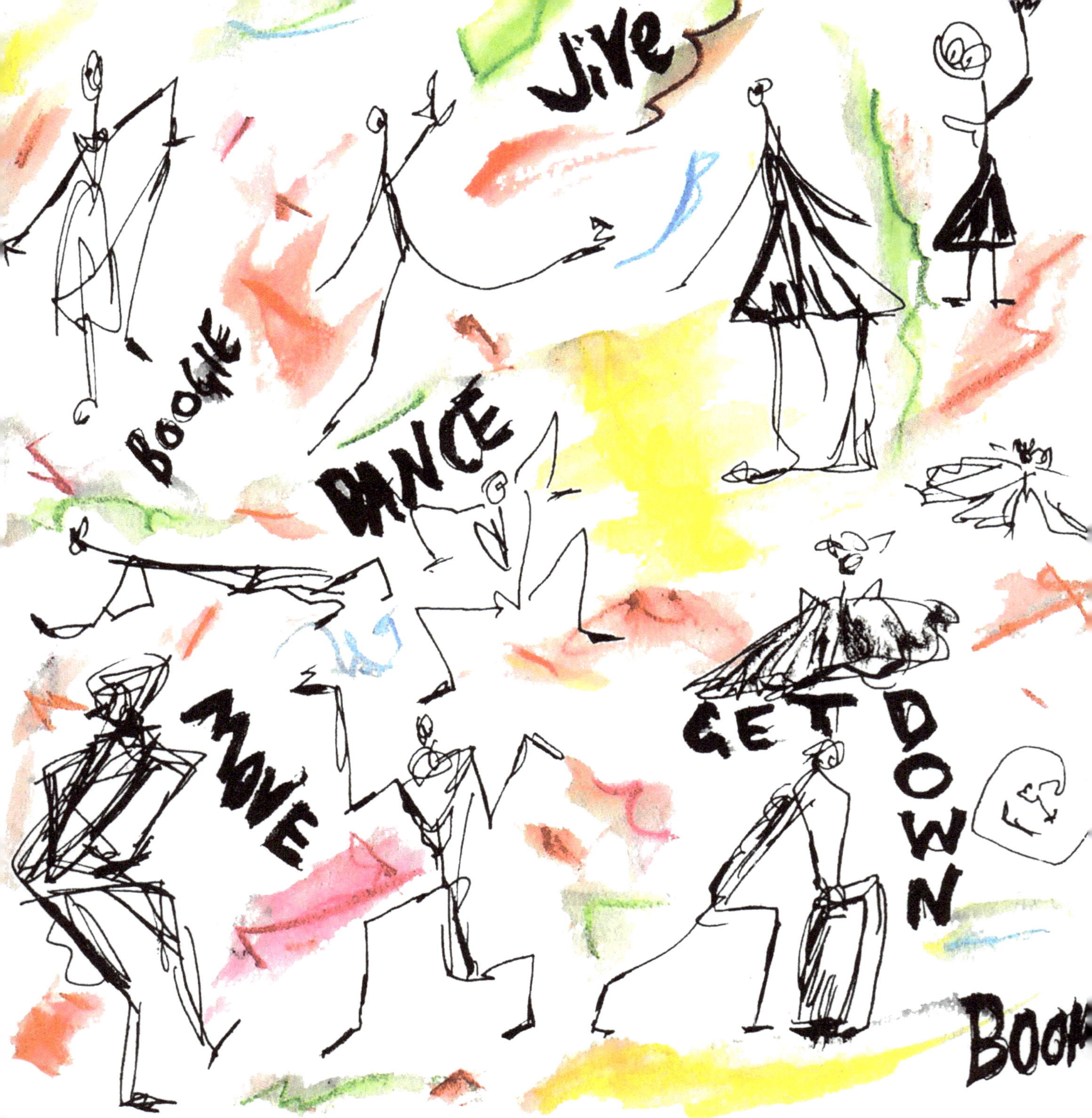

JIVE
BOOGIE
DANCE
MOVE
GET DOWN
BOOM

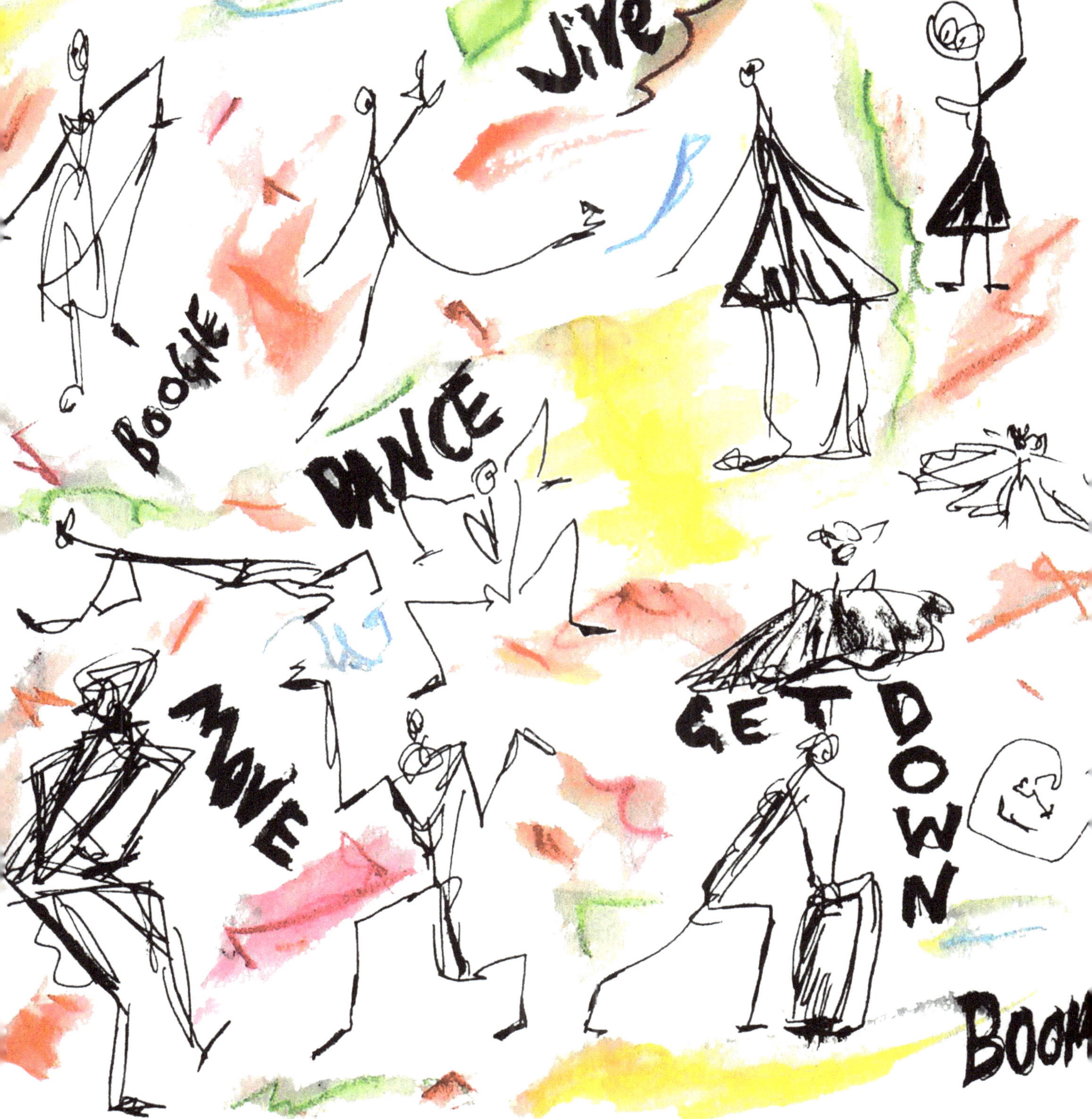

JIVE
BOOGIE
DANCE
MOVE
GET DOWN
BOOM

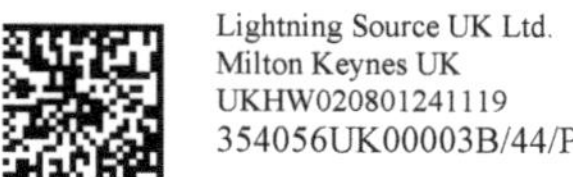

Lightning Source UK Ltd.
Milton Keynes UK
UKHW020801241119
354056UK00003B/44/P